GodStories

GodStories

New Narratives from Sacred Texts

H. Stephen Shoemaker

Judson Press ® Valley Forge

GodStories: New Narratives from Sacred Texts
© 1998 Judson Press, Valley Forge, PA 19482-0851

Cover artwork is a sculpture of Elijah. It is included at the request of the author and with permission of the Museum of New Mexico. An explanation of the sculpture's significance can be found in chapter 10 and on page 256.
Cover photograph by Blair Clark, © 1997 Museum of New Mexico. *Elijah* sculpture by Boris Gilbertson, collection of the Museum of Fine Arts, Museum of New Mexico, Museum purchase with funds donated from the Vivian Sloan Fiske Estate.

Library of Congress Cataloging-in-Publication Data
Shoemaker, H. Stephen, 1948-
    Godstories : new narratives from sacred texts / H. Stephen Shoemaker
        p. cm.
    Includes bibliographical references.
    ISBN 0-8170-1265-6 (pbk.)
    1. Bible—Introductions. 2. Bible—Criticism, Narrative. 3. Bible stories, English. I. Title.
BS475.2.S48   1998
220.6—dc21   97-29988

Printed in the U.S.A.
05 04 03 02 01 00 99
5 4 3 2

To David and Ann

who for nineteen and seventeen years, respectively,
have taught me how to become a father
and have displayed the beauty and resiliency
of God's life in us

Contents

Preface

The stories in the Hebrew and Christian scriptures belong not just to the synagogue and the church but to the world. In a speech in Fort Worth, Bill Moyers introduced his PBS series and book *Genesis* saying that we must take the Bible back from the experts and the extremists. The experts have tended to keep scripture too confined in parochial concerns, whether of church or academy. The extremists turn scripture into a weapon as they unleash their program of sacred violence in the world. French mathematician and mystic Blaise Pascal saw in the seventeenth century what we too often see now: "Men never do evil so completely and cheerfully as when they do it from religious conviction" (*Penseés*, 895).

The Bible belongs to the world as part of God's repertoire of redemption. Its own pages point to the universality of God's word: Cyrus the Persian king becomes the servant of the Lord, as does Pharaoh's daughter and Ruth the Moabite and the diminished, suffering people called Israel, and a teenaged Palestinian girl named Mary and an Ethiopian eunuch and a Hellenistic Pharisee named Saul, who became God's apostle to the Gentiles.

This book is a set of narrative essays taken from the sacred texts of Jewish and Christian scriptures. My fondest hope is that they may serve as a new entryway into these scriptures for believers and nonbelievers alike.

Beneath, beyond, and above all the characters herein, and all the stories, is a picture, however dim or fleeting, of Another—the God of all life—and of the long mercy, the wild mercy, the mercy without end.

Praising, that's it! He was as one appointed to praise,
and he came the way ore comes, from silent
rock. His heart, a wine press that couldn't last
made us an endless supply of wine.

(R. M. Rilke, *Sonnets to Orpheus*, 1.7)

When the steward of the feast tasted the water now
become wine, and did not know where it came from
(though the servants who had drawn the water
knew), the steward of the feast called the
bridegroom and said to him, "Every man serves the
good wine first; and when men have drunk freely,
then the poor wine; but you have kept the good
wine until now."

(Gospel of John 2:9-10, RSV)

Acknowledgments

Who can count or even remember all who have helped me in this book—their teaching, their sharing, their encouraging, their bequeathing of knowledge and spirit?

There are the writers, Elie Wiesel and Frederick Buechner; and pastor-theologians, George Arthur Buttrick, Samuel Miller, Carlyle Marney. And teachers, Louis Martyn, Raymond Brown, Daniel Berrigan, Wayne Oates, and Henlee Barnette; colleagues like Paul Duke and Bill Leonard. And friends like Dwight Cobb, who dreamed this book with me fifteen years ago. And schools like Union Theological Seminary, New York City, and the Southern Baptist Theological Seminary, Louisville, Kentucky. And congregations in Charlotte, Bradenton, Durham, Armonk, High Point, Falmouth, Asheville, Louisville, and Fort Worth.

I wish to thank especially Jan Richardson, who prepared the final manuscript and was a profoundly helpful first reader; and LaVonne Wilson, extraordinarily steadfast administrative assistant, who typed early versions of many of these stories with a librarian's love of books; Toni Craven and James McClendon, who offered helpful suggestions as they read the manuscript; and Broadway Baptist Church of Fort Worth, who for five crucial years has supported, sustained, and partnered with me in our common ministry; and the Agape Meal congregation of predominantly homeless people who for two years of Thursdays have brought the kingdom of God near; and Cherrie my life mate, who has cheered me on; and most especially our children, David and Ann, to whom this book is dedicated.

And to you, O God, whose steadfast love endures forever.

H. Stephen Shoemaker
April 24, 1997
Montserrat Jesuit Retreat House
Lake Dallas, Texas

Christian *Haggadah*:
Retelling Jewish /Christian Stories as Mirrors of the Human Condition and Signs of Earth's Redemption

We are story-formed creatures. Call us *homo narratus*. And we live in story-formed communities. Philosophers, ethicists, psychologists, educators, social scientists, and theologians are all coming to new awareness of the power of story in the shaping of our lives.[1] Literary critic Northrop Frye has noted that we humankind do not live directly or nakedly in nature, as do animals, but within a "mythological universe," a body of assumptions and beliefs that have arisen from our existential concerns.[2] Whether that mythical landscape is drawn by sacred scripture, Sigmund Freud, or Calvin Klein, it is a real part of our universe and it exerts considerable influence on our lives. Jesus in the wilderness said as much: "One does not live by bread alone, but by every word that comes from the mouth of God" (Matthew 4:4).

For those who have grown up in the Western world or within the sphere of Western religious belief, the biblical story is the master story that has most shaped their consciousness. The Bible is, in the words of Northrop Frye, "the Great Code." Frye got the title from seventeenth-century artist and poet William Blake, who called the Old and New Testaments "the Great Code of Art." It is hard to overestimate the power and presence of the biblical narratives on our minds and imaginations. The stories of Genesis, so wrote Willa Cather, lie "like a faded tapestry deep in the consciousness" of most of us.[3] What do we see there in the faded hues of red and gold and blue and green? A garden, a tree, two figures—one male, one female—a serpent, some fruit, a casting out. Two brothers; one lying on the ground, his blood soaking the soil. A flood, an ark, a rainbow, a tower reaching into the heavens. It is a tapestry of origins. Though faded, the images are indelibly there.

The Bible is a long, meandering book, really a collection of books. Sixty-six of them. In its pages you find primeval story, historical narrative, legal prescription and proscription, songs, short stories, poetry, prayers, parables, a new literary genre called "gospel," brought into being by the astonishing life of one named Jesus of Nazareth, letters, sermons, and apocalypse (a genre that reveals in almost hallucinatory images the end of time; the word literally means *unveiling*). The word *Bible* means "little books," and we should think of the Bible as a library of small books more than as one great book. In the ancient world of rolled-up papyrus scrolls the Bible was in fact a collection of scrolls lined up on sticks like newspapers in a library display stand.

But we see it bound in one volume—fifteen hundred or so formidable pages. If you've tried to read it straight through, you may have given up a hundred or so pages into it, possibly somewhere in the book of Leviticus with its exhausting list of ritual and legal regulations such as this: "You shall present to the LORD nothing blind, disabled, mutilated, with running sore, scab, or eruption, nor set any such creature on the altar as a food-offering to the LORD" (Leviticus 22:22 NEB). Or you've opened scripture at random and put your finger down on what you hoped would be a promising text and found yourself at some grisly battle scene or in the middle of some obscure and unpronounceable genealogy and a long list of "begats."

In spite of all its immediate difficulties, the Bible is a book of transcendent meaning; it has a unity that has shaped our culture immeasurably. It is a great running narrative of history and human existence. It begins with the creation of the universe in the book of Genesis and ends with the completion of all things in the Apocalypse of John (book of Revelation). In between we see the history and writings of a people of God called Israel and the emergence of a new people of God called the church, which arose in response to the life, death, and resurrection of Jesus of Nazareth, whom they called *Christos* (Messiah) and *Kyrios* (Lord).

If you look at its table of contents, you see that the Bible is not laid out like a philosophical discourse or a book of systematic theology. It is not a series of lessons or lectures. Its essential shape is story form, a grand, sweeping (if at times untidy) story. The unity of the Bible is in its narrative sweep and in the interplay of recurrent images, such as light, water, rock, blood, life, sheep, redeemer, and in the almost archetypal patterns in the way God operates and we operate. The Bible is the story of the creation of the universe—brilliant, glistening, new, and green—and of our own creation in the image of God. It is the story of our falling away from God and of God's repeated attempts to bring us back. This is God's story and our story and earth's story. A Scottish preacher once summarized it in his outline of the parable of the prodigal son: Sick of home; Homesick; Home.

If we asked an ancient Hebrew what God was like, we would probably not hear, "My God is omnipotent, omniscient, omnipresent," but rather a statement of the communal faith such as Deuteronomy 26:5-10: "My father was a wandering Aramean; his children wound up many years later as slaves in Egypt. Yet my God heard their cry and rescued them from Pharaoh's grip." If we asked an early Christian what God was like, we would probably not hear abstractions like Unmoved Mover, Ground of Being, or Immanent Spirit of the Universe, but more likely this summary of the story of redemption from John's Gospel: "For God so loved the world that he gave his only Son, so that everyone who believes in him may not perish but may have eternal life" (3:16). In other words, if you want to know about my faith, let me tell you a story.

Today we may be much less familiar with the biblical story than earlier generations were. It has been trivialized by its tellers, atomized by its teachers' mania for little meanings, and largely ignored by a secular world skittish about religion. Reynolds Price, novelist and Duke University professor of English, says that today his course on Milton has to be an introduction to the Bible as well, since students are largely ignorant of the rich biblical matrix out of which Milton wrote.

The purpose of this book is to reintroduce the sweep of the biblical narrative by representing key narratives of the Jewish and Christian scriptures in roughly chronological order. The approach I use is borrowed from the Jewish rabbinic tradition; I call it

"Christian *Haggadah*": a retelling of Jewish/Christian stories as mirrors of the human condition and as signs of earth's redemption. It was Elie Wiesel—Jewish writer, prophet, and Holocaust survivor—who first introduced me to this powerful and rich way of rabbinic storytelling that lets us weave together ancient and contemporary stories. His book *Messengers of God* was a revelation.[4]

Ancient rabbinic commentary on scripture consisted of (1) *Halakah*, which was the exposition of the Law of Moses into rules for daily living, and (2) *Haggadah*, which was the imaginative retelling of biblical narratives so as to teach us the way of God. In *Haggadah* stories old and new were woven together. Stories talked to each other; characters crossed centuries to converse; imaginary lines of dialogue were inserted as commentators helped us read between the lines. For instance, Jacob had as a young man deceived his father Isaac by dressing like his brother Esau, thereby stealing the blessing his father intended for Esau. Later Jacob found himself deceived by his father-in-law, Laban. Jacob awoke on the morning after his wedding night only to discover that the bride lying next to him in the bed was not Rachel, whom he loved, but Rachel's older sister Leah, whom he did not love and who was not nearly so beautiful. Laban had pulled a fast one. In the *Haggadah* the rabbis have inserted this conversation into the story: When Jacob awoke and saw Leah beside him he complained, "All night long I was calling you Rachel and you answered me. Why did you deceive me?"

"And you," she retorted, "your father called you Esau and you answered him. Why did you deceive him?"

Another story. God had called Moses to go to Pharaoh and rescue the Hebrew slaves, saying to him, "Let my people go." Moses was reluctant and kept finding excuses not to answer the call. Finally he consented. The Midrash comments that it took seven days for God to persuade Moses. *Six* days to create the world, *seven* days to persuade a man!

Elie Wiesel, contrasting *Halakah* and *Haggadah*, wrote:

> Whereas Halakah enjoins conformity by tracing guidelines to a way of life, [Haggadah], less severe and less coercive, and even at times and as circumstances require, mischievous or poetic, awakens thought, meditation or prayer.[5]

The great rabbinic scholar C. G. Montefiore says that *Halakah* was the rabbis' most ardent pursuit, but *Haggadah* "was their relaxation and amusement; in *Haggadah* their fancy and imagination found its occupation."[6] God seems not to have minded.

What does it mean for me, a Christian writer, to be using a rabbinic form, *Haggadah*? It means I write as one for whom the Christ event is the key to unlocking the scriptures. A noted novelist once said that there are three ways to write a novel. The first way is to start at the beginning and write to the end. The second is to start at the end and write back to the beginning. The third way is to start at the key, most crucial event, and write backward to the start and forward to the end. Such is the way I retell these stories from scripture. I almost inescapably see everything through the lens of the Christ event—everything back to the beginning and on to the end.

I hope to do this work without presumption. I do not seek to impose my perspective on the readers or on the stories, but rather to contribute my reading as one reading among others. I do not believe this is the only "proper" way to read the stories. The Hebrew scriptures have their own truth and saving significance for Jewish people apart from the Christ story. The biblical stories are a part of the common grace God has given to all people—people of different faiths or no particular faith.

There is a Jewish way of looking at scripture that I would like to appropriate as I explain the place of Christ in the whole biblical narrative. Most Christians have a linear view of the Bible, seeing it as moving from promise to fulfillment:

Creation—Jewish Scriptures—Christ—New Testament—Completion

Sometimes Christians have been willing to discard the Hebrew Bible altogether, forgetting that Jesus said, "I have come not to abolish the law and the prophets but to fulfill them" (Matthew 5:17).

A more Hebraic way of looking at scripture is to see it as a set of three concentric circles:[7]

The innermost circle is the Law, or Torah, the five books of Moses. This is the foundational center of all else—the oldest part and the heart of God's revelation. The second circle contains the Prophets (*nebi'im*). These include four "former" prophetic texts—

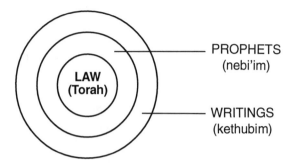

Joshua, Judges, Samuel, and Kings; four "latter" prophetic texts—
Isaiah, Jeremiah, Ezekiel, Daniel; and the Twelve so-called minor
prophets. The second circle comments on, applies, and extends the
Torah of God. It is nothing without the first circle. The third circle
is called the Writings (*kethubim*), which include books like Psalms,
Proverbs, Song of Solomon, and Job. This third circle comments
on and expands what has been revealed before in the Torah and
the Prophets. The core is always the Torah; the other circles revolve
around it.

I think of the New Testament (*euangelion*) as the fourth circle.
I use the Greek word *euangelion*, or "gospel" (literally, "good
tidings"), for this body of literature.

This fourth circle, the New Testament, is made up of witness
to the Christ it calls Messiah (*Christos*) and Lord (*Kyrios*). For
Christians it is the fulfillment of the Law, the Prophets, and the
Writings, but it has no thought of abolishing them. (In Luke the
risen Christ enumerates the three spheres of revelation—the law
of Moses, the prophets, and the psalms—and speaks of their
fulfillment in him [Luke 24:44].) Each circle has its own place and
its own integrity. In my retelling of the Hebrew stories I will refer

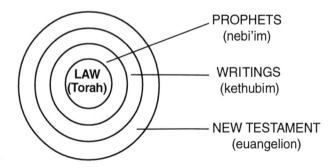

to Christ images as they reverberate in my mind with images, correspondences, patterns in these stories. But these applications and allusions do not deny the truthfulness and integrity of the stories apart from the Christ event.

So as we proceed, I have two complementary models in mind: a linear promise/fulfillment motif and a concentric circle motif, in which every layer is honored as a form of revelation.

Our lives must find their place in some greater story or they will find their place in some lesser story. Our contemporary postmodern world is a world of a thousand stories and a thousand gods. And these stories often become splintered images, brilliant, excitable, beautiful perhaps, but separated from any larger narrative to give them meaning and truth. Poet Desmond Egan in his provocative work *The Death of Metaphor* asserts that we in this century have witnessed the "dying of metaphor."[8] Postmetaphorical verse is the "poetry of the image" in which images used unmetaphorically (that is, pointing to nothing, referring only to themselves) are all we have left. If, as poet Richard Wilbur says, metaphor "is the main property of poetry,"[9] then the death of metaphor is a grievous wound to poetry itself, but more than to poetry, to our ability to picture the world in coherence and meaning. Is there a connection of things? Is there any connection between this physical world and an eternal realm of justice, truth, beauty, and goodness?

In the present culture of media and the arts there is an obsession with the image. We are overstimulated by sound and sight, a bombardment of images without cohesion or meaning—a crucifix in a Madonna video; a Mapplethorpe calla lily; Georgia O'Keefe's painting of a parish church, Rancho de Taos (a visual icon for trendy southwestern art); a Nike swoosh; a minimalist repetition of musical phrases or words in music or poetry that ends in self-referential isolation.

To give ourselves over to these lesser stories and images is to live a life diminished and fragmented. The purpose of scripture is to unite us with our Maker and to invite us into God's world of justice, grace, peace, order, hope, and mercy, where God is making us and all the world whole. It is the story itself that moves us into its sacred sphere.

In his deeply moving book on the great Hasidic masters, *Souls on Fire,* Elie Wiesel transmits this rabbinic story:

> When the great Israel Baal Shem Tov [Master of the Good Name] saw misfortune threatening the Jews, it was his custom to go into a certain part of the forest to meditate. There he would light a fire, say a special prayer, and the miracle would be accomplished and the misfortune averted.

Later, when his disciple, the celebrated Maggid of Mezeritch, had occasion, for the same reason, to intercede with heaven, he would go to the same place in the forest and say: "Master of the Universe, listen! I do not know how to light the fire, but I am still able to say the prayer." And again the miracle would be accomplished.

Still later, Moshe-Leib of Sassov, in order to save his people once more, would go into the forest and say: "I do not know the prayer, but I know the place and this must be sufficient." It was sufficient and the miracle was accomplished.

Then it fell to Israel of Rizhin to overcome misfortune. Sitting in his armchair, his head in his hands, he spoke to God: "I am unable to light the fire and I do not know the prayer; I cannot even find the place in the forest. All I can do is to tell the story, and this must be sufficient." And it was sufficient.[10]

God made humankind because he loves stories, Wiesel concludes.[11] The Hasidic masters believed in the transformative power of stories: everything becomes possible by the presence of someone who knows how to listen and love and give of themselves.[12]

Shema Y'Israel—Hear, O Israel—is the ancient call to be transformed by God. Redemption of humanity and earth hang on our discovering how to be a listening community formed by the story it hears.

Notes

1. William Bennett's program to teach character through moral-based narratives (*The Book of Virtues*) and its many spin-offs are examples of the educator/moralist approach. Steven Crites's philosophical approach to the essentially "tensed" (past, present, future) character of human existence is developed in "The Narrative Quality of Experience," *Journal of the American Academy of Religion* 39 (1971): 291-311. For an ethicist's approach, see Stanley Hauerwas, *A Community of Character* (Notre Dame, Ind.: University of Notre Dame Press, 1981), p. 9ff.; 129ff. Theologians have made narrative theology a major contemporary concern; see Amos

Wilder, "Story and Story World," *Interpretation* 37 (October 1983): 359f.; John Shea, *Stories of God: An Unauthorized Biography* (Chicago: Thomas More, 1978); James McClendon, *Ethics* (Nashville: Abingdon, 1988), to name a few.

2. Northrop Frye enumerates the seven major stages of the great narrative code as creation, exodus, law, wisdom, prophecy, gospel, and apocalypse. See Frye, *The Great Code: The Bible and Literature* (London: Ark Paperbacks, 1983).

3. As cited by A. S. Byatt, *Passions of the Mind: Selected Writings* (New York: Vintage International, 1993), p. 215.

4. Elie Wiesel, *Messengers of God: Biblical Portraits and Legends* (New York: Random House, 1976).

5. Elie Wiesel, *Souls on Fire* (New York: Summit Books, 1972), p. 260.

6. C. G. Montefiore, *A Rabbinic Anthology* (London: Macmillan, 1938), p. xvi.

7. This insight was given me by Oxford University professor John Barton in a series of lectures during the summer of 1984.

8. Desmond Egan, *The Death of Metaphor* (Gerrards Cross, England: Colin Smyth, 1990), pp. 13-20.

9. William Packard, *The Poet's Dictionary: A Handbook of Prosody and Poetic Devices* (New York: Harper & Row, 1989), p. 121.

10. Wiesel, *Souls on Fire,* pp. 167-68.

11. Elie Wiesel, *The Gates of the Forest* (New York: Holt, Rinehart & Winston, 1966).

12. Wiesel, *Souls on Fire,* p. 257.

Excursus: On the Translation and Interpretation of Sacred Texts

There are two major ways to translate a sacred text—two translation strategies. The first strategy is to make the original language of the text as easy as possible for the reader to understand in his or her own accustomed mode of thinking and talking. The second strategy is to force the reader to enter into the strangeness of the ancient text and its world. The first way helps the ancient text enter the reader's linguistic world; the second way enables the reader to enter into the foreignness of the text's linguistic world.

Both ways are important strategies of learning, and both are necessary in the interchange of understanding that is the act of translation. One strategy is to make the strange familiar; the other is to make the familiar strange. Learning uses an alternation of the two.

Think of these two ways as the opposite ends of a spectrum. The major translation tradition of the Bible into the English language—the King James Version (1611), the Revised Standard Version (1947, 1952), and the New Revised Standard Version (1989)—favors the first approach of helping the ancient text enter into our linguistic world. The proliferation of modern language vernacular translations and paraphrases, for example, the American Bible Society's Today's English Version and *The Living Bible* paraphrase, carry this strategy to its most extreme pole and move to the end of the spectrum as they seek to make the strange familiar. Let's put the latter two at one end of the spectrum.

The Jerusalem Bible and New Jerusalem Bible (which began as a French translation) move in the other direction, toward the presentation of the peculiar and strange character of the ancient texts, the use of Yahweh instead of LORD being one example. Everett Fox's brilliant new translation of the first five books of the Bible, *The Five Books of Moses*,[1] moves even closer to this other end of the spectrum as it seeks to preserve the differentness of the ancient Hebrew text. Fox forces us to enter *its* world rather than accommodating its translation to *our* world. Fox, a professor of Judaica at Clark University (who has been working on this translation for twenty-seven years), gives to us a most helpful alternative to the first (and most predominant) way of translating scripture. Novelist and professor Reynolds Price, whose own translations of scripture are a provocative blending of the two approaches,[2] says of Fox's work, "No other version since the King James Version . . . has trusted the order and music of the bare Hebrew so implicitly. . . ."[3]

Translators of scripture have struggled with these issues for at least twenty-three centuries. (The Jewish scriptures were being translated into Greek around the third century B.C.E., culminating in the Septuagint.) How do we translate a text and make it accessible to readers' understanding across centuries and cultures without accommodating its meaning to our world? Yet unless we risk the accommodation to our tongue and mind that translation risks, how can we hope to bridge the gulf of understanding?

In this book I will make use of both translation traditions, using primarily the New Revised Standard Version from the first school of thought and Fox's translation from the second. Occasionally I will use another translation or supply my own.

* * *

These issues of translation move directly into issues of interpretation. A general rule of translation is, "Every translation is an interpretation." You cannot move from one language into another without taking interpretive leaps. This is the reason that in traditional Islamic belief the *Qur'an* cannot be translated. Just as any image or representation of God is forbidden in Islam, so is translation, since translation implies an interpretive process. But such a belief employs the false literalism of fundamentalism. It assumes that sacred texts are exact representations of God's will and word. If this is one's belief, then any translation is unacceptable, and only one "approved" interpretation is allowed—and forced on all by the "keepers" of the faith.

I propose another understanding. Sacred texts are *verisimilitudes* of God's will and word. They point to the divine, but they are not themselves God. The Bible uses human words and thoughts and therefore cannot be in and of itself divine. The Bible is, to use Raymond Brown's phrase, "the human word of the Almighty God."[4]

This understanding avoids the extremes of both fundamentalism (the angry child of modernity) and postmodern deconstructionism. Fundamentalists assert that the text *is* God; deconstructionists say there is nothing but the text.[5] One equates the text with God; the other says there is no God or final realm of truth or meaning to which the text points.

My approach assumes the possibility of a text containing many meanings. Fundamentalism limits the text to only one meaning, which is of course in its sure possession. Fundamentalism must have not only an inerrant Bible but also an inerrant interpretation. The psychology of fundamentalists is that they must themselves be inerrant.

But there can be no one perfect interpretation or meaning of a sacred text, for our human minds are finite and we're reaching for infinite truth. The biblical text has many meanings—multiple layers of meaning. If we take this approach, we may begin to open the Bible again.

Bill Moyers's Genesis project on public television and in book form[6] has tapped a spiritual interest among people today for a new contact with sacred texts. It is a search for the God behind the texts, or at least for the better, truer part of ourselves that the scriptures may reveal.

Moyers's work was inspired by a communal study of Genesis that was being led by Jewish Theological Seminary professor Burton Visotzky. Those who sat with him and read and "searched out" the meanings of Genesis together were not the usual "faithful" but writers and editors from a variety of faith backgrounds. Lore Segal, one of the participants, commented in *The New York Times* (6 March 1987), "These are the best conversations going on in New York City at this moment."

Visotzky led the study using an approach to scripture outlined in his *Reading the Book: Making the Bible a Timeless Text.*[7] The rabbinic way of reading and interpreting scripture is called *midrash*, which means "searching out" the meanings of the text. I say meanings, plural, because this kind of study presupposes that there are many correct readings of scripture, and no one reading can "exclusively corner a text." Rabbinic tradition says there are at least seventy facets to each word of scripture.

Visotzky's approach, and my own, is that there is a "divine valence," or divine intention, underlying every text. But we cannot completely grasp it with our finite minds. Therefore we search out the meanings of the text in order to draw closer to the divine meaning. In Visotzky's words, "Freed from the constraints of finding one correct interpretation, they [the rabbis] uncovered the infinite truths intended by the Infinite Author of the text."[8]

Narratives by their nature are "multivalent"; they have "many meanings" that touch different levels of our lives and address the different issues brought by the hearer of the story. Too often religious communities rush to assign one meaning or moral to the story and close out other, deeper, truer possibilities. Master storyteller Marie Shedlock, in her classic work *The Art of the Story-Teller*, said this:

> Pointing out the moral of the story has always seemed as futile as tying a flower onto a stalk instead of letting the flower grow out of the stalk, as Nature intended. In the first case, the flower, showy and bright for a moment, soon fades away. In the second instance, it develops slowly, coming to perfection in fulness of time because of the life within.[9]

The rabbinic tradition spoke of *two* Torahs: the written Torah and the oral Torah. The oral Torah was as important as the written Torah. The oral Torah served, in one scholar's estimation, "the function of keeping the canonical written Bible a fluid text through endless commentary and interpretation."[10] A fluid text is less likely to become an idol. Idols are dead, fixed representations of God, and our interpretation of scripture can become an idol as surely as a carved wooden figure on a shaman's altar.

The oral Torah, that is, the Torah read and reread, interpreted and reinterpreted in community, has helped keep the written Torah alive as the living word of God. This book follows in this tradition that acknowledges a written Bible and an oral Bible; the latter, in its ongoing searching out of scripture, keeps the scripture alive.

This book invites you to enter the world of the sacred texts of Hebrew and Christian scripture. Its world is essentially a narrative world, and its stories follow the sweep of its narrative line. The narrative essays that follow invite you to a "leap of faith," which philosopher Paul Ricoeur termed "the second naiveté."[11] This second naiveté is different from the first naiveté of childhood, for it is the simplicity that lies *beyond* complexity, not this side of it. It adopts the "wager of faith" that says, I will give myself over to the truth of the narrative in the hope that I will meet the God of the story there. Jesus of Nazareth said, "Unless you become like a child, you shall not enter the kingdom of God." The second naiveté is a kind of "becoming as a child."

Welcome to *GodStories*.

Notes

1. Everett Fox, *The Five Books of Moses*, vol. 1 (New York: Schocken Books, 1995).

2. Reynolds Price, *A Palpable God* (San Francisco: North Point, 1985) and *Three Gospels* (New York: Scribner's, 1996). Price seeks a close to literal translation of sacred texts, hoping to capture the peculiar character and sound of these texts. And he is largely successful. But his own brilliant gift of simple but exceptional English vernacular speech, the uncommon use of common words, makes it more accessible to our ears than might normally be delivered by one with the same intention but with less giftedness in the English language. For example, "he saw the sky torn open" (Mark 1:10); "At once Jesus, knowing in himself that his streaming power had gone out of him" (Mark 5:30); "at once they were astonished with great wildness" (Mark 5:42) [pp. 87, 96, 97, *Three Gospels*].

3. Reynolds Price, "In the Beginning Was the Word—And They've Been Arguing about It Ever Since," *New York Times Magazine,* 22 October 1995, p. 65.

4. Raymond E. Brown, *The Critical Meaning of the Bible* (New York: Paulist, 1981), p. 1.

5. Cited in Sallie McFague, *Models of God: Theology for an Ecological, Nuclear Age* (London: SCM, 1989), p. 23.

6. Bill Moyers, *Genesis: A Living Conversation* (New York: Doubleday, 1996). This interest in sacred texts is also evidenced by a burgeoning number of books on sacred texts: Avivah Zornberg's *Genesis, The Beginning of Desire: Reflections on Genesis* (New York: Doubleday, 1996); Burton Visotzky's *Reading the Book* (New York: Doubleday, 1991); Stephen Mitchell's *The Book of Job* (San Francisco: North Point, 1987), *Genesis,* and *The Gospel of Jesus: A New Translation and Guide to His Essential Teachings for Believers and Unbelievers* (San Francisco: HarperCollins, 1991); Reynolds Price's *A Palpable God* and *Three Gospels; The Logia of Yeshua: The Sayings of Jesus,* trans. Guy Davenport and Benjamin Urrutia (Washington, D.C.: Counterpoint, 1996); *The Roaring Stream: A New Zen Reader,* ed. Nelson Foster and Jack Shoemaker (Hopewell, N.J.: Ecco, 1996).

7. Burton Visotzky, *Reading the Book* (New York: Doubleday, 1991), see esp. pp. 1-21, 225-40.

8. Ibid, p. 228.

9. Marie L. Shedlock, *The Art of the Story-Teller* (New York: Dover, 1951), p. 60.

10. Jose Faur's thought cited in Visotzky, p. 227.

11. Paul Ricoeur, *The Symbolism of Evil* (Boston: Beacon, 1969).

1

The Long Mercy:
The Biblical Story from
Genesis to Revelation

If we, and indeed all history, are the story of God, the Hebrew and Christian scriptures tell that story. Northrop Frye has divided this "Great Code" of truth and meaning into seven stages, or phases, of revelation: creation, exodus, law, wisdom, prophecy, gospel, and apocalypse. (In his mind these are primarily genres of literature that have a unity of narrative and imagery.[1])

In my own schema the consecutive phases are more than stages of revelation or genres of literature. They are also historical phases and spiritual seasons that we and all humanity traverse, past, present, and future. I enumerate nine of them as I take us from Genesis, the beginning of the Hebrew Bible, to Revelation, the close of the Greek New Testament.

To attempt this "Reader's Digest condensation" as one essay is a bit preposterous; and such a compression may tell more about this writer than about the Bible. But I take the risk. I take it with the conviction of the essentially narrative character of scripture and in the desire to get its narrative form out in some simpler form to the reader. And I write in the hope that in the end what the reader will get most is not the personality of the writer but the character of the Book and its God. In Martin Buber's *Tales of the Hasidim* we receive this guidance:

I shall teach you the best way to say Torah. You must cease to be aware of yourselves. You must be nothing but an ear which hears what the universe of the word is constantly saying within you. The moment you start hearing what you yourself are saying, you must stop.[2]

Creation

The biblical story begins at creation's dawn: *In the beginning God created the heavens and the earth.* God spoke, and from his mouth the world came to be. God spoke and life came forth from nothingness; God spoke and *cosmos* was formed from chaos. And God looked on what God had created, blessed it, and called it *good.* Our lives and the life of the universe begin in what Matthew Fox calls "original blessing."[3] The universe is not the random act of blind molecules and history or the theater of the absurd. Creation is the good act of a good God.

But the creation account is bolder still. It says that the human race is crown of God's creation, the glorious climactic work of the sixth day. It is as if the universe was made with us in mind: God made for us a garden of a home on a jeweled planet and placed us in it.

That is how the biblical story begins—with the astonishing notion that this vast universe is the creation of a good God and that God gave us this world saying, "Here is your home. It has all you need to flourish as my children. Take good care of it. It is made for you." The implications of all this are staggering: creation is to be enjoyed, not despised or destroyed. And since God has given it to us, we must take responsibility to care for it with him.

Eden's story describes our early relationship with God as communion, full and free. The One who shaped us from the clay and blew into us his own breath also walked with us in the cool of the day. Original Blessing.

The Fall

Then came the Fall and what theologians have called "original sin" (a doctrine with powerful and ambiguous consequences in the history of religion). The story of the Fall is not about just one man and one woman, Adam and Eve; it is about us all. It tells of one man and one woman who fell and of the way we all tend to fall. It depicts how we all negotiate with what Reynolds Price calls "our loyal flaws."[4]

A suggestion came to the first couple's heart, delivered by a wily serpent, that God did not really have their best interests at heart, that the rules were not fair and that God gave them only to keep Adam and Eve from gaining equality with God. "You can be like gods," said the serpent. "Just eat of the forbidden tree of the knowledge of good and evil." Adam and Eve both jumped at the chance, disobeyed God, and ate the fruit. So began the Fall, but it was far from over. It is the tumble we, all of us, take.

The fruit stands in every age as the temptation to be like God, to know everything, and to be able to do anything—in short, to live in a world without limits and to be done with this rule-making God.

From the original *shalom* (the Hebrew word meaning "peace, wholeness, well-being") of the Garden came the wilderness of warfare, the advent of discord, division, distrust, and dis-ease, the age of anxiety, estrangement, and apartheid. What God had brought together, we tore asunder. What God created we turned back to chaos. And naked we ran and hid. When God found them, the man blamed the woman and the woman blamed the serpent.

At this point God could have given up on both us and creation. But God committed God's self to be faithful to us whether we were faithful or not. God determined to do whatever had to be done, to give whatever had to be given so that we and all creation might flourish. God could have turned away but did not. The Hebrew people expressed this through their favorite verse, Exodus 34:6 (the John 3:16 of the Hebrew Bible): "The Lord, a God merciful and gracious, slow to anger and abounding in steadfast love and faithfulness."

The key word they used to describe the character of this God was *hesed*, the faithful loving-kindness of God, the steadfast, stubborn, never-giving-up-no-matter-what love of God. What God told King David would be perhaps the dearest word of all: When you sin, you will suffer human consequences, but I will never take my steadfast love, my *hesed*, from you (see 2 Samuel 7:14-15). The long mercy.

Covenant

God also showed his faithfulness through covenant, as God entered our lives and said, "I will be your God if you will be my people." God made a creation covenant with Adam and Eve, and God made a covenant with Noah marked by a rainbow, a call to end human bloodshed (Genesis 9:8-17). God made a covenant with Abraham and Sarah and blessed them and their promised descendants—not for their sake alone but that through them all the families of the earth might be blessed (Genesis 12:3). We can read scripture as a succession of covenants—with God always giving us another chance and calling us to ever deepening relationship and responsibility. Covenant stands for the free, trusting agreement between God and humankind.

Exodus and Torah

The most dramatic revelation of God's *hesed* in the Hebrew Bible was through "exodus," the story of the deliverance of the Hebrew people from slavery in Egypt. God wants none of earth's children living in the yoke of slavery, so God is eternally, forever historically at work to liberate the oppressed and to crush the oppressor, to open the door of every prison so that every person might flourish.

Next God revealed his love through the giving of *Torah*, the living law of God that teaches us how to live fully and freely. It is no accident that exodus and Torah are joined. On Mount Sinai God said, I am the God who set you free from Pharaoh; now I will teach you how to *stay* free:

> You are not to have other gods before me.
> You are not to make any graven image.
> You are not to take the name of the Lord your God in vain.
> Remember the sabbath and keep it holy.
> Honor your father and your mother.
> You are not to kill.
> You are not to commit adultery.
> You are not to steal.
> You are not to bear false witness.
> You are not to covet.
>   —Exodus 20:3-17, author's paraphrase

The story goes that the people accepted the Ten Commandments. But not easily. Rabbi Abraham Heschel comments:

> Man had to be expelled from the Garden of Eden;
> he had to witness the murder of half of the
> human species by Cain;
> experience the catastrophe of the Flood;
> the confusion of the languages; slavery in Egypt
> and the wonder of the Exodus,
> to be ready to accept the law.[5]

But the acceptance did not last long. We would not keep Torah. We called it a new slavery and ran from it. Priests did not help; they expanded the Ten Commandments into 613—365 negative ones for the days of the year and 248 positive ones for the number of bones in the male body! Neither saint nor CPA could keep count. Torah was trivialized by some, remade into a prison by others, domesticated by some, ignored by the rest.

The Rise and Fall of Nations and the Prophetic Vocation

Human pride and human anxiety being what they are, Israel's people wanted to be a nation like all the other nations of the world. So they elected Saul their first king. By doing so they largely forgot that God was their true king. "Our only king is Yahweh!" was the impassioned message of the prophets as they tried to remind the nation and its rulers of what they had forgotten. As the Bible tells the story of Israel, it tells the story of all nations. They all rise; they all fall. Here is the truth the Bible tells: God has a plan for nations and rulers—it is the way of justice and mercy. When they follow God's plan, they thrive; when they deviate from it, they self-destruct.

God would not sit passively as we turned away from the Torah. God's *hesed* sent prophets to revive its message. These prophets were not so much *fore-tellers* as *forth-tellers*. They *spoke forth* God's word. What they had in their hands was not a crystal ball but a megaphone! They called us back to the original intent of the law. The prophet Micah cut through the tangle of 613 rules and gave us the great prophetic summary: This is what God requires—to do justice and to love mercy and to walk humbly with your God (Micah 6:8). But the prophets did more than revive the law's true voice. They were sent to rebuke kings and priests who presided over God's law and perverted it, using it for their own purposes. They were sent to warn of imminent judgment unless the nation turned back to God and learned to love Torah again.

Their hearts burning with the word of God, the ancient prophets dreamed God's vision of a day when the Word of God would cover the earth as the waters cover the sea, of a day when the law of God would be written on the fleshy tablets of our hearts, when swords would be beaten into plowshares and we would learn war no more. But the prophets were beaten, jailed, and killed, their words forgotten by most, remembered only by a small company of disciples who hid their words in their hearts and kept them alive—for us.

Exile and Silence

What followed for Israel was exile—the nation defeated, the Temple destroyed. A new form of Hebrew faith was born in exile in Babylon, a faith without temple and priest, with only a "Bible" in their hands. So arose Judaism and synagogue worship.

Exile was (and is) a time of captivity and chastening, of figuring out what went wrong and why, a time of gestation, of waiting, of singing the Lord's song in a strange land, a time of hoping in what we cannot see.

God brought the children of Israel home from Babylon, but what followed was a period unlike any that had come before. It could be called the dark night of God's silence. Paul Tillich spoke of such times. They are seasons of God's judgment. We have so misused God's name and have so distorted God's word that for a time God stops speaking so that we can learn again the difference between the sound of God's voice and of our own. Tillich asks, "Could it be that in order to judge the misuse of his name within the church, God reveals himself by creating silence about himself?" Is God's silence "God's way of forcing his church back to a sacred embarrassment when speaking of him?"[6]

Such a time, so sacred history tells us, was the time between the Hebrew Bible and the New Testament, the last few centuries before Christ. The thought was widespread in the Judaism of that time that God had stopped speaking and that the Spirit had withdrawn. The age of prophecy was over. All you could hear, they said, was what they called a *bat qol*, the faint echo of a voice, the "daughter" of a voice. It was said of the great Rabbi Hillel, who lived in the century before Christ, that he was so good he would have been a prophet had prophecy not ceased. The season of silence.

Gospel*

Then a miracle happened—the miracle of all existence. The very word of God, the *Logos* through whom the world was created, "became flesh and dwelt among us, full of grace and truth" (John 1:14). As described by the first-century scholar Ignatius, he was "Jesus Christ, God's Son, who is his Word proceeding from silence." (Ad. Magn. 8:2)[7]

The Spirit of God had returned. The same Spirit that moved across the face of the deep and created the heavens and the earth moved across the face of a young teenager named Mary, and she bore a son of heaven and earth whose name was Jesus, which means "God will save his people."

The divine Word did not simply seize this man Jesus as God's word seized prophets of old. The divine Word *was* Jesus. The gospel, the good news of great joy to all people, was that the *hesed* of God had "tented" among us, bone of our bone, flesh of our flesh, in Jesus of Nazareth.

This man Jesus lived in the immediacy of God's loving care. He called God "Abba," the Hebrew child's first word for daddy, papa, and invited us to do the same.

He preached the kingdom of God (or God's reign), not as some distant hope but as an immediate, urgent, compelling, gracious possibility. The kingdom of God is *among* you, within you (*entos* you, in the Greek), in your midst, he said. In other words, the kingdom is *here* not there, is *near* not far, as near as your own breath, nearer.

Because the kingdom of God is the kingdom of *God*, it was best taught by Jesus in parables. He told hundreds of them—of a father

---

* (From the Greek word *euangelion* meaning "good news" or "good tidings." In English it evolved from *godspel* [good spiel or story] to *gospel*.

running to welcome home a prodigal son, of a Samaritan rescuing a Jew and fulfilling the law of love to neighbor and enemy alike, of the first becoming last and the last first, of lost coins found and hidden treasures stumbled upon, of foolish virgins, surprised workmen, and joyous wedding feasts, of choices that must be made, the *either/or* the kingdom places before us that means life and death to us.

Jesus not only taught the kingdom. Full of the power of the Spirit, he brought God's reign near in his very life. It came near in the way he healed the sick, opened blind eyes, and set free those locked in chains. It came near in his simple friendship with tax collectors and sinners, with outcasts, women, and children. When he ate and drank with them, the kingdom came near in joy. He was comfort to the weary, welcome to the despised, savior to all who wandered lost on the earth.

People never forgot Jesus once they glimpsed his face. Perhaps it was the compassion of his words: "Come unto me, you who are weary and heavy laden and I will give you rest." Or the glad welcome of his smile: "You're home" was what it said as it spread across his face. Perhaps it was the kindness of his eyes. Perhaps it was the authority of his voice. When he said, "Your sins are forgiven," you knew they were; they fell like dead scales from your skin, like weights from your shoulders, like tears from your heart.

Surely it was in the way he died. You might have guessed even if you had not already heard. A tumbling and fallen world would not welcome one such as he. Religious leaders hated him because his authority made theirs sound screeching and empty. Political authorities feared him because without his ever saying it, they knew he was King, and no king wants another, greater one around. So they—Jerusalem and Rome, priest and politician—conspired to kill him, and the mob wanting easy answers and quick solutions went drunkenly along. They put him to death: made of him a public spectacle, poked him up a hill, pressed into his skull a crown of thorns, and mocked him with a sign above his dying head that read "King of the Jews." Only a few heard him cry through parched lips, "Father, forgive them for they know not what they do" (Luke 23:34). And as he died, the world held its breath, or should have. We had crucified the only Son of God.

The darkness of our no to God lasted until the third day. Then came Easter morning, when God raised Jesus from the dead. God's encircling yes. It was the trumpet call of the victory of life over death, of love over all the hate we could muster. God raised Jesus from the dead to say to all who would see that God had won the victory over the powers of darkness, death, and sin.

And, yes, it was the sign of God's *hesed*, God's faithful loving-kindness. The New Testament found its own way to capture the meaning of this event, the gospel of Jesus Christ, his life, death, and resurrection: "For God so loved the world that he gave his only son that whosoever believes in him might not perish but have eternal life" (John 3:16). And the apostle Paul looked and said, "But God shows his love for us in that while we were yet sinners Christ died for us" (Romans 5:8).

The New Testament writers found their own word for God's *hesed*, the gospel come in Jesus. "Grace" they called it, *charis*, the free gift of salvation, the inconceivable mercy, the love that will not be stopped, a power within for a human kind of holiness. Jesus the Christ. In George Buttrick's words, "He is surprise of Mercy, outgoing Gladness, Rescue, Healing and Life."[8]

Church

The God who did not abandon us on the cross as we had abandoned Christ created the church as the ongoing incarnation of Christ, as his Body. On Pentecost Day the Spirit that moved across the face of the deep and created the heavens and earth, the Spirit that overshadowed Mary's flesh and brought forth Jesus, the Spirit that descended upon Jesus at his baptism and empowered his earthly ministry, let itself loose upon the church. And amid rushing wind and tongues of flame those who were gathered discovered that they were made one people out of many peoples, one tongue out of many tongues, "for in Christ there is neither Jew or Gentile, male or female, master or slave" (Galatians 3:28). The church was the miracle creation of God, a royal priesthood, all of us, a holy nation, for

> Once you were not a people,
>   but now you are God's people;
> once you had not received mercy,

but now you have received mercy.

—1 Peter 2:10

The church became the body of Christ, a community of peace and grace, *shalom* and *charis*, fashioned by God to tell his good news and to incarnate the love of Christ to all people for all time.

The story of the church is a play of shadow and light, a confounding mixture of faith and unfaith, discipleship and denial. Not only has it taken on Peter's confession, "Thou art the Christ," but also his impulsive and unpredictable nature, one moment a rock of faith, the next moment a series of shabby denials. The church has been the object of much praise and scorn throughout its history, but in truth it has been both far better and far worse than its critics know it to be. By the mystery of God's grace, it has been Christ's face to the world—his hands, his feet, and his heart. And it has also been Christ's betrayer, an anti-Christ, a mockery of his name and his face. But God in his steadfast love has been sure on his promise that the living Christ would be with us always, and this has resulted in the true church being present somewhere in all places and times.

Apocalypse

What is left? The Bible does not leave us with the halting step and faltering voice of the church. We are told the end of the story. Given visions by angels on the Isle of Patmos, John delivers to us the book of Revelation. Apocalypse means "unveiling," and what is unveiled is the end and culmination of all things.

Revelation (or the Apocalypse of John) pictures (it is filled with pictures) history as a fight to the finish between the forces of good led by the holy Trinity—God the Father, Son, and Holy Spirit, and the unholy trinity—the dragon, the beast, and the false prophet. The powers of darkness will rage until the final hour, and this reality warns against our illusion of inevitable human progress and our belief that we can bring the kingdom in by our power, intelligence, and goodness.

The book of Revelation was written during a time of great persecution, and it is God's message of assurance to us. God will win the final victory, even though there are times when this might seem impossible. Ours is a world where, as Frederick Buechner says, "The battle goes ultimately to the good . . . and where in the long run everybody, good and evil alike, becomes known by his true name."[9]

Christ shall come again, not in suffering love as in the first Advent but in shining, triumphant love. Christian and Jew shall at last join hands and welcome the Messiah.

The book depicts the Last Judgment, but we should not be afraid. The stained glass artistry of medieval cathedrals illustrates why. In the judgment scene the one on the throne is Christ. His hands, bearing the scars of the nails, are raised in blessing. The message? The One coming to judge is the same as the One who died for us.

The story pictures the end of time. In the words of J. R. R. Tolkien, it is a glimpse of "Joy, joy beyond the walls of this world."[10] There shall be a new heaven and a new earth, a new Eden where we will dwell with God and God with us. And God will wipe away every tear from our eyes and death shall be no more. Now we see through a glass darkly but then face-to-face, and we shall understand, finally understand, as we are now understood by God. Then shall be the supper of the Lamb; then shall be heard "the song of them that triumph, the shout of them that feast."[11]

It is God's plan fulfilled, Original Blessing become the Final Blessing. In the words of Julian of Norwich,

> All shall be well
> and all shall be well
> and all manner of thing shall be well.[12]

Coda

We learn in biology that "ontogeny recapitulates philogeny." This means that our body's development from fertilized egg to mature adult in some ways repeats the evolution of the species. We might also say that "biography recapitulates the Bible": our lives repeat the scripture's narrative. We live all the chapters at some point in our lives, as nations, communities, and individuals. Creation, fall, covenant, slavery/exodus and Torah, the rise and fall of nations, exile and silence, gospel, church, apocalypse—seasons in our lives as well as chapters in the Bible. But wherever we find ourselves in the story and wherever we've been, we must not forget the divine promise repeated throughout all the pages of scripture: this is a story headed toward redemption, and God and God's Christ and God's Spirit are with us, through it all, to the end.

The long mercy is what the story of God discloses about God. And long is the hope of God's faithful children who trust in God. *Hesed* (steadfast love) is the Hebrew word and *charis* (grace) the Greek word for this character of God: the steadfast, never-giving-up-no-matter-what love of God.

Langston Hughes, poet of the Harlem Renaissance, has a wonderful quatrain:

A gospel shout
And a gospel song:
Life is short
But God is long![13]

And so is God's mercy, as long as it takes . . .

Notes

1. Northrop Frye, *The Great Code* (London: Ark Paperbacks, 1983), see esp. pp. 61-62.
2. Martin Buber, *Tales of the Hasidim* (London: Thames & Hudson, 1956), p. 107.
3. Matthew Fox, *Original Blessing: A Primer in Creation Spirituality* (Santa Fe, N.M.: Bear & Co., 1986).
4. Reynolds Price, "Finding Work," in *A Common Room: Essays, 1954-1987* (New York: Atheneum, 1987), p. 18.
5. Abraham Heschel, *I Asked for Wonder: A Spiritual Anthology,* ed. Samuel H. Dresner (New York: Crossroad, 1983), p. 91.
6. Cited in James A. Sanders, *God Has a Story Too* (Philadelphia: Fortress, 1979), p. 77.
7. Cited in Amos Wilder, *Early Christian Rhetoric* (Cambridge: Harvard University Press, 1971), p. 1.
8. George A. Buttrick, *Prayer* (New York: Abingdon, 1942), p. 83.
9. Frederick Buechner, *Telling the Truth: The Gospel as Tragedy, Comedy, and Fairy Tale* (New York: HarperCollins, 1977), p. 81.
10. Cited in Buechner, *Telling the Truth,* p. 86.
11. Bernard of Cluny, "Jerusalem the Golden."
12. Julian of Norwich. This widely quoted line is adapted into modern English by the author. In context, here is her original statement: "Synne is behovabil [necessary], but al shal be wel al shal be wel & al manner of thyng shal be wele" (*Revelations of Divine Love,* ed. Grace Warrack [London: Methuen, 1950], p. 56).
13. Langston Hughes, from "Tambourines," in *Selected Poems of Langston Hughes* (New York: Random House, Vintage Classics, 1990), p. 29.

2

Genesis: The Beginnings

There are two creation stories in Genesis, not one. The first is
Genesis 1:1–2:4a. It is a poetic liturgy of creation. I can hear it
spoken to flute accompaniment. Walter Brueggemann says this
text is neither history nor myth; it is proclamation.[1] And poetry is
its tongue. "In the beginning God created the heavens and the
earth": the cadences of those words sound as natural as breathing.

The first truth of the creation story is that God is the maker of
all that is. Creation happens in six days, and for each of the six
days we hear the refrain:

> God said: Let it be
> And it was so
> And God saw that it was good.

So it happened with the creation of light, and day and night on the
first day;

> With the creation of the firmament that separated the waters
> on the second day;
> With the creation of the earth and its vegetation on the third
> day;
> With the creation of the sun, moon, and stars on the fourth
> day;
> With the creation of the creatures of sea and air on the fifth
> day;
> With the creation of land creatures on the sixth day.

God said, Let it be
So it was
And God saw that it was *tov,* good!

But that is not all that happened on the sixth day. Verses 26–27 mark the crowning climax of creation and are among the most important words of all scripture and human thought:

God said:
Let us make humankind in our image, according to our
  likeness!
Let them have dominion over . . . all the earth . . . !
God created humankind in his image,
in the image of God did he create it,
male and female did he create them.[2]

And when God made humankind, God did not look and say, as he said of the rest of creation, that it was good; God said, "It is *very* good, *exceedingly* good!"

The creation story combats false myths, ancient and modern. Creation is not the result of a war between the gods, with earth and heaven being the split body of the slain god, as in the Babylonian myth. It is not an evil material world created by an evil material lesser god, as in the gnostic myth. It is not the result of blind chance, a random accident of matter, as in the modern myth of scientism. It is *creation,* the good and purposive work of a good God.

God speaks the world into being and keeps speaking it into being in an ongoing process of creation. Genesis 1:1 tells of creation out of nothing—*original* creation. Genesis 1:2 speaks of creation out of chaos as the Spirit broods over the deep—*ongoing* creation. Listen to Everett Fox's translation:

When the earth was wild and waste,
darkness over the face of Ocean,
rushing-spirit of God hovering over the face of the waters.[3]

The story of creation underlines over and over that God liked what God saw and called it good: *tov.* God takes delight in creation. The last book of the Bible echoes the first: "Thou art worthy, O Lord, to receive glory and honor and power: for thou hast created all things and for thy pleasure they are and were created."[4] This story says that we and all creation are good and that with God's first breath God blessed us! Original blessing: in this the world began.

Where does your Bible begin? Many people whose spiritual lives have been taught according to what theologian Dorothee Soelle calls "the curse tradition" understand their Bibles to begin with chapter 3, with "the Fall" and what since Augustine has been called "original sin." But as Matthew Fox's work has reminded us, the universe began not in original sin but in "original blessing."[5]

The climactic work of creation was the creation of humankind in God's image. In our humanness we bear the likeness of God. What an astonishing thought! But this does not mean that we *are* divine. Avivah Zornberg represents the theological reserve of the Jewish tradition when she says that the image (*tselem* in the Hebrew) is "less than and not identical to the model."[6] We partake of the divine, and the divine image is in us all. But we are not—contrary to ancient and modern pantheist perspectives—in and of ourselves divine.

There has been through the years much conversation about what the image of God, or *imago dei*, is within us. Two comments are important. First, the *imago dei* partakes of both maleness and femaleness. Judeo-Christian tradition has perpetuated a male image of God, which is both unbiblical and idolatrous. It distorts and impoverishes our image of God. The creation account says that humankind's creation in the image of God necessitated both male and female.

Second, the creation of humankind in God's image as male and female suggests that the *imago dei* has something crucial to do with relationship, with communion and community. Daniel Day Williams has offered that the *imago dei* is the will to communion—our capacity to love.[7]

The first creation account moves on to say that the God who created us and blessed us also calls us to be partners with God in the ongoing work of creation. The original calling (Genesis 1:28) was twofold, first, "to be fruitful and multiply." Who said God's will was all work and no play? Our first calling is to the ecstatic communion of conception and the loving duty of child rearing. Our second calling is to "fill the earth and subdue it," to "have dominion" over the creatures of earth.

Inevitably we read this verse in the context of the ecological crisis and our willful destruction of nature. It has become a commonplace in intellectual circles to blame this verse in particular and Christianity in general for the human exploitation of the environment, as Lynn White has argued in his influential article "The Historical Roots of our Ecological Crisis."[8] But we could better argue that using Genesis to justify the exploitation of nature is a misuse of this scripture. The Hebraic tradition carries many warnings against our turning our "dominion" over creation into a destruction of it (e.g., Isaiah 5). To "have dominion" means to "order, rule, and care for,"[9] and this ordering, ruling, caring for points to the proper use of human power and knowledge.

Phillip Sherrard in his book *The Eclipse of Man and Nature* argues that modern science devoid of the dimensions of the transcendent and the spiritual leads to the dehumanization of humanity and the desanctification of nature. We humankind, he says, are called to be priests to the world, mediating between God and creation. We are truly human—we are who God made us to be—when we are like the priest who "offers the world to God in his praise and worship and who simultaneously bestows divine love and beauty upon the world."[10]

Wendell Berry, Kentucky farmer, philosopher, poet, novelist, and major prophetic voice to our times, expresses our sacramental vocation in God's creation with these words:

> To live, we must daily break the body and shed the blood of Creation. When we do this lovingly, knowingly, skillfully, reverently, it is a sacrament. When we do it greedily, clumsily, ignorantly, destructively, it is a desecration. In such desecration we condemn ourselves to spiritual and moral loneliness and others to want.[11]

The modern division between religion and science has been a tragic one, and one of the most tragic chapters in this history tells of the astronomer Galileo. When he inspected the heavens with his telescope and confirmed the new Copernican theory that the earth moved around the sun rather than vice versa, he was denounced as a heretic by the Church. On February 24, 1616, the pope's consulting theologians declared that the propositions of the sun's being at the center and the earth's revolving around it were "absurd in philosophy and formally heretical, because expressly contrary to Holy Scripture."[12] The intellectual cost to the church has been enormous. The division has placed the Bible and science in needless opposition, and it has pushed science to do its work cut off from a spiritual and moral dimension. The words of Nobel scientist Francis Crick, discoverer of the double helix structure of DNA, is an apt illustration:

> I myself, like many scientists, believe that the soul is imaginary and that what we call our mind is simply a way of talking about the functions of our brains. . . . Once one has become adjusted to the idea that we are here because we have evolved from simple chemical compounds by a process of natural selection, it is remarkable how many of the problems of the modern world take on a completely new light.[13]

Unlike that time in history when science needed to be set free from the shackles of religion and superstition, our day needs a new marriage of religion and science that allows scientific fact and moral and spiritual wisdom to work hand in hand. The creation story of Genesis should not be read in opposition to science, only in opposition to the places where science overreaches its vocation of discovering the empirical facts of existence and begins to make philosophical pronouncements about spiritual matters. (We should also mark any arrogant pronouncements that religion makes about matters of empirical science.) Science asks the *what* and *when* and *how* questions; religion asks the *who* and *why* questions.

The Genesis story goes on to say that creation was finished on the seventh day when God rested. *Shabbat,* the Hebrew word from which the word "sabbath" comes, means "to stop, to cease." God stopped working on the seventh day and calls us to do the same. The sabbath is our way of acknowledging that life is a gift and that this world and its blessings are not the result of the work of our hands. M. Tsevat says that on the sabbath he hands his life back to God, remembering that it is not his own.[14] The sabbath, in Walter Brueggemann's words, is "an antidote to the enormous anxiety we have about the fragility of the world." It shows that "God is not anxious about the world. On the seventh day, he doesn't show up at the office. He lets it be. That shows confidence on God's part that the world has coherence and vitality."[15]

The fact that God took the seventh day to rest and enjoy the work of creation also means that creation's purpose is not completed in work, but in joy. On this day we simply receive; it is the day we rest and play rather than work and produce.

> Thus were finished the heavens and the earth,
>   with all their array . . .
> God gave the seventh day his blessing, and he hallowed it,
>   for on it he ceased from all his work,
>   that by creating, God had made. —2:1-3[16]

"These are the 'begettings' of the heavens and the earth," concludes the first creation story, "when they were created." And from these origins we glimpse our own.

Notes

1. Walter Brueggemann, *Genesis* (Atlanta: John Knox, 1982), pp. 1-13.

2. Everett Fox, *The Five Books of Moses*, vol. 1 (New York: Schocken Books, 1995), p. 15.

3. Ibid., p. 13.

4. Revelation 4:11, King James Version.

5. Matthew Fox, *Original Blessing: A Primer in Creation Spirituality* (Santa Fe, N.M.: Bear & Co., 1986).

6. Cited in Bill Moyers, *Genesis: A Living Conversation* (New York: Doubleday, 1996), p. 19.

7. Daniel Day Williams, *The Spirit and the Forms of Love* (New York: Harper & Row, 1968), pp. 131-35.

8. Lynn White Jr., "The Historical Roots of Our Ecological Crisis," *Science* 155 (1967): 1203-7. White asserts: "Christianity . . . not only established a dualism of man and nature but also insisted that it is God's will that man exploit nature for his proper ends" (p. 1205). Science and technology now, in White's estimation, are out of control, and if so, "Christianity bears a huge burden of guilt" (p. 1206). So we shall, in White's words, "continue to have a worsening ecologic crisis until we reject the Christian axiom that nature has no reason for existence save to serve man" (p. 1207).

9. Brueggemann, *Genesis*, p. 11.

10. Phillip Sherrard, *The Eclipse of Man and Nature: An Enquiry into the Origins and Consequences of Modern Science* (West Stockbridge, Mass.: Lindisfarne, 1987), p. 40.

11. Wendell Berry, unpublished address, "The Gift of Good Land," p. 19. (Author's files.)

12. "Galileo," *Encyclopedia Britannica*, 11th ed., vol. 11 (New York: Encyclopedia Britannica Co., 1910), p. 408.

13. Cited in Sherrard, *Eclipse of Man and Nature*, p. 78.

14. In Moyers, *Genesis*, p. 14.

15. Ibid., p. 15.

16. Everett Fox's translation, p. 17.

3

The Second Creation Account:
Eden's Story

The second creation account begins with the second half of the fourth verse of Genesis chapter 2. It sounds more primitive than the first, like the product of tribal storytelling handed down in oral tradition. God is less transcendent here. He doesn't *speak* the world into existence; he literally gets his hands dirty with earth's soil.

"In the day that YHWH God made the earth and the heavens." A new name for God suddenly appears: *YHWH* (the name given by God to Moses). Scholars speculate that the name was pronounced *Yahweh*. In the tradition of the major English translations, from the King James Version to the New Revised Standard Version, the Hebrew word *YHWH* is translated as "LORD." Scholars refer to the writer of this second creation account as "the Yahwist," or "J," because the author consistently uses the name *Yahweh* for God.

In this second creation story the language is earthy and concrete:

> No bush of the field was yet on earth,
> no plant of the field had yet sprung up,
> for YHWH, God, had not made it rain upon earth,
> and there was no human/*adam* to till the soil/*adamah*—
> but a surge would well up from the ground and water all the
> face of the soil;
> and YHWH, God, formed the human (*ha adam*) of dust from
> the soil,

> he blew into his nostrils the breath of life
> and the human became a living being.[1]

God set *ha 'adam* (literally, "the human," or "the human creature") in a garden called Eden, which had every type of tree desirable to look at and good to eat. God called the human creature "to till and keep" the garden, words which suggest care for the earth, not exploitation of it. There was also the Tree of Life in the midst of the garden and the Tree of the Knowing of Good and Evil. God commanded that every tree could be eaten from except the Tree of the Knowing of Good and Evil. Eat of this tree, God said, and you will die.

Then God realized that there was something "not good," "not *tov*," about creation. "It is not good for *ha 'adam*, the human, to be alone." God had created other creatures to be on earth; still the human was alone with no *'ezer*, helper, companion, one "corresponding to him" (2:20, Fox). So God caused *ha 'adam* to fall asleep and took a rib from him and closed up the wound. Then YHWH, God, built from that rib a woman (*ishah*) and brought her to the human (*ha 'adam*). *Ha 'adam* said when he saw her:

> This-time, she-is-it!
> Bone from my bones,
> flesh from my flesh!
> —2:23, Fox

Renita Weems says "this is the first love song a man ever sang to a woman."[2] Love poetry began here as the human creature laid his famished eyes on the woman. The human finally had a companion, an *'ezer*:

> She shall be called Woman/*Ishah*
> for from Man/*Ish* she was taken!
> —2:23, Fox

Before there was only the human one, *ha 'adam*, translated by Phyllis Trible as "earth creature"[3] (literally, in a play on words, "the one," *ha 'adam*, formed from the soil, *'adamah*). Now there is woman, *ishah*, and there is man, *ish*. This part of the creation story ends with a beautiful picture: though two they become one, and though naked they are not ashamed.

This second creation story, much more than the first, pictures God in anthropomorphic images: God kneels in a muddy river bank shaping the human creature from the clay. One rabbinic story says God gathered soil from the four corners of the earth, white, sandy soil, red clay, rich black earth, and plowable brown earth, so that no people could claim Adam as theirs alone.

There is tension between the first creation story, in which God creates us male and female at the same moment, and the second story, which has God creating *ha 'adam* first and later creating woman, *ishah,* from one of *ha 'adam's* ribs. One may find here a suggestion of subservience, woman to man, but it appears much less in the text than in the tradition that has interpreted it. The Hebrew word used to describe the woman, *'ezer,* traditionally translated as "helpmeet" or "helper," may suggest to our ears a subservience, woman to man. But the word in other contexts in scripture means "deliverer" (Exodus 18:4. 1 Samuel 7:12, Deuteronomy 33). In this context, joined with the next word,"corresponding to him," *'ezer* suggests a relationship of equality, a companion, one who saves by completing.[4] If you look again at the Hebrew text, you see an earth creature, *ha 'adam,* that is not yet differentiated into male and female. When God creates *ishah,* woman, then *ha 'adam,* the earth creature, not only has a companion but is now described as a man, *ish.* Without woman (*ishah*) the human creature is not yet man (*ish*); he is the human (*ha 'adam*), lonely, with no companion (*'ezer*), and no one "corresponding to" or like him (2:20). As Westermann comments, "It is here that the creation of humankind achieves the goal intended by God."[5]

The second creation account does not end at this point, however. We see a man and a woman in the picture, and now we see a tree and its fruit—and a serpent with its body wrapped around the trunk of the tree.

Here begins the story of "the Fall," the fall of one man and one woman and the fall we all tend to take. Four centuries after Christ, the theologian Augustine called it "original sin," construing it as a "genetic" flaw transmitted sexually from generation to generation. The church has been wrestling with the issue ever since. I like the take on the subject that we find in the comic strip *Calvin and Hobbes.* Calvin asks Hobbes about "original sin": "Does it mean we are all born sinners?" Hobbes replies, "No, it just means we're all quick studies!"

Enter the serpent, the slyest and subtlest of creatures. The serpent begins by planting seeds of distrust and doubt, driving a wedge between *ishah* and her God. "Did God say you shall not eat of any tree in the garden?" The woman explains they can eat of any tree but one; if they eat of that tree, they will die. The serpent says, "You shall not die." He explains that the decree is God's way of keeping them in their place. "If you ate of the tree, your eyes would be opened and you would be like God." (We shall see that both God and the serpent are "right": Adam and Eve will not die physically, not immediately, but at this point spiritual death enters the world.)

The doubt has been created in her mind. We too chafe under prohibitions, commandments, boundaries, laws. We want the garden but without God; as Davie Napier put it: "No one wants the landlord with the rent, not even if the flat is free."[6] Knowledge is pleasure and knowledge is power, and we want all we can get. One scholar has translated the phrase "You shall know good and evil" as "You shall know everything from the best to the worst." This is our Faustian lust, to want to know everything, what one has called "the lure of infinity." And it is our undoing. She eats; he eats. Distrust has turned to disobedience has turned to judgment. And this judgment has a taste, a feel, a look. (Writer John Cheever says shame is the taste of a rusty blade in the mouth.)

They look at each other and see their nakedness, and, seeing their nakedness, for the first time they feel shame. They hide their bodies from each other, weaving fig leaves to cover their nakedness. When God comes walking in the garden in the cool of the day, they run and hide themselves from God.

God calls out, "Where are you?"

Adam responds, "I heard your sound and I was afraid, I was naked so I hid."

God asks, "Who told you you were naked? Have you eaten of the tree?"

Adam answers, "The woman whom *thou gavest* to be with me [is he blaming God here too?], *she* gave me [the fruit] of the tree and I did eat" (3:12 KJV). *Ha 'adam* answers by blaming the woman. No surprise here. (Contemporary conservative religion has raised this blaming to the status of a doctrine, naming Eve "first in the Edenic fall" and using this as a reason to exclude women from spiritual leadership.[7])

And the woman? She blamed the serpent: "The serpent beguiled me so I ate." The original "devil-made-me-do-it" defense.

What followed was banishment from the garden and a new existence "east of Eden." Here we see life under judgment, the terrible and real consequences of our behavior. Life east of Eden would now be like this: God would give us children, but childbearing and childrearing would be mixed with pain and sorrow; God would give us work, but work would be hard and filled with frustration; God would give men and women to one another but there would be in this primal relationship a "distortion of desire"—"Yet shall you desire your husband, and he shall rule over you" (3:16).

What God had designed to be a relationship of mutuality, equality, and joy would now be contaminated by control and domination, power struggle and mistrust, a battle of the sexes from Adam and Eve to Shakespeare's Kate and Petruchio to Hollywood's Tracy and Hepburn. And to strife even darker—family violence and sexual abuse, date rape and divorce court, Anita Hill and Clarence Thomas, O. J. Simpson and a thousand and one variations on the theme of desire and need that become mixed with domination, submission, control, abuse, rage, manipulation, and retribution. And because male and female are equally made and equals in sin, the culpability flows both ways.

The *distortion of desire:* sometimes bumbling, sometimes stupid, sometimes cruel, sometimes crazy, sometimes monstrous. It is wrapped around a very common human theme: The very people we need and love and desire (sometimes those on whom we depend on for our very lives) are the same people who can hurt us most terribly and whom we can harm most terribly.

Verse 20 says *ha 'adam*, the man, named his wife "Eve." This is the first time Eve is named. The name means "life giver," and God will be gracious to make her the mother of all the living. But one wonders whether Adam has usurped God's role in naming her. Was this an exercise of dominion God meant for us to have over the creatures but not over one another?

But God would not abandon us in this new existence; God

would still be gracious and giving. Together Adam and Eve bear children, no small mercy, and God gives to them coats of skin for clothes (3:21) and covers their shamed nakedness.

Life lived "east of Eden" is life with both blessing and curse. Rabbinic tradition tells this story as a cautionary tale to depict our two inclinations, "the good desire" (*yetzer hatov*) and "the evil desire" (*yetzer hara*) and to warn that we are given freedom to choose and must bear responsibility for our choices. Christian tradition, reading this story backward from the universal redemption in Christ, has needed to see in it a universal fall determinative for all. But it is not so much determinative for all as descriptive of all. We all live in the fallenness of creation.

We humankind long for Eden. Is it a memory encoded in our genes, embedded in our "collective unconscious," the inheritance of our whole human race? We "sigh for Eden," as Henry Vaughn, British metaphysical poet, pictured Adam:

> He sigh'd for Eden, and would often say
> Ah! what bright days were those?[8]

Frederick Buechner has captured Eve's longing: "Then sad and beautiful dreams overtook her which she would wake up from homesick for a home she could no longer even name, to make something not quite love with a man whose face she could not quite see in the darkness at her side."[9]

We also long for a way forward from the brokenness of the fall toward some redemption, some healing. Can wholeness happen east of Eden? Is there some heavenward hope? Here is the message of the New Testament: "Sin abounds but grace abounds all the more." This is the hope of poet David Bottoms in his southern lament, "In a U-Haul North of Damascus":

> Lord, what are the sins
> I have tried to leave behind me? The bad checks,
> the workless days, the scotch bottles thrown across
> the fence and into the woods, the cruelty of
> silence, the cruelty of lies, the jealousy, the indifference?
>
> What are those on the scale of sin or failure
> that they should follow me through the streets of Columbus,
> . . . What are these

that should find me half-lost,
sick and sleepless
behind the wheel of this U-haul truck parked in a field on
    Georgia 45
a few miles north of Damascus.
    *   *   *   *   *   *   *   *

Lord, why am I thinking about this? And why should I care
so long after everything has fallen
to pain. . . .
Could I be just another sinner who needs to be blinded
before he can see? Lord, is it possible to fall
toward grace? Could I be moved
to believe in new beginnings? Could I be moved?[10]

His question is ours: "Lord, is it possible to fall / toward grace?" We've heard the fearful phrase "fallen from grace." But here is God's good news: We all, you and I, the whole human running race, have, by the mercy of God, fallen toward grace.

Notes

1. Everett Fox, *The Five Books of Moses*, vol. 1 (New York: Schocken Books, 1995), p. 19.
2. In Bill Moyers, *Genesis: A Living Conversation* (New York: Doubleday, 1996), p. 12.
3. Phyllis Trible, *God and the Rhetoric of Sexuality* (Philadelphia: Fortress, 1978). I am deeply indebted to this book for a new acquaintance with the Hebrew texts of creation.
4. Ibid., p. 90.
5. Claus Westermann, *Genesis 1—11* (Minneapolis: Augsburg, 1984), p. 229.
6. B. D. Napier, *Come Sweet Death: A Quintet from Genesis* (Philadelphia: United Church Press, 1967), p. 18.
7. See Southern Baptist Convention resolution on women, Kansas City, 1984; (*S. B. C. Annual Report* [Nashville: Executive Committee of the S. B. C., 1984]).
8. As cited in William H. Willimon, *Sighing for Eden* (Nashville; Abingdon, 1985), p. 7.
9. Frederick Buechner, *Peculiar Treasures* (New York: Harper & Row, 1979), p. 35.
10. David Bottoms, *Armored Hearts: Selected and New Poems* (Port Townsend, Wash.: Copper Canyon, 1995).

4

Cain and Abel

As Willa Cather suggested, these early primeval stories lie like a faded tapestry deep in our consciousness. Our eyes catch sight of the two figures naked in the garden, a tree, its fruit, a snake, a casting out. Life east of Eden is mixed with pain; blessing and curse live side by side. Life as man and woman is marked not only by the possibility of ecstatic union but also by distortion of desire. What God created as a relationship of mutuality, equality, and joy is now intermixed with domination, manipulation, and distrust. We've moved from what Martin Buber called "I-thou" relationships to "I-it" relationships.

In this next story, from Genesis 4, we move from humankind as Adam and Eve to humankind as Cain and Abel, from man and woman before God to brother and brother before God. The story does not get prettier.

I

Chapter four of Genesis begins, "Now the man knew his wife Eve, and she conceived and bore Cain [*Kayin* in Hebrew]." The name itself describes the event from Eve's perspective: "I have gotten [or acquired] a man with the help of Yahweh." Do we sense here a distance between Adam and Eve? He "knew her"; she conceived and bore. But, "I have gotten," she says of her new son. It's as if they are in two separate rooms. The legacy of the fall continues on.

Along came a second son, Abel. One son became a tiller of the soil; the other son became a keeper of small animals. Cain the farmer, Abel the shepherd. The story has a thousand and one variations: one a rancher and the other a sod buster; one a hunter, the other a musician; one hard, the other smooth; one rugged, the other sensitive; one a pragmatist, the other a dreamer; one a warrior, the other a poet—a tale of two brothers, different as night and day.

In the course of time Cain brought an offering to the Lord from the fruit of his fields. Abel, following his brother, brought his own offering, the firstfruits of his flock. It is an elemental religious response to give to the God of blessing a portion of our blessings.

So far so good. But then we read, "And the Lord had regard for Abel and his offering, but for Cain and his offering he had no regard."

We are jarred by this sentence. Why would God accept one but not the other? Could it be that one offering was a more worthy offering? Was the spirit of one giver more worthy than the other? These are our questions but not necessarily those of the text. When reading an ancient biblical text, I keep at least these three presuppositions in mind. First, the narrator often knows more than the characters know. So to say that God preferred Abel's offering to Cain's does not mean that the two brothers got some immediate message from God to that effect. Second, the God behind the story knows more than the narrator. This means that even the narrator's main meaning is not the final meaning. The final meaning lies partially revealed, partially hidden in the mystery of God. Recognizing multiple meanings in a story is more reverencing to the holiness of God than straining after one meaning. Third, ancient Hebrew belief was founded on a radical monotheism. In that day everything was understood as coming from divine causation. The two options were polytheism, belief in many gods, or monotheism, belief in one God. A primal Hebrew theological assertion is "God is *one*." The rigorous monotheism of the Hebrew scriptures says everything that happens, happens by way of God, the good and the bad. When I read the ancient texts that say, "God caused this or that," what I hear is simply that "this happened."

Abel's offering, the text says, was acceptable to God, but Cain's was not. What if this is how it happened: Cain and Abel made their offerings. Afterward, Abel's flocks prospered and Cain's crops flopped. What we may well be observing in this story is the relative good and bad fortune of the brothers. How they read this inequality of fortune was that God accepted one's offering but not the other's.

Don't we all try to read God's action in all that happens? When things go well, we feel that God is pleased with us and is blessing us; when things go badly, we fear that God is displeased and has withdrawn blessing.

What if everything Abel touched turned to gold and everything Cain touched failed? Abel seemed to sail through life with infuriating ease; Cain worked himself to death and barely scraped by. The story is dealing with the inequity of fortune and accomplishment—and the havoc this plays with social and family relationships.

Cain looked at Abel's success and his own struggle and read it this way: God prefers Abel's offering to mine. God prefers Abel to me.

Cain's sense of being unblessed turned into the bitter fruits of envy and anger: "Golden Boy Abel," he smirked, "Effortless Abel, Able Abel, God's Pet. I work twice as hard as he does and look at the results: my crops are dry, shriveled, stunted. Abel's flocks multiply like rabbits and look like they graze on butter."

We see here the darkened heart of sibling rivalry. Mom loves you best; Dad loves you and not me. God prefers you to me. You're the blessed child; I'm the unblessed.

Perhaps we are seeing religious rivalry here too—and religious anger. We believe that God has favored another more than ourselves and that we must work extra hard to get God's blessing. Or perhaps another person may not be involved at all—we simply feel rejected by God and believe that we must go to extraordinary measures to change God's mind. This is why religious people sometimes harbor deep hostility toward God.[1] How can we not feel hostile, consciously or unconsciously, toward one who we feel has rejected us? And some religious teaching inculcates this feeling and sets up certain religious practice as a way of overcoming this elemental rejection. It is a tragic spiritual story: to try to win what God has already given, God's grace, which flows as freely as the sun that shines and the rain that falls to earth.

But life. Life is maddeningly unfair. Some people seem to lead charmed lives; others have trouble all their days. The hostility at the heart of some religion comes from the false teaching that if we worship right and believe right and behave right, then everything will turn out right. But it doesn't always work that way, and failed religion turns us bitter, bitter toward God and toward our sisters and brothers who seem to have it better. We become children of Cain.

II

The next verse notes God's awareness that trouble is brewing with Cain.

"Why is your face cast down, Cain? Why your pout?" Cain's face is long, and he averts his face from Abel's.

"If you do well, there will be a lifting up," God says. In other words, if you do well, your face will be lifted again, and you'll meet people's eyes again, most importantly your brother's eyes.

We can almost hear Cain snapping at God: "If I do well?! What do you think I've been trying to do? I work seven days a week, sunup to sundown. I'm good to my folks." (By the way, where are they, Adam and Eve, in this story? Was Cain's sense of being unblessed attached to how he felt treated by them?) "I make my altar sacrifice. And look, my crops are a disaster. What do you mean, If I do well? I'm doing all I can, thank you. Evidently that's not good enough. So don't talk to me about *attitude!*"

God warned Cain about his growing envy and anger. "If you do well, you will lift up that face." And added, "But if you do not do well, sin is crouching at the door; its desire is for you, but you must master it."

Here is a vivid picture of virulent sin: it is a power that desires to have you. Sin is a hungry lion waiting, ready to pounce. In other words, Cain, your anger is a devourer and envy will eat you alive. You must master it or it will be your master.

III

Next scene. Cain said to Abel, "Let us go out to the field." When they were in the field, Cain rose up against his brother and killed him. Up to this point in the Bible, death has been a concept, a

warning given to Adam and Eve, "Eat of this and you will die."
Here in this story death becomes concrete: a brother lies slain.

God appeared, and the exchange with Cain has echoed down
through the ruined corridors of time.

"Where is your brother?" God asked.

"How should I know?" answered Cain. "Am I my brother's
keeper?" It was a deflective, off-putting question: Am I my
brother's babysitter?

God would not be deflected: "What have you done!?" God
replied. "Listen, your brother's blood is crying out to me from
the ground."

There is no blood shed that does not cry to God from the
earth. Life and blood belong to God and God alone. And the
blood of all earth's children cries out its story to God—and to
the citizens of earth.

IV

The punishment is given: the ground soaked in Abel's blood will
not yield its sweet return of crops to Cain. He will be a fugitive
and a wanderer on the earth.

Cain said, "*My punishment is more than I can bear.* I will be open
game the rest of my life, tracked down until I am killed." Then
Cain says with tragic pathos, "I shall be driven from your face." [2]
This was not God's judgment but Cain's own self-damnation. God
heard his cry and answered, "Not so!" (God will not let us so easily
consign ourselves to damnation.) God put a mark of protection on
him. Even in judgment there is blessing. God would not take
Cain's life and repay evil for evil. God's ways are not our ways.
No "eye for an eye" from God. As Mary Gordon has commented:
"The terrible machine of vengeance is stopped."[3]

The story ends:

> Then Cain went away from the presence of the Lord
> and settled in the land of Nod—which means the
> land of wandering—east of Eden.

What was this mark God placed on Cain to protect him? Was
it as conspicuous as a tattoo, signifying: This man is God's, do not
harm? Was the mark something more subtle but just as terrible? A

vacant look in the eyes, a haunted, tormented look that said to all who came near, "No need to kill me; I'm already dead."

The rabbis say, "Cain's true punishment was this: He *unlearned* the meaning of *shabbat*," the sabbath, the experience of sabbath joy and rest in God.

He would be forever restless, living in the land of Nod, the land of endless restlessness, forever a fugitive, a wanderer, one who never expects to find home.

This story has become the human story:

> A man and a woman had two sons,
> Cain and Abel
> Isaac and Ishmael
> Jacob and Esau.
> A certain man had two sons,
> the younger asked for his inheritance
> and the older smoldered in anger out in the field.
> A certain God had two children,
> Sarah and Hagar
> Israel and Mohammed
> Jew and Christian
> Japanese and American
> Asian and African
> Hispanic and Indian.

The first murder was fratricide, and all murder since has been the killing of a brother, a sister. And the first war was a religious war: between two brothers and two altars. Some religious war is stoked with Cain's envy, "God prefers you to me," and it seeks to slay God's beloved. Other religious war is fueled by the fury of self-righteousness, "God prefers me to you." I have the truth, you do not, I am righteous, you are not—the sacred violence of Crusade and Inquisition.

V

What is the answer to Cain's anger and envy and to our religious violence? Only a religion of grace and the law of love.

Did Jesus have Cain and Abel (and their altars) in mind when he said: "You have heard that it was said to those of ancient times, 'You shall not murder'; and 'whoever murders shall be liable to judgment.' But I say to you that if you are angry with a brother or sister, you will be liable to judgment; . . . . So when you are offering your gift at the altar, if you remember that your brother or sister has something against you, leave your gift there before the altar and go; first be reconciled to your brother or sister, and then come and offer your gift" (Matthew 5:21-24)?

Did he have us in mind?

True religion is founded on the miracle of reconciliation—our reconciliation with God—and on the call to reconciliation—our reconciliation with our brother, sister, spouse, neighbor, enemy. Otherwise we, children of Cain, live in hostility toward God and in simmering enmity with others.

VI

The tapestry of origins moves to a picture of a flood, an ark, and a rainbow—and to a tower being built to heaven.

Noah's flood is a story often found in children's books, and every toy store seems to have its Noah and the ark toy set with miniature pairs of animals waiting in line. In truth this is a story with as much darkness and light as we can stand. It describes a time when the earth had become filled with violence. In deep sorrow God decided to undo creation and begin again. It is sobering to realize that not only God but also we, God's partners in the ongoing creation, have the power to undo creation, to turn our earth back to chaos.

God started over with Noah, a righteous man who heard God's call to be part of God's project of saving and remaking the earth. At God's instruction, Noah assembled his family and the pairs of animals into the ark and waited as the rains came and the waters covered everything. For forty days and nights it rained. Noah almost despaired of touching dry land again.

When the waters receded, Noah and his family knelt in the mud and made an altar. A new covenant was established. This one not only repeated the dual calling of the first covenant of creation—to be fruitful and multiply and to have dominion over the earth—but also added an injunction against violence:

> Whoever now sheds human blood
> By human hands shall his/her blood be shed

For in God's own image God made humankind.[4]

Along with the new covenant came a sign, a rainbow.

My bow I set in the clouds,
so that it may serve as a sign of the covenant between me and
the earth. . . .
Never again shall the waters become a Deluge, to bring all
flesh to ruin![5]

The rainbow. Old Testament scholar Gerhard von Rad notes
that "bow" is the same word used for a warrior's bow.[6] God
unilaterally disarmed. God put down the warrior's bow and
restrung it with all the colors of creation, the sign of a God who
was making peace, the God of *shalom*.

The tower of Babel is the last of the primeval stories in Genesis
1–11. In our folly and pride we wanted to build a tower to the
heavens. "Let us make ourselves a name," the builders said, "lest
we be scattered over the earth." (The text underlines the futility of
the plot in the details: bricks made of mud trying to reach heaven!)
Perhaps Reinhold Niebuhr was right: pride has its roots in anxiety.[7] To secure ourselves against the unknown, we build towering
cities with walls no one can break down.

But they always break down, and our pride leads to destruction. In Pieter Brueghel's sixteenth-century painting of the tower
of Babel the project of building the tower has completely dominated every aspect of the city's life. Its size completely dwarfs the
city and casts a shadow over the whole town. The tower looks like
a concentration camp. Pride and anxiety have issued into a totalitarian project. If you look carefully at the picture, you see almost
everyone conscripted into work; only three are not working.
Where is God's *shabbat*? Where is God?

What is God's judgment on the tower and its builders? God
baffles their language, and so the tower is named the tower of
"babble." And God scatters the people over the face of the earth.
It is the story often repeated: nations grow grandiose in their
design to rule the world and then self-destruct. Often their
language begins to show the signs of deterioration before the
walls and buildings. Language becomes untrue, obfuscating,

undependable—like the doublespeak of Orwell's *1984*. Its currency of truthful communication is bankrupt. It is babble.

From this moment on, the city acquires an ambiguous character in the Bible. It represents human accomplishment and human pride; our best and worst are mingled here. Sodom, Babylon, Jerusalem, Rome. They epitomize and magnify human striving, its successes and its failures.

Notes

1. See Paul Tillich, *The New Being* (New York: Scribner's, 1955), pp. 20-21.

2. I am indebted to Toni Craven (professor of Hebrew Bible at Brite Divinity School, Texas Christian University) for this translation and insight.

3. In Bill Moyers, *Genesis: A Living Conversation* (New York: Doubleday, 1996), p. 99.

4. My translation, Genesis 9:6.

5. Genesis 9:13-15; translation by Everett Fox, *The Five Books of Moses*, vol. 1 (New York: Schocken Books, 1995), p. 43.

6. Gerhard von Rad, *Genesis* (Philadelphia: Westminster, 1961), p. 134.

7. Reinhold Niebuhr, *The Nature and Destiny of Man*, vol. 1 (New York: Scribner's, 1964), p. 183.

5

Abraham: Friend of God

The God who created the world keeps creating it all over again with people who will listen to his call and his promises. He did so with Noah when the violence that began with Cain's murder of Abel escalated to cover the whole world. Now he does so again with Abraham and the calling of a people who will be named Israel.

Abraham's story is the story of the birth of a faith people. Faith will be called forth and tested through the emigration of a family, danger in new lands, childlessness, and the terror of the ritual sacrifice of a child. With Abraham faith begins and grows old, matures, and endures. A new chapter of human history begins.

I

Genesis 12:1 announces the call:

> Go-you-forth
> from your land,
> from your kindred,
> from your father's house,
> to the land I will let you see.
> I will make a great nation of you
> and will give-you-blessing
> and will make your name great.
> Be a blessing! . . .
> All the clans of the soil will find blessing through you![1]

Then the climactic words: "Abraham went as Yahweh had spoken to him."

Israel, and any people of God, are those to whom God speaks, those who stand before God and hear, and those who hearing, obey. Israel's elemental creed, recited every sabbath, begins *Shema Y'Israel*, "Hear, O Israel." Abraham responds to the voice of God like young Samuel did centuries later: "Here I am; speak, for your servant hears."

Faith begins there, in obedience, in hearing God's word and obeying—obedient *action*. Abraham became God's friend because what was important to God was important to Abraham. The book of Hebrews underlines this epochal moment:

> By faith Abraham obeyed when he was called to go out to a place which he was to receive as an inheritance; and he went out not knowing where he was to go. (Hebrews 11:8)

Along with the call came the promise, a blessing in three parts: the giving of a land, the making of a great nation, and the promise that through them God would bless all the world. Note that here is a blessing given in promise. Blessing in the ancient world was understood as good fortune already received: crops, flocks, and babies; health, wealth, and success. Abraham and Sarah begin a new kind of spiritual history—a people of faith who act in trust of a promise spoken but not realized, of a blessing promised but not yet here. It is faith as delayed gratification.

Abraham and Sarah rose and went as God called them to do. When they arrived at the new land, it was in the midst of drought. The land of promise was a land of famine. So they went to Egypt seeking food, a not uncommon story in the ancient Near East.

II

The next chapter could be called "When Faith Falters, We Falter." When Abraham and Sarah arrived in Egypt, Abraham anticipated that Pharaoh would desire his beautiful wife for his harem, even if it meant killing Abraham. So he perpetrated a cowardly deceit. He lied and passed her off as his sister. We don't like Abraham very much here. Martin Luther said of this act that Abraham "let the Word get out of his sight."[2] I think he let other things out of his sight too. Abraham stopped trusting in the promises of God to make of his descendants a great nation and tried to save his own skin by means of this deception. Sarah was taken into Pharaoh's harem. When Pharaoh discovered the ruse, he upbraided Abraham for his lack of ethics. (Pharaoh didn't like Abraham very much either. It's rather embarrassing for the pagans of the world to call God's people on the carpet for their lack of morality!) Remarkably, they were delivered from Pharaoh's grasp and returned to Canaan in safety. When we are faithless, God is faithful. And Abraham learns a new dimension of faith: resilience. In the face of our wrongdoing we admit our wrong and let God pick us up, brush us off, and put us back on the road of faith again.

III

Back from Egypt, Abraham faces a family crisis with his nephew Lot over who gets what of the promised land. Prosperity brings its problems. Multiplied flocks and herdsmen lead to a quarrel between Abraham's hired hands and Lot's. Who gets to graze where? Now we see the dimension of faith as magnanimity, a bigheartedness and openhandedness. Abraham went to Lot with a magnanimous solution. "There is plenty of land for both of us. Let there not be quarreling between family members," he said. Abraham took Lot to a place where they could see the full expanse of the land promised to them. "Look as far as you can see to the right and to the left, to the east and to the west," said Abraham. "You take your pick. If you choose the land to the east, I'll take the land to the west; if you choose west, I'll take east."

Lot looked to the west (what will become Judah) and saw rocky, desertlike expanses. Then he looked to the east at the fertile, watered plains of Jordan. He chose the rich plains of Jordan; Abraham got the leftovers.

The Yiddish language has terms that describe two kinds of people. A *schlemiel* is a person who goes through life spilling soup on people. A *schlemozzel* is the one who is spilled on.[3] A schlemiel takes advantage of people; a schlemozzel is the one who gets taken advantage of. One is a taker; the other one keeps getting taken. One's a pusher, the other a pushover. In the comic strip *Peanuts*,

Charlie Brown is the schlemozzel who keeps trying to kick the football Lucy is holding in place, and Lucy is the schlemiel who keeps pulling it away at the last moment.

When Abraham said to Lot, "You take your pick," Lot could have said, "No, Uncle Abraham, you are the eldest; you brought us here. You take your pick first." But no, Lot was the schlemiel and Abraham the schlemozzel. That's one way to read this scene, but it's not the only way. Another way is to say that Abraham trusted in God, so he could risk being magnanimous. He could be bighearted and generous because he knew that God was that way and that God would make good on his promises.

So the man whose faith faltered in Egypt proved its mettle in a family quarrel over land—no small feat if you've ever been caught in a family squabble over who gets what. As it turned out, the best-looking choice was not the best choice. A land of bounty can fall to great temptations. The plains of Jordan were populated by the cities of Sodom and Gomorrah. Their bounty led to a flabby spirituality that led to their destruction. We should take note. Alexander Solzhenitsyn, the Nobel Prize–winning Russian writer, has warned America that our easy affluence and taken-for-granted freedom have made us spiritually weak.

IV

The next scene pictures another dimension of faith, which has been called "faith as 'expostulation.'"[4] Friends trust each other enough to argue with each other. Abraham as a friend of God could argue with God over what he saw as injustice.

The dictionary defines "to expostulate" as "to reason with a person earnestly, objecting to his or her actions; to remonstrate." Abraham was the first in a long line of God's people with the boldness of faith to argue with God. When we argue with God, when we rail against God, we're searching for what Paul Tillich called the "God beyond God," the true God that's left after all our images of God are shattered.

In this scene God declares his intention to destroy Sodom and Gomorrah for their wickedness. Abraham, the text says, "stood before God"—as friends stand before each other and are free to question one another. He asked God, "Will you destroy the innocent

along with the guilty?" How can a righteous judge act unjustly?
Here is the conversation between Abraham and God:

> "Will you really sweep away the innocent along with the
> guilty?" Abraham asked. "Perhaps there are fifty innocent
> within the city; will you really sweep it away?"
> Yahweh replied: "If I find fifty innocent in Sodom, I will bear
> with the whole place for their sake."
> Abraham then spoke up and said: "I have ventured to speak
> to my Lord, and am but earth and ashes. But please listen.
> Suppose of the fifty innocent, five will be lacking—will
> you bring ruin upon the whole city because of the lack of
> *five?*"
> God replied: "I will not bring ruin if I find there forty-five."
> Abraham kept on with this line of questioning: "What O God,
> if there are forty?"
> "I will not destroy for the sake of the forty," God answered.
> "How about thirty?"
> "I will not do it if I find thirty."
> "Perhaps then there will be twenty?"
> "I will not bring ruin for the sake of the twenty."
> "Pray Lord," said Abraham, "do not be upset if I speak one
> more time. What if there are only ten?"
> God answered: "I will not destroy for the sake of the ten."
> (Based on Genesis 18:22-33)

The passage ends, "And Yahweh went his way when he had
finished speaking." But it was Abraham who had done most of the
talking, a man pleading justice in the courts of the Almighty. He
thus began a long and noble line of those who have engaged in
passionate argument with God and God's children about justice:
Moses, Jeremiah, Habakkuk, the psalmist, Job, Elie Wiesel, Martin
Luther King, Marian Wright Edelman.

Only a friend of God can stand before God in expostulation.

V

Next we come to the drama of the long-promised and long-
awaited child. Abraham and Sarah had gone many years without
a child, and Abraham was growing discouraged about their pros-
pects: "Lord, I will die childless and my house servant, Eliezer, will
be my heir!"

God hauled him outside the tent into the brilliant desert night and pointed to the heavens. "Look up at the stars, Abraham. Can you count them?!" Abraham was silent. Then God said, "So shall your descendants be." And Abraham trusted in God, and, as the next verse says, "God counted it as righteousness" (15:6). Abraham's radical faith would be echoed by Paul in Romans 4. It would be emblazoned on Reformation banners as sixteenth-century reformers struggled to renew dead faith in the church: *sola fide*—by faith alone.

Which leads us to the annunciation scene. One day three visitors appeared at Abraham and Sarah's tent. The text tells us that the three were in fact "the Lord." "Do not neglect to show hospitality to strangers," scripture says, "for in so doing some have entertained angels unawares" (Hebrews 13:2). Hospitality to strangers can become a visitation of God, an epiphany. You never know. God sometimes waits for us in the stranger, the one who is "other."

The three visitors turn out to be the Lord. *Sometimes God comes in threes!* And I'm not speaking tritely of trinitarian formulas, but of the ways God's goodness comes to us in circumstances of threes: a wife and two children or three daughters or three sons. A character in a movie spoke of three times God had saved him: when his mother died and his aunt became his surrogate mother; when he met his wife; and when the army took him in as a young man and gave him a career at a time when his life could have gone in several bad directions.

It is said that death or bad news comes in threes. Here's something better: God comes in threes, blessing comes in threes, good news comes in threes. Why not anticipate the good rather than the bad? There is a mystery of goodness in this world of God. Who knows how many blessings we've missed by not looking?

When Abraham had welcomed the three, they asked about Sarah and then made their pronouncement: we will come again in the spring and Sarah will have a son. It's the message God had delivered to Abraham in the preceding chapter, and when Abraham heard it, he "fell on his face laughing" (17:17). Here he was one hundred years old, and Sarah was ninety. Hardly candidates for parenthood! This time it was Sarah who, listening at the door of the tent, burst into laughter. "I am worn and he is old," she said to herself, trying to cover her laugh.

Here we come to the border of the possible and the impossible, which is often where faith is most alive. Sarah laughs at the incredibility of it all—and at the crazy, wild possibility of it all. She is laughing it off and laughing it up all at the same time. This reminds us of how the Gospel of Luke describes the disciples who met the resurrected Jesus: they "disbelieved for joy."

How often have we given up on what God can do? We've already decided for ourselves what is possible and impossible, having little faith in God and only the thinnest hope in our own human capacities.

But guess what happened? Sarah laughed all the way from the retirement home to the maternity ward. The only one not laughing was the bureaucrat at the Medicare office trying to process a claim for labor and delivery! Old Sarah laughed through morning sickness and late-night cravings; she laughed through swollen feet and Lamaze classes; and when she gave birth to that beautiful boy and he was placed at her breast, she said, "I will call him Isaac (which means "laughter"), for God has made laughter for me!"

> How silently, how silently, the wondrous gift is given;
> So God imparts to human hearts the blessings of his heaven.[5]

VI

Now a scene thick with mystery: there is terror and there is finally mercy. The Jews call it the "Akeda," the binding of Isaac.

It is a story we can scarcely bear to hear. Near the top of my list of questions for God is to ask God to explain the events of Genesis 22: "Why would you ask Abraham to sacrifice his son and drag him and Sarah and Isaac through all that terror only to deliver him at the end?" Is the message worth the harrowing journey? Would not they all be forever scarred by this late mercy?

The ancient stories of scripture are like old oil paintings in which you can see variations of the final version recorded there in the paint. "Pentimento" it is called, from "repent," for the artist changed his mind. Oil becomes more transparent with age, and in old paintings you can see the artist's previous versions of the scene. A figure has changed position or has been completely removed. A hand once here is there. So too the ancient texts. They are like a palimpsest, an old manuscript in which you can glimpse erasures of earlier versions of the words beneath the final copy. In scripture we catch glimpses of different "performances"[6] of the text and tellings of the story embedded there in the words on the page.

These ancient stories were told in different settings with different purposes over a wide expanse of time. The Akeda was told at one time to give the message that the era of infant sacrifice was over. Yahweh, the Lord, will never require of you as an offering the slaughter of your children. But in the last telling of the story of the binding of Isaac, the final version set in Genesis 22, the message was this: Do not ever lose faith in the promises of God. *God will provide.*

The story is terrifying and mysterious, saved only by the mercy of the end. Verse 1 announces the story's purpose: this happened as a "testing" of Abraham. Here is what is recorded:

> God called his name,
> "Abraham."
> Abraham said,
> "Here am I."

(Here are echoes of God's original call to Abraham in Genesis 12.)

> God said,
> "Take your son, your only son whom you love, Isaac, and go
> to the land of Moriah and offer him up as a burnt offering"
> (the Hebrew word is *'ola,* an offering totally consumed by
> flame, a *holocaust*).[7]

Abraham said nothing but rose early the next morning, saddled his donkey, took the wood for the fire, two servants, and his son Isaac, and they set off toward Moriah. After a three-day journey that the philosopher Kierkegaard said lasted longer than the four thousand years separating us from the event, they arrived at the foot of the mountain. In Abraham's one hand was a burning coal for the fire, in his other, a knife. The wood he placed on Isaac's back for him to carry.

> Isaac then said his first words:
> "Father."

Abraham for a second time said:
"Here am I."
Isaac said:
"Here are the fire and wood. Where is the lamb to be offered?"

All Abraham could do was choke out the words, hoping against hope:

"God will provide."

When they reached the place of the sacrifice, Abraham built the altar, arranged the wood, and bound his son atop the pyre. Abraham then stretched out his hand and took the knife. As he raised it up, a messenger of God called from heaven:

"Abraham, Abraham!"
Abraham for the third time answered:
"Here am I."
The messenger of God said:
"Do not stretch out your hand against the boy. Now I know your fear and reverence for God. You have not withheld your own son, your only son, from me."

Abraham lifted his eyes and saw a ram caught in a thicket by its horns. He cut his boy loose, bound the ram to the altar, and offered it up in place of Isaac. Thus Abraham named this place of sacrifice "YHWH-Jireh," which means *God-will-provide*.

Moriah brings to our minds stories of children spared and children not spared. I think of a parent whose child becomes gravely ill and is at the point of death, a parent who agonizes, "Will I lose my child, this love of my life? Will the God who has given her now take her?" Then after days of unspeakable anguish and terror the child gets well, and there comes unspeakable joy.

And I think of children not spared—the million-plus in Nazi death camps, children on planes that go down into the sea, children who are victims of illness, violence, and accident. And of parents whose faith is shaken to the depths as they walk through this darkest of dark nights.

And I think of how God entered our story as the Grieving

Parent and watched his own Son die in agony. And I hear the words of the apostle Paul:

> If God is for us, who can be against us? He who did not hold back even his own son, but freely offered him up for us all, will he not also give us all things with him? . . . Who shall separate us from the love of Christ? Shall tribulation or distress or persecution or famine or nakedness or peril or sword? As it is written, "For his sake, we are being killed all the day long: we are like sheep led to be slaughtered." No, in all these things we are more than conquerors through him who loved us. For I am sure that neither death, nor life, nor angels, nor principalities, nor things present, nor things to come, nor powers, nor height, nor depth, nor anything else in all creation will be able to separate us from the love of God in Christ Jesus our Lord. (Romans 8:31-39, RSV)

By faith we hold to God—through the worst that life can bring. And when we lose our hold, we are held.[8] The journey of faith makes it through the darkest and most absurd of nights because God will make good on his promises.

For by faith, Hebrews says, Abraham obeyed and went to a land he knew not of. By faith Sarah conceived even when she was past the age and Abraham as good as dead. By faith Abraham was tested and was willing to offer up the son of his promise.

And by faith we join with all who have lived by the promises of God: some who in this life have enjoyed the promises, and some who, as Hebrews says, "have died not having received what was promised but having seen it greeted it from afar"—all of whom kept on toward a land, in the words of Thomas Wolfe, "more large than earth, more kind than home," toward which we and all the earth are tending.

Notes

1. Translation by Everett Fox, *The Five Books of Moses*, vol. 1 (New York: Schocken Books, 1995), p. 55.
2. Cited in Walter Brueggemann, *Genesis* (Atlanta: John Knox, 1982), p. 126.
3. Frederick Buechner's distinction from *Telling the Truth: The Gospel as Tragedy, Comedy, and Fairy Tale* (New York: HarperCollins, 1977).
4. Bernhard W. Anderson, "Abraham, the Friend of God," *Interpretation*, October 1988, p. 362.
5. Phillips Brooks, "O Little Town of Bethlehem," (1868), stanza 3.

6. See Frances Young, *Virtuoso Theology: The Bible and Interpretation* (Cleveland, Ohio: Pilgrim, 1990), for the development of interpretations of texts as performances of the text.

7. See Elie Wiesel, *Messengers of God: Biblical Portraits and Legends* (New York: Random House, 1976), p. 71.

8. The epiphany of a Wendell Berry character in *Remembering* (New York: Farrar, Straus & Giroux, 1990).

6

Jacob: Wrestling with God

The story of Jacob is the story of a con artist who became the father of the twelve tribes of Israel. How did this deceiver become a hero? It did not happen until he received "the wound of blessing" that shadowy night in the river and was at the same moment blessed and crippled.

Jacob's story tells us that the blessing of God is not so much something that we lay hold of as something that lays hold of us. Such wildness of blessing is captured by Frederick Buechner as he puts these words in Jacob's mouth:

> When the camel you're riding runs wild, nothing will stop it. You cling to its neck. You wrench at its beard and long lip. You cry into its soft ear for mercy. You threaten vengeance. Either you hurl yourself to death from its pitching back or you ride out its madness to the end.
>
> It was not I who ran off with my father's blessing. It was my father's blessing that ran off with me. Often since I have cried mercy with sand in my teeth. . . . I bury my face in its musky pelt. The blessing will take me where it will take me. It is beautiful and it is appalling.[1]

Let us go back to Jacob's birth.

I

Jacob was born a twin. Esau first, Jacob second. There was a children's song I learned in church:

> Who was born a twin
> Many years ago?
> Who was born a twin?
> Tell me if you know.
> Jacob was his name.
> Esau was his brother,
> Isaac was his dad,
> Rebekah was his mother.

I have a modern updating of the song (to the tune of "The Beverly Hillbillies"):

> Come listen to the story of a man named Jake
> As a young man he acted like a fake
> Esau his brother he made an enemy
> Jacob belonged to a dysfunctional family.

The story of Israel is of a dysfunctional family redeemed by God. That's our story too. All God's children got dysfunction. The sins of the parents are passed down to the children and to their children, a cycle broken only as we bring our childhood wounds to consciousness to be healed by the grace and truth of God.

Father Isaac is a passive figure. It is hard to get a fix on his personality. It would have been tough being the son of heroic Abraham. And who can imagine the lifelong effects of that day of scalding terror when Abraham led him up Mount Moriah to be sacrificed: Isaac carrying the wood, being placed on the wood, seeing the knife in his father's hand, being saved at the last moment by a ram caught in the thicket. His father was prepared to kill him. God provided a ram instead, declaring the end of child sacrifice, but not before the boy Isaac had experienced himself as the sacrifice of his father's religion.

Abraham seemed not to have trusted Isaac's abilities. He even sent his own servant to pick out a wife for Isaac—Rebekah. Who knows how well or how badly this arranged marriage worked out.

Then came the twins. Esau was born first and Jacob arrived

second, clutching the heel of his brother. That's how he got his name: Jacob means "heel holder." But to catch somebody by the heel is also to trip him up, to "supplant" him; thus, this meaning of Jacob's name foreshadows what is to come.

Esau as the firstborn was entitled to special honor and double the material benefits from his father. Both birthright and blessing were due him. Culture was ordered by the law of primogeniture: the firstborn son (never daughter) got the lion's share of the family honor and family inheritance. But throughout the expanse of the biblical narrative God seems to be disrupting this cultural pattern.

Jacob came second, a close second, but as they say, close only counts in horseshoes and hand grenades. So great were the advantages enjoyed by the firstborn in those days that when twins were born, the midwife would fix a red thread around the arm of the firstborn so as to not mix them up. Esau needed no red thread—his hair was red.

The boys could not have been more different—Esau: rough, rugged, red-haired, the hunter; Jacob: mother's helper, clever, introspective, the homebody. Esau subscribed to *Field and Stream;* Jacob baked quiche. Esau played linebacker; Jacob played Mozart.

Jacob didn't remember being born clutching Esau's heel, but he realized all too well that his father preferred Esau. Perhaps that was one reason Rebekah favored him. The text says "Rebekah loved Jacob . . . Isaac loved Esau."

The mysteries of favoritism lie deep in the human psyche. Sometimes a parent almost instinctively gravitates to one child over another. Parents may love all their children, yet one especially catches their delight. It is not a matter of the will; it is a matter of deep psychological push and pull. Did Rebekah bond to Jacob to supply needs Isaac could not meet? Did Isaac prefer Esau because the boy had qualities he wished he had? Did Rebekah sense that her "different" son Jacob, not Esau, was the one who could fulfill God's promise to Abraham and to the nations?

II

One day Jacob was in the house, as usual, in the kitchen, as usual, cooking a red stew. Esau, as usual, was out in the fields. Esau came in famished and begged Jacob for some of his stew. It was a drama often replayed: Jacob getting Esau to beg.

"I'm starving to death," Esau said. Jacob answered, "What will you give me for it?" "Anything," said Esau. "How about your birthright?" Jacob asked. Esau agreed—what good was a birthright if he starved to death? The deal was made, and it wasn't until he had eaten his fill and slept the night through that he realized what he had done and what Jacob had done to him.

But the trickery wasn't over. In Rebekah's eyes Jacob deserved not only Esau's birthright but the blessing Isaac would give his firstborn. So when old and blind Isaac said to Esau, "Go kill some game and make me a stew and I will give you my blessing," Rebekah overheard and went to work. She coached Jacob in an act of deceit.

Jacob went into Isaac's room carrying a bowl of stew, dressed in Esau's clothes, and wearing animal skins so he would feel and smell like Esau. Old blind Isaac, fooled by the guise, took the stew and gave Jacob the blessing he thought he was giving to Esau.

He kissed Jacob and pronounced the blessing handed down to him from Abraham. It was *power* that was supposed to flow from father to son at the blessing. Could Jacob fully receive this blessing? Lies had gotten him this blessing, and who can trust a blessing we've cheated to get?

When Esau came in from the fields, he prepared his stew and went in to see his father. When he gave Isaac the stew and knelt for the blessing, Isaac trembled with the terrible recognition. Esau had been supplanted once again by his brother Jacob. Then Esau cried out some of the most painful and poignant words ever spoken: "Have you only one blessing, father? Bless me, me also, father!" And Genesis 27:38 concludes with: "Esau lifted up his voice and wept."

I saw a sculpture of this scene at the art museum in Glasgow, Scotland. It was a larger-than-life scene in stone. The father was reclining, his son Esau lying before him with hands imploring, eyes and mouth pleading for the father's blessing already spent, given to Jacob. The inscription reads:

> Have you but one blessing, my father?
> Bless me, even me also, O my father!

As I stood before the sculpture, I saw the pain wracking the body and face of the son, but from that angle the father's face looked oddly passive. Then I walked around the end of the sculpture past the heads of the reclining characters, along their backs, and around to the opposite end at their feet. When I saw Isaac's face from that angle, I saw a father's face ravaged with pain.

Then I knew not only the son's pain for having lost his blessing but also the father's pain for not being able to bless Esau the way he so wanted. Is this not a picture of the human condition: our desire to bless our children when we are sometimes unable to do so? This is where the blessing of God becomes our salvation; we receive from God what we cannot fully receive from our parents, and we are able to provide for our children what we ourselves cannot humanly give.

Esau's anger grew to murderous rage, and he swore to kill his brother. Rebekah got word of his vow and planned Jacob's escape. She sent him far away to her brother's home in Haran. He fled for his life, not looking back.

III

Who could have imagined it? This is the father-to-be of the twelve tribes of Israel: a young man of doubtful character who had conspired with his mother, cheated his brother, deceived his father, and now is on the run—a fugitive from home, from God, and from his own true self.

En route to Haran Jacob stopped for the night. He found a stone for a pillow, sank into sleep, and began to dream. What he might have expected was a nightmarish dream, disturbed, guilty, anxious, the kind from which you wake up exhausted and filled with dread. What God might have given him in the dream was a lecture on honesty and family values, a hellfire-and-damnation sermon holding before him the penalty of his sins.

Instead, what God gave him was a glimpse of heaven. Heaven opened and a ladder shining with God's own light stretched from heaven to earth and from earth to heaven. And there were angels without number ascending and descending. Have you ever beheld a beauty that caught your breath or brought tears to your eyes? Jacob beheld the beauty of God, the beauty, beauty, beauty.

But that was not all. A voice came out of heaven's light and instead of the "blessing out" Jacob knew he deserved, God gave him a blessing:

> I am the Lord God of Abraham and Isaac.
> The land on which you lie asleep I will give
> to you and to your descendants. They
> will number like the dust of the earth,
> north, east, south, west, and by them
> shall all the families of the earth be blessed.
> —based on Genesis 28:13-14

And with that blessing, an echo of the one given to Abraham, there came another, more personal word: "I am with you, Jacob. And I will be with you and keep you wherever you are going. And I will bring you here again and home again. I will not leave you until my promise is fulfilled."

When Jacob awoke he said tremblingly: "Surely the Lord is in this place, and I did not know it." The next morning he took the rock that had been his pillow, poured oil on it, and named the place *Bethel*, which means "house of God," for this, he said, "is none other than the house of God and the gate of heaven."

Then he did something characteristically "Jacob" and characteristically us. He took the grace of God and turned it into a bargain. He took a gift freely, unaccountably given and turned it into "Let's Make a Deal." What he said was: *If* . . .

> If you go with me and keep me and give
> me bread and clothing so that I come
> again to my father's house in peace,
> then the Lord shall be my God and this
> stone shall be God's house and I will
> give a tenth of all I own to thee.
> —based on Genesis 28:20-22

Why can't we trust the goodness, the sheer giftedness of grace? Why is it when someone unexpectedly gives us a gift, our first response is to say, "Let me pay you for it," or we scramble to think of some way to repay later on with a gift of our own?

How many years do we sing "Amazing Grace" before it sinks in? We don't sing "Amazing *works*, how sweet the sound that saved a soul like me" or "Amazing *deal*, how sweet the sound that saved a soul like me." But some days we live as if those were the words.

And we who've spent all our lives trying to win what is ours already, thinking we must earn God's blessing—God's and everybody else's—finally see that God has opened heaven for us, and there's a ladder with angels ascending and descending, almost too beautiful to watch, and there are words for our hungry ears to hear, if we will only hear them: "I am with you . . . I will go with you and keep you and never leave you. I will bless you and through you bless the world."

If, Jacob said to God, still bargaining for grace, but there would come a day when his song would be:

> Through many dangers, toils, and snares
> I have already come;
> 'Tis grace hath brought me safe thus far,
> And grace will lead me home.

But not yet. Jacob was on his way, a long meandering way, to becoming Israel.

IV

If, Jacob said, making his deal with God.

Well, vows get broken, and trying to bargain for grace is like trying to bottle the wind, so the next twenty years of Jacob's life were filled with one misadventure after another. Approaching Haran, Jacob arrived at the same well where many years before Abraham's servant had found Rebekah for Isaac. There he saw lovely Rachel and was instantly smitten.

When she approached to draw water, Jacob single-handedly rolled away from the mouth of the well the stone which normally took several shepherds to move. The old "muscles at the beach" routine. Then he kissed her and told her who he was—Rebekah's son. She ran back to tell her father, Laban.

Laban was a shrewd and mercenary man. He saw dollar signs everywhere. When he saw this strapping young man come to visit, the pupils of his eyes changed into dollar signs. "State your wages," he said.

Jacob made a proposal: "I will work seven years for the hand of your daughter Rachel in marriage." The bargain was struck. And the scripture says, "the seven years seemed to him but a few days because of the love he had for her" (29:20). As Samuel Taylor Coleridge said of Jacob, "No man who could love like that could be wholly bad."

When the seven years were up, Jacob was married, and he spent his first night of wedded bliss only to wake up the next morning and discover that the woman he had wed behind that veil—and with whom he had consummated the marriage—was not Rachel but Rachel's sister, Leah, who was not nearly so pretty and whom he certainly did not love.

Laban had pulled a fast one. He had outconned the con artist. The law required that he marry off his older daughter first. That was Leah. Laban had failed to mention that little detail seven years earlier, and Jacob had failed to read the fine print.

You can imagine the dismay Jacob felt when he awoke and discovered that the woman beside him in bed was not Rachel but Leah. In the Midrash, the Jewish commentary on the Hebrew scriptures, the rabbis have invented this conversation and inserted it into the story: When Jacob awoke and saw Leah next to him, he complained to her, "All night I was calling you Rachel and you answered me; why did you deceive me?" "And you," she retorted, "your father called you Esau and you answered; why did you deceive him?"[2]

Greater love hath no man than this: to work fourteen years for a woman. When he discovered that he was married to Leah, Jacob bargained with Laban that if he could have Rachel for his wife as well he would work seven more years. That sounded pretty good to Laban, the cash register jingling between his ears.

So now Jacob had two wives, Leah and Rachel, and some days he probably wished he had taken a vow of celibacy. He got caught in a war of jealousy between the sisters. The battles were for his attention, and babies were the ammunition. Both sisters had trouble conceiving at first. When Leah bore the first son, she named him Reuben, which means "See, a son." This no doubt echoed like a taunt in Rachel's ears.

The contest had begun. When the wives had difficulty conceiving, they brought on their handmaids to bear Jacob's weary seed and bring forth children in their stead. The race was on to see who could accumulate the most babies, and by the time the dust and bed feathers had settled, Jacob was the proud (not to mention exhausted) father of twelve sons and a daughter. That's how we got the twelve tribes of Israel!

Barren, beloved Rachel finally bore a son after a long wait. He was number eleven, after six born to Leah and two each to Bilhah and Zilpah, the two handmaids. No wonder Jacob and Rachel would dote on him so. His name? Joseph.

Psalm 76:10 says in the King James Version, "the wrath of men shall praise thee" and we might add "and the trickery of men and the contesting pride of women as well." For without Laban's trickery and the jealousy of the sisters, we would not have had all twelve tribes of Israel, nor would we have had two fairly important descendants of Leah—one named Moses, the other named David.

"God moves in mysterious ways," the saying goes, our blunders to transform.

V

For fourteen-plus years Jacob had served Laban in Haran. His work brought tremendous prosperity to them both. His flocks multiplied to an almost miraculous size. When he announced to Laban it was time for him to return home, Laban was not eager for him to go. Jacob had been good luck to him.

A contest of wills and wiles ensued between Jacob and Laban. It is almost as if God gave to Jacob a mirror of himself in his father-in-law to be part of his redeeming. Jacob and Laban's negotiated departure was filled with bargaining and trickery. They divided the flocks between them. Then the tricky Laban stole some of Jacob's share, but by some ingenious method of animal husbandry (something about peeled almond rods in front of watering holes!) Jacob's decimated flocks multiplied far beyond Laban's. And so the contest went.

Finally one day when Laban was away, Jacob gathered his wives, family, and flocks and left by stealth—yet another leave-taking for Jacob under less-than-positive circumstances.

Rachel, making matters worse, stole her father's household gods for extra good luck.

Laban came home, discovered them gone, and rushed after them. In the face-off Laban and Jacob dropped their swords and decided not to hurt each other any more. A line was drawn, marked by stones, and they vowed not to pass that line, either one of them, on the way to harm the other. It was as much of a covenant as they knew how to make. Laban's words "the Lord watch between me and thee when we are absent from one another" has been taken as a sentimental benediction. In fact Laban was saying: "The Lord keep an eye on the both of us, since we can't keep an eye on each other!" Laban then kissed his daughters and grandchildren good-bye, and Jacob went on his way, back towards home.

VI

When Jacob got to a river called Jabbok, he heard that his brother Esau was on the way to meet him with four hundred men. Jacob sent the rest of his party ahead with peace offerings of gifts for his brother. Maybe they would cool Esau's anger, at least buy some time. Now he was all alone.

As Jacob waded out into the stream, something happened. Whatever happened is shrouded in mystery. It is as dark and raw as our worst nights fuddled by wild dreams.

Something hit him, there in the water. There was a wrestling— fierce, agonized, decisive, and long, all night long. The narrative tells us that the one whom Jacob wrestled was a man; Jacob's contemporaries might have named him a river god; later scripture would call him an angel. After the battle Jacob said it was God himself. But when he went into the stream that night and was met by that force, he did not know what in heaven's name—or hell's— had hit him.

They wrestled all night. At times Jacob thought he was winning; most times he feared he was losing. Near dawn his opponent reached out and touched Jacob's hip, wrenching it out of its socket. And Jacob knew at that moment whoever or whatever it was, his opponent was playing with him, or having mercy on him, and could have won at any moment.

The Other said, "Let me go. It is daybreak."

Jacob said, "I will not let you go till you bless me."

The Other said, "What is your name?"

"Jacob," he answered, "Supplanter," the word sounding for all the world like the scrambler, the hustler, the cheat he knew he was.

The Other said, "Your name shall be Jacob no more, but *Israel,* for you have striven with God and with others and have prevailed."

Everett Fox has vividly captured the meaning of the naming in his translation:

> Not as Yaakov/Heel-Sneak shall your name be henceforth
> uttered,
> but rather as Yisrael/God-Fighter
> for you have fought with God and men
> and have prevailed. (32:29)[3]

Jacob said, "Tell me your name."

"Why do you wish to know?" the Other said elusively, then blessed him and was gone.

Jacob never got the name, but he knew the One whom he held onto that night, and the One who had hold of him. He gave a name to the place of the struggle. "Peniel," he called it ("face of God"), "for I have seen God face to face and my life has been saved" (32:31, Fox).

The episode ends with the words "As the sun rose he passed Peniel limping on his hip." He had been blessed and he had been wounded. Something had died and something had been born. Jacob had become Israel.

And that was not all. Blessing also happened the next day when the brothers met. As Jacob hobbled to Esau, bowing seven times in humility, Esau ran to meet him, grabbed him around the neck, and kissed him. Inexplicable grace.

Esau wept to be holding him again. Jacob said, "To see your face is like seeing the face of God." And now he wept too. The wrestling during the night and the embracing by day were joined as one in Jacob's mind. He had met God in the river and in his brother's arms. And God's name and face was Grace.

Composer Charles Wesley captured the moment in one of his greatest hymns:

> Come, O thou traveller unknown,
> Whom still I hold, but cannot see;
> My company before is gone,
> And I am left alone with thee;
> With Thee all night I mean to stay,
> And wrestle till the break of day.
> My prayer hath power with God; the grace
> Unspeakable I now receive;
> Through Faith I see Thee face to face—
> I see Thee face to face and live!
> In vain I have not wept and strove—
> Thy Nature and Thy Name is Love.[4]

VII

Jacob limped toward the dawn bearing the wound of blessing. Can we speak of a diminishment that blesses? A blessing that leaves us with a limp? Some wounds in life are what C. S. Lewis called a "severe mercy."

Some nights of our lives we find ourselves wrestling in the river Jabbok, in that stream called "Struggle" (for that's what the name "Jabbok" literally means). Is it a human person we wrestle with? an angel? a demon? God? Is it life itself, with all its fierce and frightening power? Is it death we wrestle with there in the waters?

Whoever it is we have hold of, or Who has hold of us, we find ourselves hanging on for dear life and crying, "I will not let you go until you bless me!"

This is not an act of defiance, but an act of *faith* in God, a faith that refuses to give up on life's goodness, and God's, a faith that believes that somewhere in the midst of the struggle, darkness, and pain, there is blessing.

Ever felt life hit you like a Greyhound bus? You thought you were in control. You'd figured out a way to get most of the things you wanted, but now you hear the word *disease* or *divorce* or *depression* or *bankruptcy* or *disgrace* or *death*. It is as if the opponent you thought you could whip has reached out and touched your hip, and now in searing pain you see your leg dangling hideously from its socket.

If this is your story, the message of the text is: Hang on! Don't let go until you are blessed. God will make you equal to your sufferings, maybe in some mysterious way worthy of them. When life is at its hardest, hang on! And say, as an act of faith stubborn, tough, and strong: I will not let you go until you bless me!

Whose face was it Jacob saw on that night of wrestling? Frederick Buechner describes it as a face more terrible than the face of death—the face of love, "vast and strong, half-ruined with suffering and fierce with joy."[5] It was a face like the one hanging on a cross, strung up between two thieves, who cried out in agony, "My God, my God, why have you forsaken me?" and with the next breath, "Father, forgive them for they know not what they do."

If we gaze at that face long enough, we will find ourselves Jacob's brother, Jacob's sister—blessed and limping, headed toward the Dawn which is the face of God. Heading home.

Notes

1. Frederick Buechner, *The Son of Laughter* (New York: HarperSanFrancisco, 1993), p. 86.
2. Elie Wiesel, *Messengers of God: Biblical Portraits and Legends* (New York: Random House, 1976), p. 115.
3. Everett Fox, *The Five Books of Moses* (New York: Schocken Books, 1995), pp. 155-57.
4. Charles Wesley, "Come, O Thou Traveller Unknown," in *Songs of Praise*, ed. P. Dearmer, et al. (London: Oxford University Press, 1931), p. 571.
5. Frederick Buechner, *The Magnificent Defeat* (New York: Seabury, 1966), p. 18.

7

Joseph's Story

Joseph's story: God and human evil.

It begins when Joseph is a young man in Canaan. It ends many years later in Egypt when Joseph is a man in his middle years. In the course of the story we see the full range of human passions: political intrigue and sibling rivalry, love and hate, jealousy, lust, ambition, heroism, and mercy.

Joseph is the hero, but the major actor is God—not directly, but indirectly, through the turns and twists of the plot. In this story we see a glimmer of the truth that somewhere behind it all there is a God who knows us and who cares, a God who makes out of all our stories one story and out of all our human maneuverings one plot.

Joseph points to that truth at the end of the story. There he stands, his brothers crouching before him, fearful now that with father Jacob dead Joseph will take revenge on them for selling him into slavery. And what does Joseph say?

"Do not be afraid. Who am I to be in God's place? No, *you meant it for evil but God meant it for good.*"

This is a brave statement of faith in the providence of God.* It is brave because it is spoken while looking evil in the face. Joseph had not lightly passed over human evil. He had passed through it.

---

*This is the theological doctrine that asserts that at the same moment God watches over and provides for the well-being of the world *and* of every individual.

I

The story begins as Joseph turns seventeen. He was the first son of the beloved Rachel, apple of his father's eye, Jacob's favorite. How ironic! Jacob himself was passed over, his own father, Isaac, preferring Esau over him. Jacob knew the pain of seeing his father favor his brother, yet he now plays favorites with his son, Joseph. How much like us: despite our protests and promises to the contrary, we repeat the mistakes of our parents. Blessing and cursing become a largely unconscious legacy passed on unless some new awareness takes place. I am reminded of Milton's famous definition of education in his essay, "Of Education": "The end then of learning is to repair the ruins of our first parents by regaining to know God aright, and out of that knowledge to love Him, to imitate Him, to be like Him."[1]

Joseph was the favored son of his father; he knew it, he loved it, and he flaunted it. Jacob gave him a special coat of many colors, and Joseph wore it like a neon sign that read, "Father loves me best." Spoiled, he craved attention; a dandy, he fancied the way he looked.

His brothers hated him, and we can understand. The story says that they would not even speak peaceably to him—they would not even extend the daily "shalom." They passed by and did not speak; their eyes would not meet.

One day Joseph went to his brothers and said: "Listen to my latest dream. We were gathering wheat in the field when suddenly my bundle stood up and all of yours formed a circle around mine and bowed down to it." His brothers didn't have to be Sigmund Freud to get the point. "What!" they retorted angrily. "You wish to reign over us?!"

Undaunted, Joseph told them a second dream—this one even more preposterous: "I saw the sun, the moon, and eleven stars prostrate before me." That was too much even for his doting father, Jacob. "What!" said Jacob, "Are you like God so your parents and brothers bow down to you?!"

Because of the dreams his brothers hated him even more. They began to plot to kill him. One day Jacob sent Joseph to Shechem to meet his brothers. Did Jacob not see how his favoritism had caused his other sons to hate Joseph? Why did he not foresee the danger? Later, the mixture of sorrow and self-recrimination over questions like these would nearly kill him.

When Joseph met his brothers, they jumped him. They tore off his ornamented coat and threw him into a pit. While they were debating over how to dispose of him, Judah, the eldest, spotted a passing caravan and talked his brothers into selling Joseph into slavery.

They meant it for evil, but God meant it for good.

According to the Genesis text, Joseph was silent throughout the brutal attack. No pleading, no bargaining. Silence. Like a sheep led to slaughter.

Why the silence? The Jewish imagination of writer Elie Wiesel asks: Did it cross Joseph's mind that his father might be behind all this? Had not Jacob sent him to his brothers!?[2]

Did the memory of Mount Moriah sweep over Joseph—the memory of Abraham's binding of Isaac? Was his father Jacob trying to match the heroic faith of Abraham? Was he offering his own favorite son? The terror Joseph must have felt—not just at the violence of his brothers but at the thought, just the thought, that Jacob might be behind it all!

The two episodes, Moriah and Shechem, both speak to the providence of God. Both begin in terror and end in a miracle: Isaac saved by the sudden appearance of a ram; Joseph, by a passing caravan. Joseph's life is saved, but the terrible questions inside his mind must have persisted throughout the years that followed.

The memory of Moriah and Shechem sparks Christian imaginations as well, shifting us to another place, Golgotha, to another son led to slaughter, like a lamb mute before his shearers—this one not saved as the other two, but slain, slain that we and all the world might be spared.

The brothers, meanwhile, returned with a lie for their father. They dipped Joseph's coat of many colors into goat's blood and took it to Jacob. Jacob jumped to the conclusion that the brothers intended: "A wild beast has killed my son!" What cruel irony! Again. Jacob, who as a young man dressed up like Esau and deceived his father Isaac, was now deceived by his own sons. The guilt and grief would almost destroy him. He cried out, "I will wear my mourning clothes until I die." And he nearly did.

II

Joseph in the meantime was brought down to Egypt a slave. The scriptures say, "Yahweh was with him," just as the Lord is always with the bruised and oppressed. God hears the cry of his children wherever they cry, from any bondage or trial.

"The Lord was with Joseph." From his unlikely beginnings as a slave, Joseph achieved stunning success, first, as an interpreter of dreams and second, as a statesman, the king's right-hand man.

Joseph, like a cat, always landed on his feet. He succeeded in whatever tasks he was handed. First of all, he became high-ranking Potiphar's trusted servant, the manager of his house. Being an extraordinarily handsome young man, Joseph also attracted women, and they brought temptation. The text says, "Now [Joseph] was fair of form and fair to look at" (39:6).[3] The plot thickens.

The Talmud has a story about Joseph in Potiphar's house. One day a group of high-society ladies came to lunch. Madame Potiphar served citrus fruits and gave each lady a knife to peel them with. In walked Joseph. So moved and bedazzled were the ladies that they went into a state of shock and cut their hands with the knives. Madame Potiphar breathlessly moaned: "This is what I must endure day after day, hour after hour."[4]

Madame Potiphar is often pictured as a femme fatale, but in Bill Moyers's *Genesis: A Living Conversation,* author Nessa Rapoport suggests with delicious irony that the real "femme fatale" in the story is Joseph![5] Seductions are rarely simple.

Joseph had turned the head of Potiphar's wife. The next verses in the Bible read like a soap opera. Potiphar's wife fell head over heels for her young servant. She made many overtures to him. Repeatedly, however, he refused her advances. (That part is quite *unlike* the soap operas.)

Then one day, when the house was empty save the two of them, Madame Potiphar, sick with longing, moved aggressively to win him. He ran away in a panic, leaving his outer garment in her hands. It was evidence enough.

She called the other workers in and, using the word "Hebrew" as a racial slur, said, "This *Hebrew* tried to lie with me."

But it was his Hebrewness that gave Joseph the wherewithal

to resist—to resist not only her but also what she represents in the story, all the temptations of the Egyptian way of life. Joseph would not accommodate to his adopted culture or to its ways of sin.

In particular, Joseph would not violate the trust his master had put in him (39:9). Madame Potiphar, humiliated by his rejection, took vengeance by accusing Joseph of her own sin (a familiar human defense mechanism). The Bible says that God provides a way of escape from temptation (1 Corinthians 10:13), but the way is not always easy. For Joseph it meant going back to jail, this time falsely accused of going after his master's wife.

She meant it for evil but God meant it for good.

Joseph in jail. The text again says, "And the Lord was with him." And again Joseph made the best of a bad situation. He made friends with his jailers. Before long he was the administrative director of the jail! Have you known people like that? Joseph the cat had again landed on his feet.

Next he became the king's private psychoanalyst and interpreted the famous dream of the seven fat cows and seven skinny ones. "There will be seven bountiful years of harvest," said Joseph, "and seven years of famine. You had better get prepared." "You've got a job," said Pharaoh. Joseph's practical wisdom so impressed Pharaoh that he made Joseph his right-hand man, prince, chief bureaucrat (with one difference from many state bureaucrats—Joseph's plans worked!). Because of Joseph's shrewd administration, Egypt was prepared for the famine—not only surviving it but serving as the caretaker of the neighboring nations. By God's will this country of industry and plenty provided food for all the starving nations around its borders. This is the way of the righteous nation, whose leaders rule with God's justice. That is the way the biblical God uses the nations he blesses and blesses the nations he uses. God uses the strong to bless the weak, the rich to bless the poor, the smart to bless the simple. And guess what happens? The rich find themselves blessed by the poor, the strong by the weak, and the smart by the simple. Such is the way of blessing in the kingdom of God.

During those years Joseph became a powerful prince, married an Egyptian princess, and had two sons: Manashe, which means "For God has made me forget all my tribulation," and

Ephraim, which means "For God has made me bear fruit in the land of my misery."

In Jewish tradition Joseph is called *tzaddik,* Joseph "the Just." He epitomizes the justice and the righteousness of God: he resists temptations, he keeps his word, he administers God's justice, and he is able to show God's own mercy. This last quality comes into focus in the next chapter of his life.

III

The predicted famine brings an unexpected turn in the story. Joseph's brothers—minus the youngest, Benjamin—arrived at Joseph's court seeking grain. The family was close to starvation, and they had come to Egypt for help.

Had Joseph forgotten them? Had he forgiven them? When they came and bowed before him, scripture says that he "remembered the dreams which he dreamed of them"—their stalks of wheat bowing down to his stalk, and so on. We get no glimpse of *how* he remembered the dream—did he chuckle to himself at the sweet justice of it all? Did he look on with rueful acknowledgment of the grandiosity of his dreams now tragically and ironically played out before him? What we do know is that with the passing of the days ahead, Joseph won victory over bitterness.

Joseph did not then tell them who he was, but he set to work trying to reunite the family. He maneuvered a way to get his brothers to bring back his brother, Benjamin, and then his father, Jacob. On the first trip back they brought Benjamin. Later, as they set about to leave for home, Joseph planted a silver cup in Benjamin's saddle bags. He then sent his soldiers to confiscate the cup and bring his brothers back. Accused of stealing the cup, they were brought before him. Joseph gave the verdict: Benjamin had to stay and become his slave.

Judah, the eldest, came before Joseph and pleaded that he might take Benjamin's place. He told Joseph (whom he still did not recognize) that his father, Jacob, had nearly died over the death of his son Joseph and that if Benjamin were taken away that would finish him for good. Judah cried out, "I cannot bear to see this disaster come upon my father."

With this show of love, Joseph could not conceal his identity any longer. He sent everyone out of the room except his brothers. He broke down and wept and told them who he was: their brother Joseph whom they had sold into slavery.

IV

You can imagine that the first response of the brothers was fear. Wouldn't Joseph go ahead and demand revenge? Instead, Joseph showed that he had conquered vengefulness and bitterness and forgave them. He called for a family reunion and had Jacob brought to Egypt.

His response to their fear was remarkable. His vision transcended family, tribe, and nation. It took in the universal, overarching providence of God: "Do not be pained that you sold me here," he told them. "For it was to save life that God sent me on before. God sent me here to save the lives of many, even your lives," he went on, "to keep you alive as a great body-of-survivors" (45:7).[6] "So do not waste yourself in grief," Joseph said. "Go get Father Jacob and bring him here." And so they did.

His brothers would be afraid of him once more—when Jacob died. Joseph had promised his father that he would forgive his brothers and do them no harm. But now Jacob was dead. Would Joseph keep the promise?

The brothers came to Joseph and trembling with fear said, "Please forgive us the evil that we did to you." When Joseph heard them, he wept and said: "Do not be afraid. For am I in the place of God?" Was there the hint of penitent self-knowledge in his voice? That is exactly how he had seen himself when he was a boy and dreamed the dream of the sun and moon and eleven stars bowing down to him. But now as one remarkably wise, mellowed by years and God, he said, "Do not be afraid. Am I in God's place? You plotted evil against me but God turned it into good."

You meant it for evil, but God meant it for good. I like Everett Fox's new translation: "You planned ill against me (but) God planned-it-over for good" (50:20). That is a vision from an eternal place. That is an affirmation of faith in the power and purpose of a good God. In the words of the gospel song, "His eye is on the sparrow, and I know he watches me."

V

The story of Joseph evokes from us and confronts us with a series of questions that get to the heart of our existence.

Can we believe that God can take evil and turn it into good? Can we believe that God can take the evil done to *us* and turn it into good? Can you believe that God can take the evil *we* have done and turn it into good?[7]

This "believing" is no simplistic notion that the evil we see in the world is not truly evil, but some form of hidden good. Rather, it is the stubborn faith that there is no evil dark enough that God somehow, someway, sometime cannot redeem. The faith that no matter how dark it is, the darkness will not overcome the light. Grace shall prevail. It is the tenacious faith the apostle Paul expressed in Romans 8:28: "We know that in everything God works for good with those who love him, with those called according to his purpose" (RSV).

What kind of God is this who allows suffering, then uses it for good? What kind of God is it who can take evil done us and turn it into good? What kind of God is it who can take the evil of our hands and use it for our salvation?

It's the kind of God who *went with Joseph* into slavery and into jail; the kind of God who was with a baby hidden in the bulrushes and who used that baby, Moses, to free the Hebrew people from Pharaoh's grip; the kind of God who two thousand years ago appeared in a makeshift crib in a shepherd's cave outside Bethlehem; the kind of God who hung on a gallows outside Jerusalem; the kind of God who held back not even his own son.

What kind of God is it who can take our crucifying of his only son and turn it into our salvation? It's the God of Abraham and Sarah and Isaac and Jacob and Joseph and Mary and Jesus.[8]

We say it bravely. We say it sometimes with tears. We say it sometimes with hardly any breath at all because the breath has been knocked out of us. We say it sometimes without seeing it, without feeling it, for "we walk by faith, not by sight."

Still, we say it:

They meant it for evil; you meant it for evil; I meant it for evil. *But God means it for good.*

Joseph's story teaches us to offer God all that happens to us, both the evil done to us and the evil we ourselves have done, and to say, "God, please, somehow use it for your redemptive good!" Not as a denial of our responsibility, but as an admission, bowing before the Mystery, that hands bigger and better than ours are required to redeem our lives.

They planned ill, you planned ill, I planned ill, but *God planned-it-over for good!*

Notes

1. As cited by Reynolds Price, *A Common Room* (New York: Atheneum, 1987), p. 16.

2. Elie Wiesel, *Messengers of God* (New York: Random House, 1976), pp. 165ff.

3. The translation of Everett Fox, *The Five Books of Moses*, vol. 1 (New York: Schocken Books, 1995).

4. Wiesel, *Messengers*, p. 148.

5. Bill Moyers, *Genesis: A Living Conversation* (New York: Doubleday, 1996), p. xiv.

6. Everett Fox's translation.

7. This turn of questions was suggested to me by James S. Sanders, *God Has a Story Too* (Philadelphia: Fortress, 1979), pp. 53ff.

8. Again I'm indebted to Sanders, ibid.

8

Tamar: Unlikely Redeemer

One of the spiritual gifts of our age is the emergence of women biblical scholars[1] who are giving us new eyes through which to look at old biblical stories, some of them familiar, some long ignored. One little-known story is from Genesis 38, the story of Tamar.

It is a story rated R in its original form, but, if told at all, is usually edited to PG for modern congregations. And not without precedent. According to rabbinic tradition,[2] some passages in the Hebrew Bible deal with such sensitive subject matter that they may be read in the synagogue service in the original Hebrew but are not allowed to be translated—a decision sure to prod all Jewish boys and girls to polish up their Hebrew skills! Such stories include Reuben's philandering with his father's concubine in Genesis 35 and the story of David's adultery with Bathsheba in 2 Samuel 11:2-17. Other passages are neither to be read in the Hebrew nor translated, such as the tragic story from 2 Samuel 13 of David's son Amnon, who raped his half-sister. Not only are these stories sensitive in nature, but they also could lead, it was thought, to the destruction of personal relationships as well as the social fabric. It's interesting, however, that the story of Tamar in Genesis 38 is to be both read and translated. Why? Because for all its R-rated action, it is at its core a story of redemption. Listen to the ancient tale of Tamar—survivor, tenacious believer in life, "unlikely redeemer."[3]

I

The opening scene rushes us through a generation full of action at breakneck speed. Judah left his family and "went down" into Canaanite territory. There he met a friend named Hirah. Judah soon fell in love with a Canaanite woman named only "the daughter of Shua," and they had great success in producing sons, three of them: Er first, then Onan, and Shelah third. Soon Judah picked out a wife for his firstborn son, Er. Tamar was her name. Judah prided himself on his taste in women. Tamar would be a fine daughter-in-law to bear children who would carry on the family name and thus fulfill God's covenant promise to Judah's great-grandfather Abraham, that Abraham's descendants would number as the stars in the sky and be a great blessing to all the nations. In the first scene of our story, the years fly by for the whole family, marked with good times, love, marriage, babies, and hope for future generations.

II

The next scene, however, turns heavy with tragedy. Judah's son Er died. Our storyteller attributes the death to his wickedness, but Judah, like all parents, was probably blind to any hint of wickedness in his son. Boys will be boys. Now the boy was gone.

What complicates the tragedy is that Er and Tamar had produced no children by the time of Er's death. This left Tamar in a most vulnerable position. In that ancient patriarchal world, a woman had only two proper roles: to be an unmarried virgin in her father's house or a child-producing wife in her husband's home.[4] Once Tamar left her father's house to be married, she no longer belonged there but in her in-laws' house; her name, place, and lifelong security depended on her ability to bear children. The law of the day said that if a husband died, none of the inheritance went to his wife; all of it went to his children. So Tamar's social security depended on her having children. A childless widow had no place. She dropped through the cracks of society's floor. Such was the rationale for what seems to us the odd practice called "levirate marriage." According to this law, if a married son died without children, it was the next brother's duty to be husband to the widow in order to bring forth children in the dead man's name.

This accomplished two things: it provided the widow a lifelong place in the family, and it helped ensure the production of children to preserve the family lineage into the next generation.

Picture Judah's plight. His first son Er has died without children. God had promised to Abraham and Jacob to number their descendants as the stars in the sky, as the grains of sand in the sea, as the dust that covers the earth. But it hadn't happened with Er, and second son Onan was next in line. So Judah, following the levirate law and still believing in the covenant promise, told Onan to go to Tamar and do a brother-in-law's duty to raise up offspring for his brother. Onan knew that the offspring (or "seed" in the King James Version) and their inheritance would carry his brother's name, not his, so he did a selfish, disobedient, and deceitful thing: he refused to impregnate Tamar. The text says that he "spilled [his seed] on the ground" (v. 9).

Tradition throughout the years has misguidedly focused on Onan's method of refusal. Some may well remember scalding warnings against "onanism" from their adolescent years! But in fact the sin of Onan did not consist of the method he used in his refusal to impregnate Tamar, but in the refusal itself to obey the law and help carry on the family name. The sin would have been the same had he just skipped town.

Suddenly, much to the terror of Judah, Onan died. (Unlike the biblical storyteller, Judah probably did not connect Onan's death with his disobedience. Judah may not even have known about it.) So here was Judah with two sons suddenly and tragically dead, a childless daughter-in-law, and one young son left to carry on the family name. It must have been overwhelming for Judah. Did he feel that his family was cursed? Did he blame Tamar for being a jinx? Probably. He himself had picked her out and given her to both sons; now both sons were dead. What Judah did was to retreat from life and from God. He lost faith in God's covenant promise and lost confidence in life itself.

We can sympathize. When life has been bad enough, we are tempted to give up on it, to let go of the hope that anything good can come in the future. We circle the wagons, lower our expectations, refuse to take any risks. Our bodies may not be in the grave, but we have stopped living.

So it was with Judah. He was supposed to give his third son,

Shelah, to Tamar as a husband. But Judah had given up on God, had abandoned the covenant promise of innumerable descendants. We see this in his refusal to offer his third son to Tamar. He will not take the risk. Better that the family name be lost and the covenant broken than to have another son torn away from him in death.

So Judah did wrong by Tamar. He told her that Shelah was too young to be her husband and sent her back to her father's home, promising that when Shelah was old enough he would bring her back into the family. But in fact Judah never intended to risk his third son. He deceived Tamar, banishing her to her father's house, where she no longer really belonged. He deprived her of the chance to become a mother—which in that culture was her only means to have a proper place, name, and security. She would be "odd person out" for the rest of her life.

To this point in the story Tamar's only role has been that of victim. She has been victimized by the death of her husband, by her childlessness, by the oppressive customs of her patriarchal world, by a brother-in-law who refuses to do his duty, and by a cowardly, deceitful, and irresponsible father-in-law who has given up on his life (and thus robbed her of hers). To this point in the story we have heard nothing from Tamar. She has no voice. Nor has she acted except at the beck and call of the men who have complete control over her life.

It wouldn't surprise us if the story ended here. A thousand other Tamars have had their stories end like this—in our day as well as hers. But not so. In the next scene Tamar spins into action. The silent victim is given a voice and becomes the redeemer of the tribe of Judah. (I know a woman who, in reading this story for the first time, became so enraged at Tamar's victimization that she hurled her Bible against the wall and broke its binding. But then she picked up the Bible with the broken back and read the story again and again—until today Tamar has become for her a figure of empowerment and redemption.) How could redemption emerge out of a situation like Tamar's? Scene 3 will show us.

III

The story tells us that in time Judah's own wife dies. After a proper period of mourning—after he had been "comforted"—Judah went and got his old friend Hirah and together they set off to the sheep-shearing festival. This was a favorite occasion of their day, a time of hard work and harder play, a kind of Mardi Gras for herdsmen.

Tamar, meanwhile, had not been idle in her father's house. Nor had she given up hope for the future. She had kept up with the news from Judah's household. Now that Shelah was plenty old enough to marry and it had become obvious that Judah had no intention of giving him to her, Tamar went to work on a plan.

She heard that Judah was going to the sheep-shearing festival. She put aside her widow's clothing and put on the clothes of a harlot, covering herself with a veil. Then she went and sat down at the gate in town where the men passed by on their way to the festivities. When Judah passed by, he noticed her. She caught his eye, though he did not recognize her as Tamar—to him she was just another harlot.

"How about a night together?" he asked. "How much?" she asked. "A kid from my flock," he offered. "Fine," she answered, "but what pledge will you give me until I get paid in full?" "What pledge do you want?" asked he. "Your signet ring, cord, and staff," replied she. Judah agreed, even though this was the equivalent of leaving all his credit cards with her![5] We get the drift of his situation: He's away from home, it's a festival night, and it has been a long time since his wife died. Yet he had let Tamar languish much longer and more severely than that.

The deal was made, the night was had, and lo and behold, Tamar conceived. By her actions the goal of levirate marriage was accomplished and the covenant promise fulfilled. But that's getting ahead of the story. The story says that after the encounter Tamar took off her harlot's clothes, put her widow's clothing back on, and returned to her father's house.

IV

Scene 4 is a comedy of errors and embarrassment. Judah woke up the next day with the obligation to pay hanging over him, not to mention his worry over the "credit cards" he had left in the harlot's possession. He asked his good friend Hirah to go make the payment and retrieve his ring, cord, and staff.

Good ol' Hirah went to town, kid in hand, but he couldn't find the mystery woman anywhere. Clearing his throat with embarrassment, he asked the townspeople, "Anybody seen a 'sacred prostitute' around here since yesterday?" (He's using the term for a higher-class form of the profession than "harlot.") "No," they replied, "there's been no prostitute here." So Hirah returned to Judah and reported, "I couldn't find her, and the townspeople said there was no prostitute around there." Judah replied, "Then let her keep the things, lest we make fools of ourselves." Hirah probably shot back, "What do you mean, *we?!*" Judah said, "I sent her this kid and *you* couldn't find her!" We can imagine Judah bopping Hirah on the head like Oliver Hardy used to bop Stan Laurel.

V

Three months pass and the report comes to Judah: Your daughter-in-law Tamar has played the harlot, and now she is pregnant. Judah rendered the father-in-law's verdict, which by culture was his right. It is brutal, short, and quick, just two Hebrew words in the original: "*Bring* her out. *Burn* her." Following his order, she was brought out. But before she was immolated, she sent a message to Judah. Now Tamar finds her voice! "The man responsible for the child left behind his ring, cord, and staff. . . . Observe them," she says, "and see if you know whose they are."[6]

Our story says that Judah "took a close look." I'll bet he did. Tamar had caught him. The Jewish commentary from the Midrash on this passage has God say these words to Judah: "The Holy One be praised; you deceived your father with a kid [remember the brothers dipping Joseph's coat in goat's blood in order to fool father Jacob?]. Now Tamar has deceived you with a kid."[7] Just as surely as the prophet Nathan trapped David with his own condemnation, Tamar has trapped Judah. He is the one truly guilty—he had cast her off and he had propositioned her.

What Tamar did was to put the responsibility for her plight back where it belonged—in Judah's lap! What she did was to call him to take responsibility for the long pattern of neglect and abuse toward her. He identified *her* as the guilty party, yet she had the strength to turn a mirror on *him* so he could take a look at himself.

What was Judah going to do when faced with the truth? He

could deny it and go ahead and have her executed. It was a man's
world. Instead, the truth drove home and he said an astonishing
thing: "She is more righteous than I for it was I who refused to
provide my son, Shelah, for her" (see v. 26). She is more righteous
than I! From this moment on, Tamar became an honored member
of the family, and Judah acted honorably by her.

Six months later Tamar delivered her children—twins!
Judah's two sons had died, but now two new sons are born to carry
on the family line. Their names were Perez, which means "burst-
ing forth," because he burst ahead of his brother to be the firstborn,
and Zerah, which means "shining forth," for on that day God's
light did shine on the family of Judah.

And guess what happens? Perez has a son who has a son and
so on down the line till a man named Jesse has a son named
David—the king. Without Tamar, the tribe of Judah would never
have produced David. And that's not all. In the genealogy of Jesus
of Nazareth there are four women mentioned: Bathsheba, Ruth,
Rahab, and our hero, Tamar. This woman was the foremother of
David and of the one called the Christ.

So Tamar changed her clothes again, from a widow's clothes,
to a harlot's, to maternity clothes. And we can imagine the day she
put on party clothes—the day her sons were married, when she
and Judah stood side by side marveling at the strange goodness
of God who had fulfilled the covenant promise through it all, a
God who had taken a victimized woman and made her the
redeemer of the tribe of Judah. How Tamar must have danced
that day!

It may seem a bit strange to put the word "redeemer" with
Tamar, but in the Hebrew scriptures the word "redeemer" means
"to take responsibility for" and refers to persons who take responsibility for others and who call people to responsibility. A redeemer, then, is one who keeps life and love alive, who sees that
people do right by each other, who keeps the family going and the
community intact. Women have been doing that for a long time.
By the providence of God, the story of such a woman was remembered in the Bible.

Tamar's story is the story of a survivor who kept going, kept
living, loving, hoping—despite her victimization by men in a
man's world. Sometimes survival is the best we can do; it is itself

a triumph. God not only understood what Tamar had to do to survive; he called her righteous. She had done nothing evil in the sight of the Lord. Such is the story of many a woman, from Tamar's time until now.

Tamar's story is the story of a Canaanite woman whose passion for life was her own covenant with God. She would not give up on life, even when the men of the covenant had. While Judah was abandoning God's covenant, Tamar was plotting to fulfill it. What a risk she took as she disguised herself as a harlot! She could have been recognized and disgraced. She could have been executed by burning. Almost was. But she took that risk—and in the risk of her own body became the mother in whose redeemed body the promise of God was made good.

Tamar's is the story as well of Celie in *The Color Purple*,[8] who rose from victim's status to embrace life and restore a broken and brutal family history. Tamar's is the story of every sexually abused woman-child given voice to tell the truth and confront her abuse, and given power to start life all over again and receive a homecoming in her own body. Tamar's is the story of Sojourner Truth and Coretta Scott King and Maya Angelou and a multitude of women who have suffered yet endured in the way of truth and love.

Yes, the townspeople were right when they answered Hirah: there was no prostitute there. They spoke more truth than they knew. Tamar was indeed no harlot. She was a woman fighting to restore responsibility within a broken family and to reclaim her rightful place within it.

And Judah was right when he said, "You are more righteous than I." Tamar kept on living when Judah had quit. She kept believing in the promises of God when Judah had stopped believing. Years before, when the Lord had told Abraham that his descendants would number as the stars in the sky, the Bible says that Abraham "believed the Lord and he reckoned it to him as righteousness" (Genesis 15:6). So it was with Tamar: she believed in God, in life with its promised goodness, and God reckoned it to her as righteousness. Through all that was done to her and all she had to do, God said to Tamar: "You are righteous, my child. Walk with newness of life. Lift your head and walk into the future with all the goodness I have in store for you." Such righteousness is believing in God and God's promises to the point that you never give up on God or life. This kind of righteousness is not perfection so much as *perseverance*. It is stubborn hope in the goodness of God.

God speaks the same word to us as well, inviting us to enter into life—a life that despite its pain and risk is brimming with goodness. We are invited to lay down fear, to lay down despair, to lay down guilt, to lay down hate—so that we may rise and choose *life*.

Notes

1. For example, Phyllis Trible, Union Theological Seminary, New York City; Johanna Bos, Louisville Presbyterian Seminary; Toni Craven, Brite Divinity School at Texas Christian University. See especially Trible's *God and the Rhetoric of Sexuality* (Philadelphia: Fortress, 1978) and *Texts of Terror* (Philadelphia: Fortress, 1984). See also Toni Craven, *The Book of Psalms* (Collegeville, Minn.: Liturgical Press, 1992), and *The Women's Bible Commentary,* ed. Carol A. Newsom and Sharon H. Ringe (Louisville, Ky.: Westminster/John Knox, 1992).

2. Susan Niditch, "The Wronged Woman Righted: An Analysis of Genesis 38," *Harvard Theological Review,* April-June 1978, p. 149.

3. Johanna Bos, "Tamar: The Story of an Unlikely Redeemer," unpublished paper; author's files.

4. Niditch, "Wronged Woman," pp. 144ff.

5. Robert Alter, *The Art of Biblical Narrative* (New York: Basic Books, 1981), p. 9.

6. Bos's translation.

7. Alter, *Art of Biblical Narrative,* p. 11.

8. Alice Walker, *The Color Purple* (New York: Pocket Books, 1988).

9

Moses: YHWH's Hero

Here is the story of Moses. There is no more heroic figure in all scripture. Moses: the one who freed a nation of people from slavery in Egypt. The one who brought the law of God down from Mount Sinai. Moses: the one whose grave was hidden by God so no one would worship him and make of his final resting place a shrine. Moses: a man so great that, according to the book of Jude, when he died the archangel Michael and the devil fought over his body.

I: Prologue

We begin at the end. There is probably no more poignant picture in all scripture than the last days of Moses. After eighty years' wandering in the wilderness, Moses had finally led the Israelites to the Jordan and the boundary of the Promised Land. Now God took him to the top of Mount Pisgah, and from that peak God showed him the Promised Land. Moses saw it all: the River Jordan, the Dead Sea, the Sea of Galilee, even a glint of the great Mediterranean. It took his breath; his heart was a pounding drum.

But then came the words that broke his heart: "Moses, this is the land I promised Abraham, Isaac, and Jacob. I have let you see it, but I will not let you enter it." From breathtaking joy to heartbreaking sorrow all in a moment. He would not be allowed to lead his people in. For reasons difficult for us to understand, his people would go on without him, the younger leader Joshua at the helm.

One hundred twenty years old, with a lump in his throat as big as Texas, Moses thought back as far as he could remember over his long, turbulent, God-driven life.

Actually it began before Moses—in the heart of God. Before he knew God, God knew him. Before he picked God, God had picked him to accomplish his purpose: to free his people from slavery in Egypt and to found a faith based on the law of God, a covenant faith.

God prepared the way for Moses even before Moses left his mother's womb. Paranoid Pharaoh, fearful of the growing ranks of Hebrews, ordered the midwives of Egypt to strangle at birth all Hebrew boys. But scriptures say: "The midwives feared God and did not as the King of Egypt commanded." There's an arresting thought. *The obedience to God in the heart of a nurse-midwife is greater than all the pharaohs of the world.* God's pyramid of power is different from ours. As the apostle Paul would later say: God has chosen the weak things of the world to confound the things that are mighty (1 Corinthians 1:27).

Pharaoh, undeterred by the midwives' civil disobedience, ordered all Hebrew baby boys thrown into the Nile. This is where Moses' story begins.

II: Moses—His Beginnings

When Moses was born, his mother hid him at home as long as she could. Then she wove a basket of papyrus, waterproofed it with pitch, and made of it a little ark. She placed the basket in the Nile behind some bulrushes and stationed the baby's sister, Miriam, to watch out for him.

Pharaoh's daughter just happened to be bathing in the river one day when she discovered the basket with the crying baby inside of it. Her heart went out to him. Then Moses' sister appeared out of nowhere and offered to find a Hebrew woman to nurse the child for her. She was given permission and ran and fetched Moses' mother, who was paid to nurse her own baby— Pharaoh's daughter's new adopted son. Only God could make such events happen. Moses was allowed to nurse at his Hebrew mother's breast until he was weaned and went to live in the royal palace. Out of the wondrous workings of God's purpose this fine, handsome boy found himself raised in Pharaoh's house and given the best education Egypt and the ancient world had to offer.

However, his being raised in the privileged ruling class of Egypt did not cause Moses to turn his back on his own people. He could have lived a long and easy life of leisure and wealth. Instead, as the scriptures say, "He grew up and went out to see his people." And seeing them, his heart went out to them in the suffering of their captivity. He risked everything to intervene. It is the drama repeated throughout history: people moved by divine sympathy and divine justice to act on behalf of others—the Buddha, Saint Francis, Dietrich Bonhoeffer, Dorothy Day.

The Jewish commentary on scripture, the Midrash, tells us that Moses first tried to work within the system to help his people. Then one day he saw an Egyptian overlord torturing a Jewish slave. Rage consumed him, and he threw himself on the Egyptian and killed him. Moses the murderer. This act changed the course of his life and of all history. With a death sentence hanging over his head, Moses fled far away to the desert around Midian.

In Midian he came to a well and saw seven daughters of a priest named Jethro who had come to draw water for their flocks. Some hoodlum shepherds appeared and began to harass the young women. Moses intervened and drove them away. Then he helped the girls water their flocks. They took him back to their father Jethro. Before long Moses married one of the daughters, Zipporah, fathered a baby boy, and became keeper of Jethro's flocks.

III: The Call of Moses

One day as he was tending the flocks, Moses saw a bush that was burning but was not consumed by the flame. He went closer to investigate. A Voice said, "Moses." "Here am I," Moses replied. "Come no closer; take off your shoes, this is holy ground," said the Voice.

"I am the God of Abraham, Isaac, and Jacob—your God. I have seen the affliction of my children in Egypt and have heard their cry. I send you, Moses, to Pharaoh to bring my people out of slavery."

There is no secret in the Bible whose side God is on in the historical equation of tyrant/captive, oppressor/oppressed, master/slave, dominator/dominated. God is freedom to the bound, comfort to the bruised, reproof to the tyrant, strength to the weak. The question is not whose side God is on but whose side we are on.

When God called Moses from the burning bush, Moses objected all he could: Who am I to go up against Pharaoh? You know how I stutter. Why not my older brother Aaron, who can t-t-talk? Objection upon objection. God answered patiently with the quiet refrain: I will be with you. The Midrash says it took seven days for God to persuade Moses. Six days to create the world; seven days to convince a man!

When Moses said, "I am heavy of mouth and slow of tongue," God said, "Who made the mouth, the tongue?"

When Moses said, "I have not the power," God told him to throw down his shepherd's staff. Moses did, and it became a serpent writhing on the ground. "Pick it up," said God, and it became a stick again. The message? Moses, you will not conquer by a sword or by your own human strength, but by a shepherd's staff and the power of God.

When Moses said, "Who shall I say sent me . . . what is your Name?" God said,

> EHYEH ASHER EHYEH
> *I Am Who I Am* [the most widely accepted translation].
> Thus you will say to the children of Israel
> *YHWH* sends me to you.
> —Exodus 3:14

The Name of God. In Hebrew, *YHWH*.* We guess at the pronunciation, *Yahweh*, and its translation, *I am Who I am*. Jews to this very day will not pronounce the Name of God; such is their reverence. It is a name whose meaning is wrapped in mystery, suitably elusive and untranslatable, standing for the Holy One whose ways are not our ways and whose complete nature is hidden from our sight. I love how Professor Toni Craven interprets the meaning of God's giving of this name: Call me *Yahweh*, and I will teach you what it means![1]

---

*The Hebrew alphabet is made up only of consonants. The vowels are supplied by the long tradition of usage.

So Moses went to lead God's people—with a staff and a Name. Jewish tradition tells this story: Once when Moses was tending his father-in-law's sheep, one young kid ran away from the flock. Moses left the flock and searched for it until he found it in a deep ravine drinking water from a well. Picking up the young kid, he said, "I did not know you were thirsty. Now you must be weary," and he carried him back to the flock. Then God said, "Because thou hast shown pity in leading back one of a flock belonging to a man, thou shalt lead *my* flock Israel."[2] It is God who calls and God who qualifies. Moses was a murderer, but God would now refine his passion for justice. Yes, he stammered. But as Martin Buber said, "It is laid upon the stammering to bring the voice of Heaven to Earth."[3]

IV: Exodus

The book of Exodus describes in feverish pace what happened next: Moses pleading with Pharaoh, "Let my people go"; Aaron having to convince the Hebrew people to let *Pharaoh* go and leave Egypt. How frightening freedom can be and how comfortable slavery can seem!

Pharaoh's heart was hard; he refused. And so God sent ten plagues, with only the last one finally breaking through the hardness of Pharaoh's heart. We can feel in our bones the terror and the excitement of that last night in Egypt, darkness and light all amix. The firstborn of every Egyptian family slain; Hebrew homes passed over and spared; Pharaoh grieving the death of his son, finally consenting to let God's people go. We can hear the mournful wailing of Egyptian parents, the jostling and shouting as Moses' lieutenants urge the people out and on: "Let's go, fast, faster, before Pharaoh changes his mind!"

Soon after leaving the city the Hebrews found themselves boxed in, the Red Sea just ahead, Pharaoh's troops behind. Pharaoh *had* changed his mind!

The people panicked, but Moses said, "Stop your crying, the Lord will save you." Then he stretched out his hand, a strong easterly wind blew back the waters, and the people crossed the sea on dry land. Then as Pharaoh's horses and chariots followed, the waters swept back and the Egyptian soldiers drowned beneath the waves.

Then Moses, the stutterer, let loose with a song of deliverance:

He has covered himself in glory
Horse and rider he has thrown into the sea
YHWH is my strength, my song
YHWH is my salvation.

Then Miriam, his sister, took a tambourine and continued the song of praise. It was probably she who wrote the song for both. As she sang, women followed with tambourines and dancing:

The Lord is my captain
His helmet the sun, the moon his shield

*   *   *

Hallelujah
The hands of the Lord were with us.
They pushed the water aside and aside
Like the hands of a farmer dividing grain.
Hallelujah
The horse and his rider were cast into the waters.
The Lord is just, quick to smite the tyrant.
Quick to heal the oppressed, comfort the afflicted.
He dips his sword in honey, in balm his spear.

*   *   *

Hallelujah, Hallelujah.[4]

The people crossed the desert to Mount Sinai where God gave them the Ten Commandments. "I bore you on eagle's wings," God said, "and brought you to myself. If you obey my voice, you will be my possession on earth" (19:4-5).

Then God said, I am your God who brought you out of slavery. Now, to stay free, hear my commands:

Thou shalt not
Thou shalt not
Thou shalt not . . .

Ten of them in all. Ten commandments that formed a series of questions that God has asked from that day to this:

Will you remember that I am the Lord your God who

brought you out of bondage in Egypt? Will you promise to worship no other God? Nor to make graven images to worship them?

Will you keep the sabbath holy? Preserve the holiness of the family, honor your parents, respect the sanctity of the bonds of marriage? Do you promise never to steal, never to murder, never to lust after what is not yours? Will you cleave to my words and follow my way?[5]

After Moses received these commandments on top of Mount Sinai, he went back down the mountain. What he saw when he got back to camp, he could not believe. His people were dancing and singing around a golden calf that had been formed by melting down their jewelry and ornaments carried out of Egypt. Moses had been gone so long that they had turned to a god they could see and touch and fashion with their own hands. And who was leading them? None other than Moses' brother Aaron. When times get hard and God seems nowhere to be found, the consolations of what we can see and touch, taste and smell are awfully appealing: the feel of gold, the taste of skin, the smell of the soil, the sea. Golden calves often beat out the impalpable God.

Moses was so angry when he saw what was going on that he threw down the tablets containing the commandments and broke them into a hundred pieces.

Moses had had just about enough. This was close to the last straw. What was he to do with this stiff-necked, bellyaching, faithless people? No sooner had they left Egypt than they were already complaining: Why did you make us leave? Did you lead us out of Egypt so that we would die in the desert?

Three days after the miraculous crossing of the Red Sea, they were complaining about something to drink. And a month later they were complaining about something to eat: "Let's go back to Egypt—at least there we had plenty to eat!" Even after God sent them manna to eat, they bellyached. At one point Moses cried out, "O God, what am I to do with this ungrateful people? One more incident and they will stone me to death!" On another occasion he had to remind them that he had taken nothing from them and that he had not gotten rich at their expense. You only say that when you've been accused. "Who knows," suggests Elie Wiesel, "perhaps God's decision not to let him enter the Promised Land was meant as a reward rather than as punishment."[6]

And yet as troublesome and disappointing as they were, Moses would not forsake his people. He even defended them against God's anger.

When God saw the people dancing around the golden calf, he was so angry that he wanted to destroy them and told Moses so. But Moses pleaded with God, saying that God should not free his people only to turn around and kill them. To make his point further, he reminded God of God's promise to Abraham and Isaac and Jacob—to make of them a great nation.

Then Moses' heart broke and he said to God: "If you refuse to forgive them, and you destroy them, then go ahead and wipe my name out of your Book of Life too!"

Moses became like one parent defending his child to the other parent. God said to Moses: "Your people have sinned." And we can almost hear Moses saying: "When they are good, they are *yours*, but when they are bad, are they *mine?*"[7]

Moses pleaded and prayed and prayed and pleaded. And God Almighty heard the prayer of this Jew and changed his mind! He did not destroy them.

We get the picture of this great hero trying to pull God to his people and trying to pull his people to God. Moses: trying to pull heaven and earth together with his bare hands. We react with equal amazement: that Moses would stay faithful to such a people and that God would forgive and save us!

How did Moses keep on? Occasionally, just to keep going Moses would ask God for some sign, some assurance that he was still doing what God wanted. And God obliged. Remember that day when God showed Moses his Glory? God swept by, hiding Moses in the cleft of a rock, sheltering him with his hand. It was a new experience of God, one never before recorded. "I will make all my goodness pass before you," said God. It was the experience on which is based perhaps the most beloved verse of the Hebrew Bible, Exodus 34:6: "The Lord is a God merciful and gracious, slow to anger and abounding in steadfast love (*hesed*) and faithfulness." Grace. It was but for a moment, and all Moses saw was God's back; yet this brief, shining glory was enough to keep him going for the rest of his life.

Until that day when God showed him the Promised Land from Mount Pisgah and then called him home.

V: The Death of Moses

When Moses heard the word from God about his death, he spent his last hour blessing the tribes of Israel, one by one: Reuben, Judah, Levi, Benjamin, Joseph, Zebulun, Issachar, Gad, Dan, Naphtali, Asher.[8] Then he began his climb up Mount Nebo. Slowly he entered the cloud that covered its summit and waited for God. Looking back, he could no longer see his people. Emotion filled his eyes.

Jewish tradition describes the death of Moses this way:

> When he reached the top of the mountain, he halted. You have one more minute, God warned him so as not to deprive him of his right to death. And Moses lay down. And God said: Close your eyes. And Moses closed his eyes. And God said: Fold your arms across your chest. And Moses folded his arms across his chest. Then, silently, God kissed his lips. And the soul of Moses found shelter in God's breath and was swept away into eternity.[9]

As scripture says, "So Moses died . . . by the mouth of YHWH" (Deuteronomy 34:5).

And at the foot of the mountain the people of Israel wept for thirty days; partly out of guilt for the way they had treated him, partly out of grief for the loss of their leader and the part of God he had brought into their midst. They grieved the death of this man, this lonely and passionate and powerful prophet of God— Egyptian prince, murderer, shepherd, spokesman, liberator, YHWH's hero.

And from that time deep within their hearts was born a hope, a hope that defied all circumstances: a hope that another would come, a New Moses greater than the first, who would bring a new law, this one written not on stone but on hearts, this one based not on frail human will but on the Grace of God.

And come he did, the New Moses, with a New Covenant—not to abolish Moses and the prophets but to fulfill them.

Notes

1. Toni Craven, Professor of Hebrew Bible, Brite Divinity School, Texas Christian University from an address at Broadway Baptist Church, Fort Worth, Texas, August 1996.

2. C. G. Montefiore and H. Loewe, eds., *A Rabbinic Anthology* (London: Macmillan, 1938), p. 45.

3. Martin Buber, *Moses: The Revelation and the Covenant* (New York: Harper & Row Torchbook, 1958), p. 59.

4. Miriam's song revised by Anthony Burgess, *Moses* (New York: Stonehill Publishing, 1976), pp. 82-3. This verse is a collation of both Moses' and Miriam's songs.

5. This series of questions suggested by Burgess, *Moses*, pp. 120-21.

6. Elie Wiesel, *Messengers of God: Biblical Portraits and Legends* (New York: Random House, 1976), p. 199.

7. From the Midrash, cited in Montefiore and Loewe, *Rabbinic Anthology,* p. 243.

8. Simeon is for some reason missing in the text; scholars and Hebrew tradition must come to the rescue.

9. The prose version of Elie Wiesel, *Messengers of God*, p. 204.

10

Elijah the Prophet

Sometimes the light of God's word seems like a flickering lamp about to go out, but God's lamp never goes out. God will always find women and men to carry it. Some days it is carried by a single, lonely prophet.

Such a one was Elijah. If Moses is the most heroic figure of the Hebrew Bible, Elijah is a close second. Moses and Elijah came to personify the two major ways God revealed himself in scripture: the law and the prophets. Their names became synonymous with them. To say "Moses and Elijah" was to say "the law and the prophets."

To this day in the Jewish Passover meal a glass of wine is set in honor of Elijah and in the expectation of his return to prepare the way for the Messiah. In Jewish tradition, when a stranger appears with greatness, people ask, Is this Elijah? When Jesus walked on earth, people asked about him, Is he Elijah? In the gospels it is Elijah whom God brought along with Moses to talk with Jesus on the Mount of Transfiguration.

Who was this formidable figure whose huge life was recorded in eight scant chapters in the First and Second Kings? Come along and see.

I

We are abruptly introduced to Elijah in the first verse of chapter 17:

Now Elijah, the Tishbite, of Tishbe in Gilead, said to Ahab,
"As the Lord, the God of Israel lives, before whom I stand,
there shall be neither dew nor rain these years, except by
my word."

He seems to have come from thin air, and at the end of his life
he seems to vanish into thin air.

We catch Elijah at midcareer, no background information. But
this is no surprise. Backgrounds do not make prophets; neither do
parents nor Ph.D.s. Prophets are men and women seized by the
living word of God, its truth burning in their bones. They are those
who see through appearances and see the world as it really is.

Elie Wiesel says of the vocation of the prophet and of Elijah:

Who is a prophet? . . . Someone who sees people as they are,
and as they ought to be. Someone who reflects his time, yet
lives outside time. . . . A prophet is forever awake, forever
alert; he is never indifferent, least of all to injustice. . . .
Restless, disquieting, he is forever waiting for a signal, a
summons. Asleep he hears voices and follows visions; his
dreams do not belong to him. . . . Often persecuted, always
in anguish, he is alone—even when addressing crowds,
when conversing with God or himself. . . . There is sometimes
a theatrical aspect to him; he seems to recite lines written by
someone else. And yet, in order for him to be a prophet, he
must descend into the very depths of his being. In order for
him to be inhabited or penetrated—or invaded—by God, he
must be truly, authentically himself. . . . He is God's sounding
board. But, at times he is the last to know: Elijah spoke and
occasionally did not know what he had said.[1]

II

Elijah spoke forth God's word. And to whom did he speak? To
Ahab, king of Israel, a man not so much wicked in his intentions
as in his acquiescence to every evil influence around him. Ahab
had two major headaches to deal with. To use the words of an old
commercial, Excedrin headache number one was Elijah. "If generally speaking," Buechner quips, "a prophet to a king was like
ants to a picnic, Elijah was like a swarm of bees."[2]

Excedrin headache number two was Ahab's wife, Jezebel.
Jezebel knew that Yahweh and Baal worship were incompatible,

and she clearly took the side of Baal. Ahab married her to secure a political alliance with Phoenicia, and when she moved in she took over. One of her crusades was to force the worship of the fertility god Baal on the people; she set up idols and temples to Baal all over the countryside. She instituted and ordained a whole legion of priests of Baal, and she authorized the systematic execution of all of the prophets of Yahweh. It was not one of the happier chapters of state-sponsored religion!

Of course, Baal religion was not just an imported religion of an imperialistic queen; it was also the native religion of the country's not-so-distant past.

What was Baal worship? To this agrarian culture Baal was the god of fertility, his worship the worship of nature with its rhythms of rain and sun and seasons. It was the religion of the full harvest, the house full of kids, the life of security and pleasure and plenty. Here is the religion of a god you can see rather than one you can't see. It swaps faith for instant gratification.

We don't have to scratch deep beneath the surface of our piety today to see this kind of religion at work in us, to recognize our own versions of Baal worship. It is the native religion of our soil too. It is the religion of success (if it works—do it), self (if it serves me—do it), and sensuality (if it feels good—do it), that is, of pragmatism, egoism, and the pleasure principle. Our Baal gods have only changed names. Instead of the weather, we worship Wall Street; the precincts of politics become our sacred temples. We fall down before idols of beauty and fame.

Baal worship takes human goods and goals and elevates them to the place of God. We must be clear. Success, self, and sensuality are not evil in and of themselves; they are part of God's good creation. But when they take the place of God, they take on an evil proportion.

What names are given to our baals? Will Campbell, a prophetic baptist figure, left the South as a young Mississippian and took in a liberal theological education at Yale University. He was a leader in the civil rights movement, a convert to liberal Protestantism, but he also saw some of its temptations. In a book called *Up to Our Steeples in Politics*[3] he challenged the American church's temptation to make a god of politics. "Politics as Baal," he called it. Today it is the Religious Right that flirts with "politics as Baal."

These people have traded the moral persuasion of Christ for the moral coercion of the ballot box. The intoxication of political power is dressed up in Sunday clothes. Not unlike Jezebel. It is easy to forget that Jesus of Nazareth died on a Roman gallows, executed by the collusion of religion and state, enemy of both Caesar and the Moral Majority.

Baal worship is the worship of human desires as God. Our totem poles are carved with our own little gods, not the one true God. What is carved there? An American flag, a dollar bill, a hauntingly beautiful form? Our totems are mirrors of our human wants and pretensions. Yahweh's Ten Commandments come in a distant second.

III

By way of Jezebel's religious campaign and the compliance of Ahab, Baal worship had once again become the dominant religion of Israel. The Israelites had forgotten who had brought them out of slavery and ignored the sacred demands Yahweh made on their lives. Darkness covered the land as God's word flickered like a lamp about to go out.

Then crisis hit—in the form of drought and famine. Crisis is always a call to clarify one's faith. It brings a defining moment. It is God's call to wake up and choose what is important.

Elijah made sure that Ahab knew that this economic crisis was also a spiritual crisis. "No dew nor rain except by my word and God's." It was not a pronouncement that endeared Elijah to the king.

During the long drought God led Elijah to a brook named Kerith where he was sustained by its water and fed by ravens. Some modern scholars have tried to make this miracle more plausible to our "modern" minds, with absurdly comical results. By changing a couple of vowels the Hebrew word could read instead of ravens "Arabs," or the same Hebrew word can mean "merchants." Or, another proposal: since the root word for "ravens" means "to be black," why not assume that Elijah was fed by *blacks?* Imagine blacks or merchants or Arabs tramping through the wilderness to share their Big Macs with Elijah! I agree with

Davie Napier: "Blacks feeding a white? Arabs feeding a Jew? Merchants feeding a prophet? Ravens is better."[4]

When the creek itself dried up, Elijah followed God's lead, moved far north, and was sustained by a poor widow. She shared her meager rations with him, and miraculously her jars of flour and oil never ran empty.

One day the widow's son took sick and was at the point of death. The distraught widow said to Elijah, "Why did you come, you man of God, to expose my sin and kill my son?" Her grief led her to the same deep self-questioning we all go through: Is my misfortune the result of my sins?

"Give me your son," Elijah said, and, taking the boy to the upper room, he prayed a prayer of protest to God, a long and noble tradition in Hebrew scripture:

> Moses: Why do you treat your servant so badly? (Numbers 11:11 JB)
> Jeremiah: Yahweh, you have deceived me. (Jeremiah 20:7)
> Habakkuk: How long, Yahweh, am I to cry for help while you will not listen? (Habakkuk 1:2)
> Job: You use me for target practice! (Job 16:12-13)

What Elijah prayed with the boy in his arms was this wrenching cry: "Yahweh, my God, can it be your will to inflict this catastrophe on the very widow who opened her home to me?"

God heard his cry. Elijah then took the child to his mother and said, "See, your son lives." And so he did.

IV

All the while the drought continued. Three and a half years. Finally the word of God came to Elijah: Go face Ahab. I am ready to let it rain over the land. Elijah went.

When the two met, Ahab said, "Is it really you, you troubler of Israel?" Elijah responded, "It is not I who troubles Israel, but you and your kin—you are the troublers of Israel."

That conversation is a familiar refrain throughout history between prophet and king, the world and the Word.

Martin Luther King Jr. was called a troubler of America. We ourselves may have thought him so back in the sixties. But he replied like Elijah: It is not I who troubles America, but those who build "colored" and "white" drinking fountains, who maintain a separate and unequal educational system, who deny us a seat at Woolworth's and show us to the back of the bus. King was not the troubler. He exposed the demon of racism in our land, and as he exorcised it by the Spirit of God, it rushed out with violence. The violence inherent in our land, the subtle, systemic violence of racism, was brought painfully to the surface. Still today we suffer the legacy of centuries of racism. *The parents eat sour grapes and the children's teeth are set on edge, and their children's children.* These days our educational system bears the most public pressure for years of accumulated social sin, but the problem and the solutions touch every aspect of our common life, including our churches.

"You troubler of Israel," Ahab said. "No," replied Elijah, "you are the troubler."

V

The stage is now set for the dramatic showdown between Elijah and Ahab, between the 450 prophets of Baal and the lone prophet of Yahweh. Elijah issued a challenge to the prophets of Baal to meet him on Mount Carmel. (There were also 400 female prophets of the goddess Asherah, but these dropped out of the scene after their introduction. Did Elijah spare them in the slaughter to come? Were these female prophets not worth counting as casualties?)

Here is the scene. Two altars were erected on the mountain, one to Baal, the other to Yahweh. Elijah lifted the challenge: A choice must be made. It's either/or, not both/and. You cannot worship Yahweh *and* Baal. You must choose. If Yahweh is God, follow him; if Baal is God, follow him!

This temptation is always present within the human spirit. We want it both ways. We want Yahweh *and* Baal. We want to follow our human desires and God's desires. We want to trust God's power, but we also resort to the compulsive uses of our own power. Sometimes a choice has to be made. "No one can serve two masters," Jesus said. "You can't serve God and wealth" (Matthew 6).

As Elijah lifted the challenge, the crowd grew quiet. Elijah had held up a mirror, and they saw who they were, an equivocating people. This how Elijah put it to the people:

> How long will you go limping with two different opinions?
> (RSV)
> How long do you mean to hobble first on one leg then on the
> other? (JB)
> How long will you sit on the fence? (NEB)
> How long will you hobble on this faith and that? (Moffatt)

How long can we live divided up inside? How long in double-mindedness? It will wear us out and wear us down, and it will eventually destroy us. *"Blessed are the pure in heart,"* Jesus said. It was Kierkegaard who best captured what purity of heart means: "willing one thing." It is the end of double-mindedness. It is choosing who you will be.

"How long will you go limping in one direction, then the other?" Elijah said, probably hopping back and forth himself from one leg to the other in a parody of their spiritual condition. "Choose this day whom you will serve. If Yahweh is God, follow him; if Baal is God, follow him."

Then Elijah laid down the terms of the contest. Bring two bulls. You prepare an altar for one; I'll prepare one on my altar. You pray to your god and I'll pray to mine. The one who answers by sending fire to light the altar is the true God.

The people responded with a shout. "Play ball!" The contest was on.

The priests of Baal built their altar. From morning till noon they prayed. But there was no sound, no response, no fire. Then they began to do a crazy half-limp, half-dance around the altar designed to get Baal's attention. Still no action.

Then Elijah, in his full-fledged humanity, got carried away. He began to taunt them: "Cry louder to your god. Maybe he's meditating, or maybe he's gone on a vacation, or maybe he's asleep and needs to be awakened." Then Elijah got even more carried away and said, "Or maybe he's gone to the john!" (1 Kings 18:27). How embarrassed God must be at times with the ways we defend him. Most translators have camouflaged Elijah's embarrassing taunt in more polite language. So the RSV translates it, "he has gone aside"; the NEB, "he is engaged"; the JB, "he is busy"; and the KJV in its stained-glass voice, he is "pursuing." Today's English Version is all too clear: maybe he's "relieving himself." (I think I prefer the old translations!)

Carried away with the promise of victory, Elijah is like an obnoxious football fan whose team is ahead by twenty-one points at half-time.

Hearing these taunts, the prophets threw themselves into a frenzy trying to get Baal's response. They cried louder and louder. They cut themselves with swords and spears. But there was no answer from Baal.

Elijah then asked the people to come in closer. He built Yahweh's altar with twelve stones (representing the twelve tribes of Israel). He dug a trench around the altar and flooded the altar with water to magnify the miracle to come.

Then he prayed, "Answer me, Yahweh, answer me, so that this people will know that you, Yahweh, are God, and that as you let them go from you, it is yours also to bring them back."[5]

Immediately the fire of Yahweh struck the altar! The offering was consumed in flames, and the people fell on their faces and cried, "Yahweh is God; Yahweh is God!" (Which is, in fact, the meaning of Elijah's name: *Yahweh is God.*)

VI

With the rush of victory running through his veins and seeking to be obedient to the law of Moses that false prophets are to be put to death (Deuteronomy 13:5), Elijah said, "Seize the prophets, let none of them escape!" Here's how the scene ends: They seized them; and Elijah brought them down to the brook Kishon and killed them there.

It's not a pretty scene. We cringe at the violence. We like our politics bloody, but not our religion! That is, until we are really threatened, then we baptize our politics with our religion. And our wars take on the unholy zeal of holy wars.

Is there a higher revelation? The gospels tell of an episode on the Mount of Transfiguration when Jesus suddenly gleamed with God's glory, and God brought Moses and Elijah back from eternity to talk with Jesus there. While they talked, a cloud of God's presence appeared and a Voice said, "This is my son, listen to him!" Moses and Elijah, the law and the prophets, were being fulfilled in this figure called Jesus. And one distinguishing mark of Jesus' teaching was the call to peace and the prohibition of violence in God's name, for God's sake.

Recall this episode in Jesus' life. He had set his face to go to Jerusalem. They had to pass through Samaria, enemy territory for Jews. The disciples tried to find a place to stay in a Samaritan village, but they were turned away. James and John returned all angered by the rejection and said to Jesus, "Jesus, you've been rebuffed. Can we call down fire *as Elijah did* and destroy them? Can we, Jesus, can we?" No wonder James and John were called Sons of Thunder. Rambo I and Rambo II.

But Jesus rebuked them and said, "You do not know the spirit you are of. The Son of Man did not come to destroy the lives of human beings but to save them" (Luke 9:51-56). The higher way. *This is my son,* God said, *listen to him.*

VII

Elijah's triumph ends with a poignant scene. God had won the victory on Mount Carmel and now our attention turns to the crisis with which the story began: the drought. There had been no rain for three and a half years. Forty-two months. The ground was cracked and parched. Now according to God's promise the drought ends.

Elijah said to Ahab, "Get moving; it's about to rain." Elijah climbed to the top of Mount Carmel and crouched down on the ground with his face between his knees.

He said to his young servant boy: "Go and look out to sea." The boy went and looked. "There is nothing at all," the boy said. Seven times Elijah sent him to look. On the seventh time the boy excitedly reported, "Yes, I can see a cloud no bigger than a man's hand rising up out of the sea." Elijah said, "Go tell Ahab." And as he went, the sky grew dark, the winds came, and then the rain, the sweet, heavy rain.

And Elijah ran in front of the chariot, seventeen miles he ran, outrunning the horses, all the way back to Jezreel. After all that, you could have too.

Elijah: Part II

Elijah had just returned from the dramatic contest at Mount Carmel: the two altars, the 450 prophets of Baal, and the lone prophet of Yahweh. It was one of the most dramatic acts of God's power in all the Bible. It is glorious to follow God when God acts so openly, plainly, powerfully on our behalf.

But what if God is silent? What if there is no powerful, merciful, gracious intervention from God? The second half of Elijah's story could not be more different from the first half.

We have gone with Elijah to Mount Carmel, where God acted in such a visible, demonstrable way that we feel anyone would be a fool not to believe in God. Now we go with this same prophet to Mount Horeb, where God is silent, and we wonder if anyone *but* a fool could believe in God.

The last half of the story is set in three places: the juniper tree, Mount Horeb, and Naboth's vineyard.

The Juniper Tree

When Ahab arrived at Jezreel from Mount Carmel, he told Queen Jezebel all that had happened: the contest, Baal's impotence, Yahweh's power, Elijah's slaughter of the prophets of Baal, and the end of the drought—just as Elijah had spoken it.

If Ahab felt tempted now to believe in Yahweh, Jezebel soon changed his mind. When she heard what had happened, she swore to avenge the death of her prophets with the death of Elijah. Within twenty-four hours, she vowed, she would have his head on a stick.

She sent the death sentence to Elijah. The words were short, but Elijah got the message: "If you are Elijah, I am Jezebel!"[6] Get the point? "You may be prophet, but I am queen!"

If Elijah's humanity showed itself earlier when he taunted the prophets of Baal, it showed itself now in fear and spiritual despair. The text says, "Frightened for his life, he ran away." And where he ran was far south to the desert and to a juniper tree. Trembling with fear, sick with despair, overcome by self-pity, Elijah sat down under the juniper tree.

"It is enough," he cried. "I've had it. Take my life, O God. I'm only human. I alone am left who serve you, and now they want me dead. Just end it all now."

Have you ever felt the darkness of despair like his? He had thought the victory at Mount Carmel would turn the tide and ensure a return to Yahweh by palace and people—and his own sweet success as Yahweh's prophet. But that's not what happened. Ahab and Jezebel did not repent. The powers of evil in fact intensified. Jezebel was out to kill him, and a people who need Mount Carmel miracles to believe do not long stay faithful.

Have you ever felt like Elijah? You thought you'd finally turned the corner to some kind of victory, but now it feels like just another dreary bend in the road. Elation quickly sinks to despondency.

We've all sat under one juniper tree or another: of a sadness so deep you don't think you'll ever be happy again; of a depression ravaging your mind and spirit and body; of despair and hopelessness; of failure, shame, and self-doubt.

What happened next to Elijah was the quiet intervention of grace. First, he was given sleep—sometimes itself a remarkable gift. God "gives to his beloved sleep" (Psalm 127:2). As he slept, someone came and woke him and said, *Eat.* He looked up and saw a biscuit and some water. He ate and regained his strength.

Who was it there in the bleak southern wilderness who woke and fed him? Who was this someone? A stranger? An angel? God?

Sometimes grace enters in common, lowly, everyday clothing, the quiet intervention of God. Sometimes when we are at our lowest what comes to turn the tide is something small and simple: a call, a letter, a visit from a friend, a conversation over a cup of coffee, a good night's sleep, a dream hopeful, happy, and green. So God comes.

Mount Horeb

Revived by the sleep and food, Elijah traveled farther south to Mount Horeb, which was none other than Mount Sinai, the holy mountain of God where amid wind, earthquake, and fire God had given Moses the Ten Commandments and had revealed his holy Presence.

Elijah traveled to this sacred place the way we go back to our sacred places—hoping that the God who acted in the past will come and act again in our lives. We come hoping that what we felt before we will feel again; we come with desperate instinct, hoping against hope that the God who has saved us in the past will save us again.

Elijah climbed the formidable red, craggy mountain and lodged in a cave. God came near and asked, "Elijah, what are you doing here?" Elijah responded, "I have been zealous for Yahweh, Lord of hosts; yet the Israelites have forsaken thy covenant, ruined thy altars, and killed thy prophets. I alone, I alone am left and now they seek my life."

God said, "Go stand on the mountain before Yahweh." What happened next is one of the holy moments of sacred history. We bow before its mystery. In the stark simplicity of the Hebrew language, here is what happened:

> And there was a mighty wind,
> Not in the wind was Yahweh.
>
> And after the wind, an earthquake,
> Not in the earthquake was Yahweh.
>
> And after the earthquake, fire,
> Yahweh was not in the fire.
>
> And after the fire
> The sound of crushed silence.[7]

"And after the fire, a 'still small voice'" has been the translation we've learned. The "still small voice" has become almost a spiritual cliché. But what happened was the opposite of a cliché; it was the annihilation of all spiritual expectation, stated in three Hebrew words, *voice, silence, crush*. In a translation both literal and poetic, what happened was "the sound of crushed silence." A silence that was at the same time empty and full, an utmost silence that was at the same time the opposite of what was expected and more than was expected, a deafening quiet.

There Elijah was, hoping for God to reveal himself as before. In the wind like the wind that parted the Red Sea and rescued the Hebrew people from Pharaoh's army, but the wind came and Yahweh was not in the wind. In the earthquake like the earthquake that shook this very mountain where God gave Moses the Ten Commandments, but the earthquake came and God was not there. In the fire like the fire Elijah himself had seen come from heaven on Mount Carmel, but the fire came and God was not in the fire. All the expected modes of revelation came and went and God was not there.

Then the silence, the crushed silence, and Elijah covered his face with his robe. For in the silence, *God.*

With perfect spiritual instinct, the Jewish and Christian composer Mendelssohn in his work *Elijah* has inserted here an aria by mezzo-soprano that is based on Psalm 37, "O rest in the Lord, wait patiently for him, and he shall give thee thy heart's desires."

Wait on the Lord, the scriptures tell us over and over. Wait on the Lord through injury and illness, through sadness and despair, through tragedy and disappointment. Wait on the Lord, wait through the emptiness of soul and dryness of religion, through silent years, wait as long as it takes, for God will be there.

All of the most sacred experiences of God's presence came by Elijah: the wind, the earthquake, the fire. But God was not there. Have you gone back in spiritual desperation to some religious place or religious action, back to a place of retreat or worship, hoping for God to act now as God acted before, but nothing happened? You sing your favorite hymn, pray your most trustworthy prayer, reread your favorite scripture—and nothing. *Nada.* Nothing. Nothingness. The old words do not stir you; prayers seem to rise no higher than the ceiling; the symbols are empty. Not in the wind was Yahweh, not in the earthquake, not in the fire. Then silence, crushed silence.

Wait on the Lord.

Recommissioning and Reassurance

And now, out of the silence God spoke. He spoke the twin graces of recommissioning and reassurance.

First, the grace of a new call. God gave Elijah something to do. Something to do is sometimes itself a grace. God called him to reenter the political arena and anoint two future kings, Hazael and Jehu. And he called him to anoint his own successor as prophet, Elisha.

Then came the word of reassurance. In his spiritual depression Elijah had felt like the only one left who still followed Yahweh. The "Elijah complex" is the religious person's delusion that he or she alone is faithful, a martyr's grandiosity. God said to Elijah: Go back to your people. There are *seven thousand* left in Israel whose knees have never bent to Baal nor whose lips have kissed him! (So much for grandiosity!)

There are days we lose heart, when we believe we alone are left who love and follow God. But God comes to reassure us and gently chide us: Look, there are thousands who follow me and who have not bowed to Baal. The reach and strength of God's kingdom is far greater than we can see. The kingdom of God comes, Jesus said, "not with observation" (Luke 17:20).

We decry the lack of honest people in high places, but there are always people like Obadiah, in Ahab's court—someone I've not introduced yet. Obadiah was a high official in the king's court who feared Yahweh. While Ahab was trying to kill all the prophets of Yahweh, Obadiah was hiding a hundred of Yahweh's prophets in caves, protecting them and providing them with food throughout the famine. We worry about corrupt preachers, but God has promised that where shepherds are corrupt God will personally take control of the flock. We worry about the lack of courage in our own witness, but Jesus said, "If these disciples be quiet, the very stones of the earth will cry it out."

So on Elijah goes, recommissioned, reassured, and the vocation of the prophet turns a new page.

Epilogue: Naboth's Vineyard

The last scene takes place in Naboth's vineyard. It is a confrontation between Ahab and Elijah.

Ahab wanted a pretty piece of property adjoining his. The problem was it didn't belong to him. It belonged to Naboth, and Naboth refused to sell it to the king. He was one of the seven thousand who had not bent his knee to Baal nor kissed his lips! To sell the land of his fathers would be to break the law of God (Leviticus 25:23; Numbers 27:1-11; 36:7). He said so to the king, "Sir, forbid it to me to sell the inheritance of my fathers" (1 Kings

21:3). When Naboth refused to sell, Ahab went into a sulk. "Vexed and sullen," as the text puts it, he went to bed and refused to eat. When Jezebel asked him why he was sulking, he whined: Naboth won't sell his land to me. She replied, Who is King—you or Naboth? Are you a man or a mouse, "a king or a cup [of] custard?"[8] Jezebel then promised Ahab she would get the land for him as a gift. So she had Naboth framed: two false witnesses were bribed to say Naboth had cursed God and the king. Naboth was quickly sentenced to death by stoning. Then Jezebel went to Ahab and said, "Go take possession of the vineyard. Naboth is dead." (Note her words. No actor is implicated here, only a victim. It is the syntax of official obfuscation.)

Ahab went to take possession of the vineyard. While he was on his way, the word of Yahweh came to Elijah and told him to deliver the message to Ahab: "Having murdered, do you even now take possession! In the place where dogs licked Naboth's blood, they shall lick your blood" (21:19). When Elijah met Ahab in Naboth's vineyard, Ahab said to Elijah: "Have you found me, O my enemy?" Elijah replied, "I have found you."

With that last confrontation Elijah closed out his work. As prophesied, Ahab and Jezebel went to their grisly deaths. Ahab was killed in battle, and when his blood-filled chariot was washed out, the dogs lapped up his blood, and the temple prostitutes of Baal came and washed in it. Jezebel lasted a bit longer but met a similar fate. She was thrown from a window, and when the dogs had finished with her, all that was left was her skull, the palms of her hands, and her feet (2 Kings 9:35). "The grass withers, the flower fades," said another prophet, "but the word of God stands forever" (Isaiah 40:8).

The story has a surprise ending. Elijah did not taste death as other mortals had but was taken up into heaven amid a whirlwind, a chariot of fire drawn by horses of fire. (This time God *was* in the fire.) His end points to a hope of life beyond this one, a resurrected existence. "Swing low, sweet chariot, coming for to carry me home," is how the African American spiritual appropriates the scene. These two hopes together, that God's word will stand forever, and that life will find a fulfillment beyond life, are perhaps why Elijah is called "the Prophet," and why Malachi prophesied that Elijah would appear again, preparing the way for the Messiah.

Only one who had seen God in the lightning on Mount Carmel and waited for God in the crushed silence of Mount Horeb could prepare the way for One who would come partly revealed, partly concealed in human flesh, God's own son, who came to show God's face and by means of a terrible cross opened heaven's door.

Notes

1. Elie Wiesel, *Five Biblical Portraits* (London: University of Notre Dame Press, 1981), pp. 38-39.

2. Frederick Buechner, *Peculiar Treasures* (New York: Harper & Row, 1979), p. 9.

3. Will D. Campbell and James Y. Holloway, *Up to Our Steeples in Politics* (New York: Paulist, 1970), pp. 59ff.

4. B. D. Napier, *Word of God, Word of Earth* (Philadelphia: United Church Press, 1976), p. 28. These are his Beecher lectures based on the Elijah cycle.

5. Napier's translation, in *Word of God, Word of Earth*, p. 37. See also F. W. Krummacher, *Elijah the Tishbite* (reprint; Grand Rapids: Baker Book House, 1977); Elie Wiesel, *Five Biblical Portraits*, pp. 33ff.

6. See Davie Napier for this translation, *Word of God, Word of Earth*, pp. 58ff.

7. My translation is aided by the scholarship of Davie Napier, *Word of God*, and especially Samuel Terrien, *The Elusive Presence* (New York: Harper & Row, 1978), pp. 232, 270.

8. Buechner's phrase, *Peculiar Treasures*, p. 10.

11

Ruth: Embodiment of *Hesed*

Ruth is a story about intermarriage and cultural barriers, religious conversion, and the interfacing of mission and culture. It is the story of religious, tribal, racial, and social differences and how God is working with the colorful quilt of humankind to make us all one. And it is the story as well of how God's redemption operates on the smallest and most intimate of scales: in households trying to survive and do what is right.

Most of all it is the story of God's *hesed*. The Hebrew word *hesed* is perhaps the most important attribute given to God in the Hebrew scriptures. It means steadfast love; it describes God's faithful loving-kindness, the patient, persistent, never-giving-up-no-matter-what love of God, the love that will not let us go. It is the closest Old Testament word to what the New Testament calls "grace." The word *hesed* was often repeated in the singing of psalms and in Hebrew worship. The refrain of Psalm 118 (v. 1) is to the Jews what the hymn "Amazing Grace" is to Christians:

> O give thanks to the Lord, for God is good
> God's steadfast love (*hesed*) endures forever.

In our story, Ruth herself is the embodiment of *hesed*. She learned it from her mother-in-law, Naomi, and was able to return it to Naomi later, when Naomi was in great need. Ruth sets *hesed* in motion and when she does, it sets off a chain reaction of *hesed*, a "contagion of kindness," as one has phrased it.

Astonishingly, it is a foreign woman, Ruth the Moabite, who teaches the Hebrew characters of the story what their God is like. The word "Moabite" brought instant loathing to the hearts of those ancient Hebrew people. In the law set down in the book of Deuteronomy, Egyptians and Edomites, though foreign, are allowed to join the people of God, but as for Moabites:

> No . . . Moabite shall be admitted to the assembly of the Lord. Even to the tenth generation, none of their descendants shall be admitted to the assembly of the Lord because they did not meet you with food and water on your journey out of Egypt, and because they hired against you Balaam . . . to curse you. . . *You shall never promote their welfare or their prosperity as long as you live.* (Deuteronomy 23:3-6, emphasis mine)

Centuries of hurt and spite lie buried in those words. All that the Hebrews knew of Moabites was what others had told them—which is how prejudice and animosity persist.

The perfectly told story of Ruth has charmed poets and authors like Dante, Milton, Bunyan, and Goethe, but its most powerful influence has been in shaping the lives of Jews and Christians for almost three millennia. It is told in its entirety every year at Shavuot, the Jewish festival celebrating spring crops and the giving of the Torah. God's *hesed* is shown in the gracious provision of bread, scripture, love, and family.

Act 1: Death

The story begins with a series of tragedies. There was famine in Bethlehem (the town whose name means "House of Bread" now has no bread). A "certain man" named Elimelech left and traveled to the country of Moab with wife Naomi and their two sons. (Through the centuries rabbinic commentary has hinted that Elimelech's move might show a lack of mercy on his part: here a man of means decides to take his family to a more prosperous place, turning his back on the destitute of his village. The text itself does not suggest this, but later commentary asks the question, seeking, as is the human quest, some moral meaning in the misery of life.)

Fleeing death, however, they run into death. First, Elimelech died, leaving Naomi a single parent of two sons in a foreign land.

The two sons, Mahlon and Chilion, eventually took Moabite wives, Orpah and Ruth. But within ten years both sons were dead, leaving their wives childless as well as husbandless. Like the story of Job, Ruth's story begins with an unrelenting chain of tragic events.

Act 2: Homecoming

Act 2 begins as Naomi decides to leave Moab and return to Bethlehem. The famine there was over, and so she headed home, taking her two daughters-in-law with her. But along the way she stopped and tried to persuade Ruth and Orpah to go back to Moab. Naomi's speech was full of the kindness of God:

> Go, return each to her mother's house.
> May God do with you the same kindness [*hesed*]
> Which you have done for the dead and for me.
> May Yahweh give you recompense,
> In that you find security,
> Each in the home of her husband
> —1:8-9[1]

Naomi was willing to release them to go back to their homes and their gods so that they would have a chance to find new husbands and bear children. She prayed for her God, Yahweh, to take care of them even there in Moab, the land of strange gods.

Hearing her words, the daughters "wept aloud." They insisted, "No, we will return with you to your people." Naomi then intensified her pleas: "Turn back, go your way. I am too old to marry and have sons, and even if I were not, would you wait to get married until they were grown? No, you must go back. It will be better for you. Things are bitter with me here" (see vv. 11-13).

With that, Orpah turned to go back home, but Ruth still clung to her mother-in-law. Naomi intensified her plea once more: "See, your sister-in-law has gone back to her people and her gods; return with her" (v. 15).

Ruth then gave her timeless speech:

> Entreat me not to leave you or to turn back from following you! For wherever you go, I will go; where you lodge, I will lodge; your people will be my people, and your God my God. (1:16)

We may not at first glance recognize the extraordinary risk this young woman took and the astounding declaration of faith she made. Imagine the courage it took to emigrate to a culture that despised her people, knowing there was little or no hope she would marry and have children. Picture a young African woman, her face marked with tribal scars, choosing to return with her adopted mother-in-law to a white American subculture.

Her declaration of faith in Yahweh—your God shall be my God—was as courageous as any found in scripture. Old Testament scholar Phyllis Trible says, "Not even Abraham's leap of faith surpasses this decision of Ruth's."[2] Jewish novelist Cynthia Ozick calls her "a second Abraham."[3] The presence of God was on Ruth's lips as she made her declaration. Naomi's religious teaching—and God's *hesed*—had caught fire in Ruth's heart. And she was willing to risk everything a woman might want and need for that.

The final scene of act 2 is the homecoming. The text says Bethlehem was "abuzz" with excitement as the travelers entered town. "Naomi!" the women gasped. "Is it really you, Naomi?" But Naomi answered them: "No, do not call me Naomi—that means Sweet One. Call me Mara—Bitter One. For Shaddai-God has made me bitter indeed. I was full when I went away, but God has brought me back empty. God, the Judge, has testified against me. Shaddai-God has sentenced me to misery."

Her grief has thrown her into dark bitterness, which is where grief often lodges. It is interesting that the name Naomi used for God in her lament was the ancient name from pagan roots, "Shaddai-God." Sometimes old pagan images of God sweep through us, especially in desperate times, and we fear God is angry with us, paying us back for some wrong we have done. The face of God as Provider and Redeemer is obscured. Judgment religion takes over. "Where is your *hesed*, O God?" the Jews cried out as captives in Babylon, as do we in our extremity.

So Naomi's homecoming is spoiled by grief lodged in anger, bitterness, and fear of God's judgment. This sets the stage for the next act.

Act 3: Gleaning in the Sheaves

Act 3 begins with the two women on their own, starting over in Bethlehem. As Naomi slumped into passivity and depression,

Ruth sprang into action. She went to the fields to find enough grain to keep them alive. There was a gracious provision in Israel for the poor. Workers were not to clean up the loose barley and wheat dropped in the harvest. These "gleanings," instead, were to be left for those who were poor, indigent, and foreign.

Ruth went to glean in the field of Boaz. Boaz was a wealthy landowner who worked side by side with his workers in the field. He would greet the reapers with, "The Lord be with you," and they would answer, "The Lord bless you." On this particular day his eye caught sight of Ruth, and he asked who she was. The workers told him, "She's the Moabite woman who came back with Naomi. She's been on her feet since early morning, gathering enough for the two of them."

Then Boaz went over to her and welcomed her to keep gleaning in his field. He instructed the reapers to drop an extra measure of grain for her. Ruth asked why he, Boaz, was treating her, a "foreigner," so well. Boaz replied: "I have heard of all you've done for Naomi. For your kindness may God reward you, 'under whose wings you have come to seek refuge'" (2:12). Remember that line. We'll hear it again.

The contagion of kindness. The *hesed* of Ruth brings out *hesed* from Boaz. Love begets love. Then Ruth bowed and said,

> May I continue to find favor in your eyes, my lord,
> Because you have comforted me
> And because you have spoken to the heart of your
>   maidservant.
>
> —2:13

Something's heating up here.

That night Ruth returned home with a big bag of barley and some extra bread Boaz had given her. Naomi was startled: "Where did you get all that?" "I went to the field of Boaz," Ruth replied.

With this news of Boaz's kindness to Ruth, Naomi's grief begins to break up like ice floes melting in the spring. Her speech moves from cursing to blessing. The way she pictures God changes altogether: from harsh Judge to Giver of Life. Naomi now says of Boaz:

> Blessed be he by Yahweh
> Who has not forsaken his *hesed*

With the living and with the dead!
—2:20[4]

Then Naomi explained to Ruth how Boaz was a close relation to the family, one of their "circle of redeemers" (2:20). As we've seen, a redeemer in the Hebrew scripture was one who took responsibility for another. Members of the extended family were called to be redeemers for those whom life had left helpless. Now the compassion of Boaz the redeemer has begun to lift Naomi out of her grief. The chain reaction of *hesed* is in full swing.

Act 4: Encounter at the Threshing Floor

It's now Naomi who moves into action. She has perceived what Ruth and Boaz perhaps refused to admit—that romance was brewing. Could it be? Why, Boaz was old enough to be Ruth's father! Another piece of this puzzle was the Hebrew practice of "levirate marriage," part of their repertoire of family care. If a married man died without children, a kinsman could act as husband to his widow and make it possible for her to bear children. The purpose was twofold: to carry on the family name and to provide protection for the widow. Without children widows had no "social security," no place in the family. Naomi saw a way for this provision to benefit Ruth.

She concocted a plan. She counseled Ruth: "Boaz is sleeping at the threshing floor tonight. Bathe yourself, anoint yourself, and go there. After he has finished eating and drinking and lies down for the night, go lie down at his feet. He will tell you what to do."

Obediently, of course, Ruth went! She arrived at the threshing floor. Full of food and drink, Boaz had settled down for the night. Ruth slipped in through the darkness, lifted the covers about his feet, and lay down. About midnight Boaz reached for his covers. Lo and behold, a strange woman! Startled awake he cried, "Who are you?" "I am Ruth, your maidservant," she replied. Then she proposed to him on the spot. This is how she said it: "Now spread your wing over your maidservant, for you are a redeemer" (3:9).

She called his hand! Remember how he had said to her the day they met, "May God reward you and spread his wings over you"? Well, now Ruth says in effect: Practice what you preach.

Spread your own kind wings over me! In other words, Marry me, Boaz!

This midnight scene is masterfully crafted. It is full of electricity about all that could happen. But the story makes it clear: Ruth and Boaz are people of honor, and this is to be a night of high honor.

How did Boaz answer the young woman from Moab there at his feet? Here are his words:

> Blessed may you be by Yahweh, my daughter.
> You have made your latter *hesed*
> Better than your former,
> In not going after the younger men
> Be they poor or rich.
>
> —3:10

By choosing me, he was saying, your kindness for this old man is even greater than the kindness you've shown Naomi. So do not fear. You are a worthy woman; I will take care of you.

Then Boaz introduced a bit of suspense into the story: a legal detail. It seemed there was one "nearer redeemer," one kinsman closer in line, who must first be offered the chance to be redeemer to Ruth and Naomi. "If he will not redeem you, I shall," said Boaz.

When Ruth returned and told Naomi all that happened, Naomi said, "Just sit tight, my daughter. Don't fret. Things will work out, for Boaz will not rest until he has accomplished what he set out to do."

Act 5: Business at the City Gate

Boaz was true to his word. He went to the city gate, where business was transacted. Just then the nearer kinsman came by. Boaz said to him, "Stop and sit down, Peloni Almoni." *Peloni Almoni*, he called him. It's a Hebrew phrase that meant someone with no identity, a "John Doe." Why did Boaz call him that? Did he not know his name? Not likely. In a small town everybody knows everybody.

I think it was a mild rebuke: "Come and sit down, Mr. Invisible!" This man had made himself scarce when Ruth and Naomi came to town. He didn't want to step up and be the redeemer of an older widow and a Moabite woman. Perhaps Boaz's jab was meant to underline the man's flight from familial responsibility. At any rate, Boaz offered him the chance to buy Naomi's land with the proviso that he also assume responsibility for Naomi and Ruth.

Peloni Almoni did want the land but *not* the responsibility for the women. Such is the way with Peloni Almonies! So he refused. And right on the spot, in front of ten witnesses, Boaz executed the legal covenant to buy the land and take responsibility for Naomi and Ruth. Then he made the real announcement: Ruth would be his wife! Happy Boaz had a smile on his face, as the expression goes, even an undertaker couldn't get off.

All who were around the gate joined in a song of blessing: "May Yahweh make Ruth like Leah and Rachel [mothers of the twelve tribes of Israel] and give to Boaz the power to father children." Because Ruth had been childless in her first marriage and Boaz was old enough to join the local association for retired persons, this was no idle blessing!

Act 6: A Baby Boy!

If the first act was all darkness and death, the last act is all joy and excitement. Boaz and Ruth get pregnant (Boaz's smile gets even bigger) and are blessed with a boy!

The spotlight, however, turns from the happy couple to an even happier grandmother, Naomi. Her story began with death but ends with new life. Empty, bitter Mara is full and happy Naomi again.

Ruth turns her son over to Naomi to be his nurse—echoes of the birth of a royal son! The women of Bethlehem gather around Naomi and say: Blessed be Yahweh, who has provided a redeemer for you. This child will restore your life and will sustain you in old age. And as for Ruth, your daughter-in-law, who loves you and has borne him, *"she means more to you than seven sons!"* (4:15). Quite a statement in this patriarchal culture that placed far more value on sons than daughters!

The joyous cry of the women closes the book: "A son is born to Naomi!"

Conclusion

So Ruth's story ends, but God's story goes on and on. At the end of the book of Ruth there is a genealogy—a family tree. The son born to Ruth and Boaz is named Obed. And Obed has a son named Jesse who has a son named David. King David! Imagine. David had "foreign" blood in his veins, the blood of a Moabite woman named Ruth who taught the Jews what their God was like and gave us a picture of the *hesed* of God, the nurturing, never-giving-up love of God, perhaps best embodied in the feminine. This story gives no comfort to xenophobia or misogyny: an outsider, a woman, is hero, image of the invisible God.

Of course, even that's not all of the story. In Matthew's genealogy of Jesus we discover that Ruth is not only David's ancestress but Jesus' as well. When we look at Jesus' family tree, we see figures faithful and flawed, heroic and human, like Abraham and Jacob and David; a prostitute named Rahab; Bathsheba, David's other half in sin; and a Moabite woman named Ruth.

We glimpse the mystery of God's grace. How God works through the good and bad within each of us! How God humbles the proud in us and lifts the humble, takes the commonplace and makes it uncommon. How God took a bereft, widowed immigrant woman named Ruth and made her the foremother of King David and of Christ. How God took a hole-in-the-wall village named Bethlehem and made it through Ruth's actions a place of *hesed*. And how God took that same village a thousand years later and made it the center of the universe as a star stood in homage to a child nestled there in the straw, a child who would one day, for all time, become the Redeemer of the world and take responsibility for us all.

Notes

1. I am indebted here and throughout to the translation of Edward Campbell in his extraordinary commentary, Ruth, in *The Anchor Bible*, vol. 7 (New York: Doubleday, 1975).

2. Phyllis Trible, *God and the Rhetoric of Sexuality* (Philadelphia: Fortress, 1978), p. 173.

3. Cynthia Ozick, "Ruth," in *Congregation: Contemporary Writers Read the Jewish Bible*, ed. David Rosenberg (New York: Harcourt Brace Jovanovich, 1987), p. 378.

4. Campbell's translation, p. 88.

12

David: Blessing Given, Lost, Regained—Forever

Two great narratives tower over the Hebrew Bible: the Moses/Exodus narrative and the David narrative. The Hebrew people could not get David out of their minds. They had a love and fascination for this man, and in his life there is a reservoir of truth, terrible and wonderful, to which they have often returned to learn.

Who was this man who has so captivated the heart and mind of God's people throughout the years? This shepherd boy, musician, warrior, king? From his spiritual genius flooded forth the psalms. He was a man of extraordinary personal power. We would call it "charisma," but this charisma was more than the sum of his human gifts; his charisma was what the word first meant, a gift of God's spirit which blew upon him. He was the unabashed lover of Yahweh and the anointed one of God.

Perhaps above all, he reminds us of something central about us as human beings—that our capacities for good and evil are inextricably entwined and that with the increase of personal power and our capacity to do good comes the increase in our capacity to do evil. Take the powers of human speech: the better we are at revealing the truth the better we are at concealing the truth. David's story teaches us this truth and gives us a clue to how to live with these ambiguous human powers. It has to do with "having a heart after God's own heart."

This is what saved David (and finally saves us all), even amid the sin and wreckage of his life, and this is how God could continue to use him: he was "a man after God's own heart."

I

The story starts when David was a boy. He was red-headed and beautiful. He loved watching his father's sheep. It gave him a chance to be by himself, to dream, and to write songs inside his head. That was when he was most at home with himself.

He was the youngest son of his family, number eight, and still a lad when the story begins. The prophet Samuel came to his house to anoint Israel's next king. God had given Samuel the orders. Saul's time as king was about over. Though he was a man of prodigious physical gifts and an impressive leader, Saul's kingship hadn't worked out as he had hoped, or as Israel had hoped, or as God had hoped.

God instructed Samuel to go to Jesse's house and anoint one of his sons to be the future king of Israel. As Samuel announced the reason for his visit to Jesse's house, the firstborn son, Eliab, came forward. He was impressive, tall, and strong, like Saul, but God said, "No, he is not the one; you look on the outside, I look on the inside." One by one in order of birth they came, and each time Samuel was not given the go-ahead by God to anoint any of them. After seven sons the line ran out. "Is there no one else?" Samuel asked. "Yes, there's one more, the youngest. He's out looking after the sheep," Jesse answered. "Go get him," said Samuel, and they did. When young David walked into the room, Samuel knew he was the one.

Samuel took his horn of oil and anointed him to be king of Israel. And, as the text says, "the spirit of the Lord blew mightily upon him, from that day on." *David anointed* is the major picture of David's early life. "Life under blessing," one scholar has called it. As Samuel anointed him, the text comments, "He was red-headed, had beautiful eyes and was handsome." From the beginning the Israelites couldn't take their eyes off this David. The first time they saw him they loved him. Moses they respected, Abraham they admired, God they feared, but it was David they loved.

David's joy was his strength and his strength was his joy. As

Nehemiah says, "The joy of the Lord is your strength." If there was ever one who was born knowing God's pleasure in him, it was David. This is the state of grace called blessedness.

It came out in his songs. Psalm 18 was one of David's earliest psalms. "I am in love with you, Yahweh!" it began. Our translations have subdued the language, but there it is. The verb David uses is from *rachem,* or womb, the word for the deepest kind of heart love. So Terrien rightly translates: "I am in love with you, Yahweh." Such was the spiritual passion of this young shepherd, warrior, and poet.

> I am in love with thee, Yahweh, my strength!
> Yahweh, my rock, my fortress, my rescuer!
>   * * *
> For it is thou, O Yahweh, who gives light to my lamp,
> thou, O my God, who illumines my darkness.
> For by thee I can outrun an armed band
> and by my God I can leap over a wall![1]
>   —Psalm 18:1, 28-9

David, feeling his oats and God's too.

This early life of David was indeed life under blessing. Everything David did seemed charmed. When David was just a boy, King Saul was tormented by headaches. The servants called young David to play his harp for the king, and as he did, Saul's pain eased. Now David is being anointed to take Saul's place.

Remember the story of Goliath? The war between the Israelites and the Philistines had come to a standoff. The offer was made: let each side choose a champion. They would fight, and the nation's victory would go to the winner. It seems almost enlightened. The only problem was that the Philistines had Goliath, who looked like a giant on steroids, a "ringer" recruited from some high-security prison to represent the Philistines in the contest. He was nine feet tall, his armor weighed 220 pounds (twice David's size wringing wet), the shaft of his spear looked like a fence post, and the spear head itself weighed thirty pounds. When the challenge was made, with Goliath in full view of everyone, a Hebrew volunteer was nowhere to be found. For forty days Goliath made his challenge, and for forty days the Israelites shuffled their feet and looked around in vain for someone to answer.

Just then David showed up carrying some food from home to his brothers. David heard Goliath's challenge and went to King Saul and volunteered to fight. Saul was incredulous and balked. It was like sending Barney Fife to challenge Hakeem Olajuwon, or Sammy Davis Jr. to fight Muhammad Ali—and no points given for dancing and singing. Saul relented, however, and gave permission for David to go. He offered David armor, but David said no and went to face Goliath armed only with a slingshot and a few stones.

The story has become a permanent part of our collective memory. Goliath roared at the sight of David and trash talked him: "What!" he jeered, "You think me a puppy dog and you come with a switch?! Come on, young man, and I'll feed you to the birds and beasts."

David returned his own sanctified trash talk: "You come to me with sword and spear, but I come to you in the name of the Lord of Hosts. God will deliver you into my hands and I will kill you and cut off your head. This will be so the world will know that the Lord saves not with sword and spear, for the battle belongs to the Lord." Then David slung a stone, hit Goliath in the forehead, and killed him.

It was like that for David.

After David's defeat of Goliath and after his exploits as a warrior in Saul's army, Saul became insanely jealous of David. Perhaps it started with a song the people began to sing in the streets: "Saul has killed his thousands, David his ten thousands." Anthropologists have discovered a five-note musical line that is transcultural; in practically every culture it is a taunt. The words may be different but the sound means the same everywhere:

Nyah-nyah nyah-nyah nyah nyah!

I don't know what tune the people used to sing their little song, but I bet it began to sound like that musical taunt in Saul's ear:

Saul has slain his thou-sands, Da-vid his TEN thou-sands!

Saul tried to have David killed by sending him to the front lines. It didn't work; David returned a military hero. Soon thereafter David became a fugitive and an outlaw, a Robin Hood kind of figure, living by his wits and surviving all obstacles. Once when he came upon Saul sleeping and could easily have killed him, he refused to do so. One reason, no doubt, was the deep friendship and love he had with Saul's son Jonathan.

This part of David's life—as a young renegade warrior—ended when Saul and his sons were killed by the Philistines in battle. Among the sons killed was the beloved Jonathan. David composed a lament, as beautiful a lamentation as has ever been written, and asked that it be taught to the people of Judah:

> Thy glory, O Israel, is slain upon thy high places!
> How are the mighty fallen!
> Tell it not in Gath,
> publish it not in the streets of Ashkelon;
> lest the daughters of the Philistines rejoice,
> lest the daughters of the uncircumcised exult.
>
> *   *   *
>
> Saul and Jonathan, beloved and lovely!
> In life and in death they were not parted;
> they were swifter than eagles,
> they were stronger than lions.
> O daughters of Israel, weep over Saul
> who clothed you with crimson and richness,
> who put ornaments of gold on your apparel.
> How are the mighty fallen
> in the midst of the battle!
> Jonathan lies slain upon thy high places.
> I grieve for you, my brother Jonathan;
> greatly loved were you to me;
> your love to me was wonderful,
> passing the love of women.
> How are the mighty fallen,
> and the weapons of war perished!
> —2 Samuel 1:19-20,23-27 RSV, adapted

Such was the landscape of David's heart.

When David became king, he moved the capital to Jerusalem, a brilliant and shrewd political move that united all Israel behind him. The ark of the Lord was brought to Jerusalem, and dreams of a great temple to be built there were born in David's head. As the ark of the covenant was brought into Jerusalem amid a great procession, David stripped to his gym shorts and danced before the Lord with all his might. Can you imagine the king of Israel dancing ecstatically, unashamedly before the Lord and in front of the whole city? "Praise God in dancing!" (Psalm 149:3) he would write, and dance he did. Praise of God sometimes cannot be contained in word or song. It calls the whole body into praise— unaffected, unself-conscious praise. His wife Michal, however, was not happy at his display; neither was the worship committee. Things must be done decently and in order; isn't that what the Bible says? Let's not get too carried away. But the singer of Israel had become the dancer of Israel, critics be damned. God is to be praised and blessed with all you are, not politely appreciated as a piece of art people say you're supposed to like.

David under blessing. There was this swift current of praise and blessing flowing from God to David and through David on into the life of the people of God—David, a pure vessel of God's *berakah*, blessing and strength.

II

But then comes the next chapter of David's life, "David under curse," someone has called it. Second Samuel 8 records his heady rise to power with this ominous combination of verbs: *smite, take, subdue,* and *make holy* (or dedicate).[2] It is the language of holy war. His war efforts, sanctified by theology, overreached themselves. Too much bloodshed, too many lives and too many resources forced into the service of warfare. These realities would later prohibit David from realizing his dream and building God's temple.

But there was another episode, this one more intensely personal. David was at home in the palace while the troops were out fighting—that in itself was uncharacteristic of David. As David awoke from a midafternoon slumber and walked around the palace walls, he saw an image so beautiful it overwhelmed him: a woman bathing below. His better self would have rejoiced in the sight of her and offered this beauty to God in praise. As Gerard

Manley Hopkins would later write: "Give beauty back, beauty, beauty, beauty, back to God, / beauty's self and beauty's giver."[3] But David had long since lost that place where his best self was in view, and he knew when he saw her that he had to have her.

Discreetly but plainly the scene is laid out, captured, as Brueggemann notes, in the verbs. David *arose* and *walked* and *saw* (parenthetically, "she was beautiful"), he *sent*, he *inquired*, he *sent*, he *took*, he *lay*, she *returned*.[4]

And a child was conceived. There are some things even a king cannot control. Then comes the attempted cover-up and the murder of Bathsheba's husband. As Augustine said, "Sin is the punishment of sin." David panicked. He tried to entice Bathsheba's husband, Uriah, who was in combat, to take a few evenings off and spend some time with his wife (so to cover David's sin). Uriah would not indulge himself this luxury because of his loyalty to his men. Once David would have been so loyal. So David (picking up a trick from Saul) had him sent to the front lines of the battle to be killed. And so he was. "But the thing that David did was *evil* in God's sight" (2 Samuel 11:27). (Brueggemann points out that traditional translations are much too mild when they say that David's actions "displeased the Lord"; literally, what David did was "evil in God's eyes."[5]) The Lord loves this man; David loves Yahweh; the people love David. But David did what was evil. And if David can, so can we all.

The tragedy unfolds. Nathan the prophet came to David with a parable about a king who had many flocks but took the one lamb of a poor neighbor for his dinner. David condemned the king's action, and Nathan said, "Thou art the man." David broke down and acknowledged his sin. His heart after God's own heart was still pliable enough to know the truth and change his life. Sometimes our hearts are not so pliable. They are hardened by bitterness or pain, surrounded by psychological systems of defense, unable to respond to God and to truth.[6] But David cried out,

> Have mercy on me, O God,
>   according to thy steadfast love; . . .
> For I know my transgressions,
>   and my sin is ever before me.
> Create in me a clean heart, O God,

and put a new and right spirit within me.
Cast me not away from thy presence,
and take not thy holy Spirit from me.
—Psalm 51:1,3,10-11 RSV

God's forgiveness of David saved David's life. But it did not
avert the consequences of his sins. Sin, forgiven or unforgiven, has
its train of consequences. A life once blessed is now filled with
tragedy. I do not think "life under curse" is the best description.
Self-curse, maybe, but not God's curse. Perhaps "life in the tragic"
or "blessing lost" is a better description. David was no longer
living under blessing. He no longer felt God's pleasure in him.
There was no pleasure anyplace. I do not think we should see all
the tragic happenings of David's life as God's direct punishment
of his sins. Some were the cause-and-effect consequences of his
sin; some came from no one's sin or from someone else's sin. It is
important to say: all sin brings suffering, but not all suffering
comes from sin. It is also important to say: while God's forgiveness
does not rescue us from all the consequences of our sin, it can
rescue us from spiritual death, from self-damnation and self-
destructiveness that tempt us in the wake of our sin.

David's trail of tragedy includes unspeakable sorrow, including the death of the infant child he and Bathsheba had conceived,
a rape in the family, the rebellion of his son Absalom, who gathered
forces to defeat his father and was himself killed in the battle, and
God's forbidding David to build the temple because he had spilled
too much blood in military exploits. Call this portion of his life
"blessing lost" or "life in sin and tragedy." But the blessing was
not lost forever.

The redemption of David began even in the depths of his
darkness, with his capacity to face his sin—and with the conception of another son, Solomon, who would complete David's
dreams of the Lord's temple. It happened this way.

The child born to David and Bathsheba lived for only seven
days. During those days David prayed and fasted and pleaded for
God to spare the child's life, but God did not.

When the child died, the servants were afraid to tell David.
David overheard them whispering and guessed. The child is dead,
isn't he? Yes, he is dead.

The text then reports David's actions in nine consecutive verbs: he *arose, washed, anointed* himself, *changed* his clothes, *went* to the house of the Lord, *worshiped, went* to his house, *asked* for food, and *ate.*

The servants couldn't understand his behavior. We can never understand the ways of another's grief, and we're fools to judge. David said, "I have been fasting and praying and weeping, saying, 'Who knows, God may be gracious and the child live?' But now he is dead, and my grieving will not bring him back. I shall one day go to him, but he will not come back to me."

Then he went to Bathsheba to console her in her grief. His act of consolation became an act of physical love as they consoled each other with their bodies. And in this act of consolation a new son was conceived named Solomon, and the text says, "Yahweh loved him." Solomon's name means "peace," and while "peace" would never be a fitting name for Solomon, it was a fitting name for the moment of conception when forgiveness and peace and grief and consolation mingled in their embrace and brought forth new life.

III

As we look over the life of this man, these questions come: What does it mean to have a heart after God's own heart? Why does Israel love him so? What new thing does God reveal about the divine character in David's story? And why did the people not let David's story die with David, but started looking for another anointed one, a son of David, a Messiah?

What does it mean to have a heart after God's own heart? To be in love with God as David was in love: "I am in love with thee, Yahweh!" he sang. Imagine John Wayne saying something like that! But such was the spiritual passion of David. Such a passion means to love God so ecstatically that one would strip down to linen shorts and dance before the Lord and in front of the whole city and a disapproving wife. And it means this: having a heart that remained so receptive to God's spirit that even after so much sinning he could hear the prophet's accusation and say, "I have sinned against Yahweh." A heart in love, a heart of ecstatic praise, a pliable heart.

But there is more, and a few scenes from David's life give us a deeper glimpse.

The Water of Bethlehem

It was wartime. David was sitting around the campfire with his "main men." "The Three" they were called, and everybody knew who they were. David's reverie turned to his boyhood hometown Bethlehem and he said dreamily, "Boy, would I love to have a long, cool drink of water from the well in Bethlehem." Because that well was located behind enemy lines it was only a fantasy.

But "the Three" took David's wish as a challenge and took off on a secret mission to sneak through enemy lines and bring back a canteen of water from that well. At the risk of their lives they did so and came back to David. Their faces full of pride, mischief, and love for their leader, they presented the water to him. "Your water, *sir!*" they said, saluting him and handing over the canteen.[7]

If this had been an ordinary war movie, David would have thrown back his head with a roar, taken a long draw from the canteen, and then passed it around . . . and they would have laughed and laughed and laughed. But that's not what happened, not even close. David's face turned serious. His hands shook as he held the water, and with trembling hand he poured it out on the ground as an acted-out sacrament of his men's devotion. "Far be it for me to drink this water secured at the risk of my men's lives," he said. Anything gained at the risk of human life is holy, too holy to drink. When his men saw him do this, they would have followed him anywhere. And we can understand. The love that grows up between men in combat, who depend upon each other for their very lives, is a rare and precious and fierce love indeed. Add to that David's keen sensitivity to the devotion and sacrifices of the people around him.

The people of Israel would not forget this scene. It is placed at the end of David's story in Samuel, but the Chronicles put it at the beginning, as if to say, Look, this is what this man was like! (1 Chronicles 11:15ff.).

The Ark

David was fleeing Jerusalem with his priests as his son Absalom was mounting a revolt to capture the throne. As they fled, the priests came bearing the ark of the covenant. The ark was the chest containing the tablets of the Ten Commandments. It was the symbol of God's power and protection. Every military commander wanted the ark with him as he went into the battle. It was like the national flag and the Bible all rolled up in one. When David saw the priests hauling the ark with them, he said an extraordinary thing: "Carry the ark back into the city. If I find favor in the eyes of the Lord, he will bring me back and let me see it and its habitation, but if he says, 'I have no pleasure in you,' behold, here I am, let him do to me what seems good to him." It was a free, uncoerced yielding to the will of God, refusing to turn religion into magic (the attempt to coerce God's hand by religious words or actions) or to presume that God was on his side.

David's posture of bowing beneath the mystery of God's will is not unlike that of Abraham Lincoln, who as president of the United States was also a leader who had deep spiritual and theological convictions. Caught like David in a civil war that turned brother against brother and son against father, Lincoln fought for what he felt to be right but ultimately knelt before God and the mystery of God's will. On March 4, 1865, in his second inaugural address spoken in the last days of this terrible war he said,

> Neither party expected for the war, the magnitude, or the duration, which it has already attained. . . . Each looked for an easier triumph, and a result less fundamental and astounding. Both read the same Bible, and pray to the same God; and each invokes His aid against the other. . . . The prayers of both could not be answered; that of neither has been answered fully. The Almighty has His own purposes. . . . With malice toward none; with charity for all; with firmness in the right, as God gives us to see the right, let us strive on to finish the work we are in; to bind up the nation's wounds; to care for him who shall have borne the battle, and for his widow, and his orphan—to do all which may achieve and cherish a just and lasting peace, among ourselves, and with all nations.[8]

In David and Lincoln we see the pathos of great leaders, a conviction to do right, the humility to know what they see as right may not be God's ultimate right, and the reverence to bow beneath the mystery of God's will.

It was not unlike the Gethsemane words of Jesus facing execution on a Roman gallows: "Abba, Father, all things are possible to thee; remove this cup from me; yet not what I will, but what thou wilt" (Mark 14:36).

The Prayer of Thanksgiving

A final scene. David had wanted to build God a temple. God had told him no, that it would be left to his son Solomon. David had waged too many wars and had shed too much blood. David did not rebel. Instead, he set about to raise huge amounts of money, gave his own personal fortune, and offered these gifts to the Lord for the building of the Temple. As he and the people brought these gifts, David knelt and prayed:

> Thine, O LORD, is the greatness . . . for all that is in the heavens and in the earth is thine. . . . And now we thank thee, our God, and praise thy glorious name. But who am I and what is my people, that we should be able thus to offer willingly? For all things come from thee, and of thy own have we given thee. (1 Chronicles 29:11-14 RSV)

This scene shows a man who knew he was a child of grace and that every good gift, be it music or physical prowess or personal power, or wealth or wisdom, was a gift of God, freely received and freely given.

Do we not see the ways of the "heart after God's own heart" in this singer of Israel, and dancer before God, and charismatic warrior, and leader of great pathos, and preparer of a temple for God? Here was a man who, when going to make a sacrifice to God at the threshing floor of a man named Araunah, offered to buy the man's oxen, land, and wood for the sacrifice. When the man recognized him as the king, he bowed and asked to give the land, ox, and wood to the king for the sacrifice. But David said, "No, I will not offer to the Lord my God that which costs me nothing" (2 Samuel 24:24; repeated in 1 Chronicles 21:24). And it was upon that spot (and in that spirit) that years later the Temple was built, a place where people would come from all over the world to make true and worthy sacrifices to God.

Can you not see why Israel loved him so?

Is there a new thing that God reveals about God's self in

David's story? I think there is, and I think it is one reason the people could not let David's story die with David.

The pivotal scene is 2 Samuel 7. Nathan is here again—this time not in judgment but in consolation and promise. Nathan delivers these words from God to David: I took you from shepherd boy to king. I have been with you always and have given you victory over all your enemies. You may not build me a house, but I will build you a house (literally, "dynasty"), a son, and a family, and I will establish that kingdom forever. I will be his father and he shall be my son. When he commits iniquity, I will chasten him with the rod of men, but [and here is the new word] I will not take my steadfast love (*hesed*) from him. . . . And your house and your kingdom shall be made sure forever.

There it is: *if you sin you will suffer human consequences, but I will not take my steadfast love from you. Grace will abide.*

No wonder David knew himself to be a child of grace, blessed, unblessed, blessed anew. Perhaps this is why David, after the death of his newborn son, could rise, break his fast, get dressed, go to the house of worship, and go on with his life. And this is what sustained him through the awful train of tragedy and death that was to afflict his family. This is also why he would give himself to planning a temple he could never build.

Here is a man who could say, unembarrassed, "I am in love with you, Yahweh!" Here is one who could face his terrible sin, who was able to fight through a toxic shame that condemned him as worthless and tempted him to despair, and who then experienced a true guilt that let him go to his knees in repentance and rise forgiven.

Here is a man who in boyhood, in battle, in victory, and in disgrace, times of exultation and desolation, yielded himself to God for whatever God in God's pleasure would bring. Here is a man who in his last breath blessed the Lord and called Israel to do the same. Perhaps Psalm 103 is his most characteristic psalm:

> Bless the LORD, O my soul;
> > and all that is within me,
> > bless God's holy name!
> Bless the LORD, O my soul,
> > and forget not all God's benefits,

who forgives all your iniquity,
    who heals all your diseases,
who redeems your life from the Pit,
    who crowns you with steadfast love and mercy,
who satisfies you with good as long as you live
    so that your soul's youth is renewed like the eagle's.

The LORD works vindication
    and justice for all who are oppressed. . . .
The LORD is merciful and gracious,
    slow to anger and abounding in steadfast love.
God will not always chide,
    nor will he keep his anger forever.
God does not deal with us according to our sins,
    or requite us commensurate with our iniquities.
For as the heavens are high above the earth,
    so great is God's steadfast love to those who kneel before him.
As far as the east is from the west,
so far does God remove our transgressions from us.
As a parent loves a child,
    so God loves those who fear him.
For God knows our human frame;
    God remembers that we are dust.

As for us, our days are like the grass;
    we flourish for a time like a flower of the field;
the wind passes over it, and it is gone,
    where it blooms remembers it no more.

But the steadfast love of the LORD is from everlasting to
    everlasting
    upon those who fear him,
    and God's power unto righteousness to
their children and their children's children.

        *   *   *

Bless the LORD, all you angels,
    all you mighty ones who do God's word,
    who love the sound of God's voice!
Bless God, all the hosts
    all his servants who do God's will!
Bless God, all creation
In every place where God's reign rolls.
Bless the Lord, O my soul![9]

It was the promise of God's *hesed* that would never be taken away that would not let David's story die with David. Israel held on to the promise of a son of David, an anointed one who would come and bring a day of completed justice and peace, where grace was all and in all.

"Where is your *hesed*, your steadfast love?" they cried in exile and whenever their hearts were in the wilderness of despair. And God would come again and again with the divine *hesed*.

It was this promise that the crowds at Jerusalem remembered when they, one thousand years later, saw a man ride a lowly donkey into Jerusalem. Waving palm branches and strewing them on the street, they cried: "Hosanna to the Son of David! Blessed is he who comes in the name of the Lord."

Still he comes.

Notes

1. Samuel Terrien, *The Elusive Presence* (New York: Harper & Row, 1978), pp. 284, 288.

2. See Walter Brueggemann, *David's Truth* (Philadelphia: Fortress, 1985), pp. 81-82.

3. Gerard Manley Hopkins, "The Leaden Echo and Golden Echo," in *The Poems of Gerard Manley Hopkins*, ed. Gardner and Mackenzie (Oxford: Oxford University Press, 1982), p. 92.

4. See Brueggemann, *David's Truth*, p. 56.

5. Ibid, p. 62.

6. In *People of the Lie*, M. Scott Peck says we become evil when we refuse to admit our own darkness and project it onto others. David did evil, but his confession kept him from becoming evil. See *People of the Lie: The Hope for Healing Human Evil* (New York: Touchstone, 1983).

7. I am indebted to Roger Paynter, pastor of First Baptist Church, Austin, Texas, whose sermon on this scene enlivened it for me.

8. Abraham Lincoln, *Speeches and Writings, 1859-1865*, The Library of America (New York: Literary Classics of the United States, 1989), pp. 686-87.

9. Arranged and adapted by the author.

13

Jonah: God's Comedy

The book of Jonah is God's little comedy placed in the last part of the Hebrew Bible in the section traditionally called the "minor prophets." The designation is a bit confusing. Are we to pay less attention to these books than to the more familiar Isaiah, Jeremiah, and Ezekiel? You may feel like the clever but unprepared college student taking a Bible exam. To the question that said, "Name the minor prophets," the student answered, "Who's to judge?!" In fact, the designation "minor" has to do with the length of these books, not their importance. So take a look. There it sits between Obadiah and Micah.

Why call Jonah a comedy? It's a story that pokes fun at our human foibles and has a happy ending. Tragedy is about the inevitable, says novelist Frederick Buechner, and comedy is about the unforeseeable.[1] Jonah is full of the unforeseeable.

This is the story of the first foreign missionary—the first and the worst. But even though Jonah may have been the worst missionary, God figures out a way to use Jonah the preacher to fulfill the divine purpose—just as God figures out a way to use us in all our peculiar quirks of personality and character.

Jonah has been called a man of "negative disposition."[2] Temperamentally the opposite of Norman Vincent Peale, Jonah would have written "The Power of *Negative* Thinking." Jonah didn't like people a whole lot, especially Ninevites. In fact, you could have said about Jonah what was said about Matthew Arnold, a writer and literary critic known for his cranky disposition. Of his death and trip to heaven the quip was made: "He won't like God much."

So how did a cranky, misanthropic preacher wind up furthering God's plan to save all people? Let's go to the story and find out.

Act 1: Call and Flight

The tale begins with God's call to Jonah: "Arise, go to Nineveh, cry out against it; tell them their wickedness has come before me." Jonah was dumbfounded. *Nineveh?* The very name brought fear and revulsion to the ancient Hebrew heart. Capital of dreaded world power Assyria, Nineveh personified all that was evil: opposition to Yahweh, sin, cruelty, and ruthless power. It was the epitome of what five-point Calvinists call "total human depravity." (I know some four-and-a-half-point Calvinists: they believe in "partial total human depravity." That is, they believe that everybody's totally depraved—except themselves.)

Jonah could not believe that God wanted him to go preach to Nineveh. They deserved no mission of mercy. "Nineveh!" Jonah said. "Me, preach your word to Nineveh!?" his voice cracking. "Talk about pearls before swine. *No way, Yah-weh!*"

We can relate, can't we? What cities of our century have roused our fear and loathing? Berlin, Tokyo, Moscow? What cities in our country push your hot buttons of prejudice? New York, San Francisco, Miami? I was sitting with twenty thousand Southern Baptists at a meeting in Indianapolis a few years back and heard widespread, obscene laughter when someone at a microphone compared a couple of American cities to Sodom and Gomorrah and suggested an equal fate for them. There's a "pride of place"— and a prejudice.

Prejudice is a funny thing. Its focus shifts from face to face; it's the projection of our own shadow side, the fear of the "other." Some hate blacks, some hate Mexicans, some hate whites, some hate Japanese, some hate gays and lesbians, some hate the rich. Some just hate *bigots!* That's probably our bigotry of choice. It's all a self-defeating game. Augustine asked the question fifteen centuries ago: Why do we think our *enemy* can do us more harm than our *enmity?*

What did Jonah do when told to go to a place he loathed? Prophets are supposed to "stand before the presence of the Lord." Instead, Jonah "fled the presence of the Lord" (1:3). God said, "Go east—to Nineveh." Jonah went due west—to Tarshish, a faraway place where he could forget and disappear. Margaritaville. If you're fleeing from Yahweh, go where nobody's heard of Yahweh. Isaiah 66:19 names Tarshish as one of the places where no one had heard Yahweh's name or seen God's glory. Tarshish—the proverbial South Seas island, the land of forgetting. Sounded good to Jonah. He bought a ticket and boarded a boat sailing toward Spain and Tarshish.

Act 2: The Trip

While the ship was on its way west, away from Nineveh and Yahweh, a storm arose. The sailors were frightened for their lives. Meanwhile, Jonah was fast asleep down in the belly of the ship. The sailors woke him and asked him to pray to his god. When their prayers didn't work, they resorted to magic (as do we in our extremity when religion doesn't work). They cast lots to see who was responsible for the storm. The dice fell to hapless Jonah. "What's your story?" they asked. "I'm a Hebrew," Jonah answered, "I worship Yahweh, who controls the land and the sea (not to mention the dice you just threw). It's all my fault. Throw me overboard!"

Was this an act of gallantry on Jonah's part? Was it suicidal spite aimed at God—I'd rather die than live in a world where God loves Ninevites! Was it the final vanity of a man wallowing in despair? Montaigne wrote an essay on "vanity" and described such a state of mind: "When I am in a bad way, I grow bent on misfortune; I abandon myself to despair."[3]

There's a thought to ponder: despair as a form of vanity. A martyr complex has vanity in its mix. What a piece of work we are.

The sailors obliged Jonah and tossed him into the sea. The sea calmed, and the sailors converted to Yahweh on the spot! The text says they worshiped Yahweh, making sacrifices and vows. So here's Jonah, a missionary success despite himself. God can use even our vain despair.

One delightful rabbinic telling of the scene has the sailors repeatedly throwing Jonah overboard. Over he goes and the sea calms. They retrieve him back on board, and the storm starts again. Into the sea he goes again, and the storm stops. They pull him back in and the storm gets going again. This is repeated several times until the great fish ends the foolishness and gobbles Jonah up. Enough already!

Act 3: The Fish

Act 3 happens inside the whale. The text doesn't actually say "whale." It says *dag gadol*, or "great fish," species undefined. We've filled in the word "whale," the biggest sea creature we can imagine.

This part of the story has been subjected to some of the most foolish speculation in the history of Bible scholarship. Perhaps no other text in scripture has given rise to so many rationalizing attempts to explain how Jonah could have survived three whole days in the belly of a whale. In his novel *Moby Dick*, Melville satirized them mercilessly.[4] One explanation: Jonah found a hollow tooth inside the whale's mouth and hid there. Just think, if the whale had a good dentist, Jonah wouldn't have made it. Another explanation: Jonah hid in the carcass of a dead whale for three days. There's an appetizing thought. A third explanation: Jonah was picked up by a ship named "The Whale."

In the past hundred years, some liberal biblical scholars have tried to find a natural, rather than a supernatural, explanation. Other, more conservative scholars have countered with, "If Jonah didn't live in a whale's belly for three days, then you can't trust a single word of scripture and you're calling Jesus a liar 'cause he said Jonah was in the whale's belly for three days. You calling Jesus a liar?"

Both camps seem to miss the point. We concentrate on the chemical composition of the digestive juices inside the whale and we miss the drama going on inside Jonah.

Here's the crux: Jonah, who could not believe God would love Nineveh, would rather die than live in a world like that; and God, who loves both Nineveh and Jonah, would not let Jonah so easily consign himself to damnation and death.

We see the drama of salvation at work. As Jonah descends to

the bottom of the sea, God sends a great fish to catch him and haul him back to life. It's God's odd mercy in action: Jonah, who's done his best to flee the presence of Yahweh, finds himself inside a giant fish, alone with himself and the inescapable presence of Yahweh. Psalm 139 probably came to his mind—and not without irony:

> Where can I go from thy Spirit?
> Where can I flee from thy presence?
> If I ascend to heaven thou art there.
> If I make my bed in the depths of Sheol, thou art there.
> If I take the wings of the morning and dwell in the uttermost
>   parts of the sea,
> Even there thy hand shall lead me
> And thy right hand shall hold me.

In truth, the fish was not Jonah's punishment but Jonah's salvation; a monster of the deep became an angel of the deep—the whale, an ark.

Act 4: Jonah Recalled

Three days later the fish spat Jonah back on shore—which goes to show, as someone has quipped, you can't keep a good man down. But that wasn't really the case. Jonah still had an attitude sour enough to curdle a whale's stomach. (How do you picture Jonah here, newly spat out on shore? Aldous Huxley said once that the people in El Greco paintings looked to him like they'd been inside the whale: thin, elongated, wan, a bit green.) What's interesting is the lack of change in this freshly regurgitated prophet. The fish had changed Jonah's *destination* but not his *disposition*, had changed his *geography* but not his *theology*. Anyone who thinks Jonah had a change of heart has not read the text in a while.

God called Jonah again: Get up, go to Nineveh and proclaim the message I give you. Same song, second verse. This time Jonah went, not happily but grudgingly, not because he was filled with compassion for Nineveh but because once you've tried to escape in a ship, been caught in a storm, identified by dice, tossed overboard, ingested by a giant fish, and unceremonially deposited back where you started, you figure you don't have a whale of a choice left. (His story reminds me of the wry entry in *The Oxford Dictionary of the Christian Church* of a ninth-century theologian named Gottschalk who was forced into a monastery by his parents, fled, was captured, and was assigned to a monastery in Soissons, where, in the words of his biographer, he "devoted himself to the study of theology and elaborated on an extreme doctrine of Divine predestination.")

So off Jonah went to Nineveh delivering his message of judgment, hoping against hope that God really would destroy them. He delivered the message in five Hebrew words:

> Forty
> Days
> More,
> Nineveh's
> Toast.

Can't you picture Danny DeVito cast in the role of Jonah, waltzing through town delivering his terrible message, barely able to disguise his glee? If Jonah had delivered his sermon in "proper" homiletical form, that is, three points and a poem, his three points would have been: (1) God is just, (2) you are sinners, and (3) Sayonara—Bye-Bye!

And the poem? Something like this:

> In forty days, you Ninevites,
> The Lord will rain down fire.
> Like ham on a spit
> You'll turn bit by bit.
> You've roused the Almighty's ire.
> For your sins you'll die, I prophesy,
> They are many, more than a few.
> It is forty short days
> Till your buildings he'll raze
> And God makes you a Bar-B-Que!

We can hear the secret glee in Jonah's voice as he preaches hellfire and brimstone to the Ninevites. He didn't give an altar call, didn't sing "Just As I Am," not even one verse. He simply laid the message on them, left town, and sat down on a nearby hill, waiting for God's fireworks to begin.

Act 5: Repentance

What happened? The unforeseeable. Repentance happened, much to Jonah's dismay. All over the great city of Nineveh we see the miracle of turning, from the king all the way down to the cattle. And their repentance was more than words: the people truly turned from their evil ways. Everyone put on sackcloth and ashes, ritual sign of the penitent heart. Even the bandannas around the dogs' necks were blackened with ashes. Righteousness reigned.

The king's call to repentance bore the mark of true reverence: "Who knows, God may yet repent and turn from his fierce anger so that we perish not" (3:9).

"Who knows": language that bows before the holiness of God. These are not words of one trying to make a deal with God. This cry does not presume what God will do. This is repentance based solely on what God wants and what is right, regardless of what may come. "Who knows, God may yet . . ."

And with the city's repentance, God repented. God changed his mind because the people changed their hearts. What a staggering thought! The God of the universe is no "unmoved mover," no God of fixed fate. The God of freedom has inserted radical freedom into history. We have choices before us . . . and an open future. This God is affected by what we do. What you do makes a difference to God and to the universe. God is not the God of the inevitable but of the unforeseeable.

Act 6: Jonah's Fit

Jonah is not happy with this beautiful turn in the story. Besides sparing the evil city, God just made Jonah a false prophet. Jonah preached destruction; God spared the city. He spoke as God told him to, and God made him look like a fool. Moreover, in Jonah's mind God's reckless, prodigal mercy undermined the moral order.

Jonah raged at God, quoted scripture at God: "Why do you think I went to Tarshish? I knew you wouldn't do it. I knew that you were, and I quote, 'a gracious God and merciful, slow to anger and abounding in steadfast love, who repentest of evil.' [Exodus 34:6]. I've heard it; I've been to Bible drill. You speak of *hesed*, your sickeningly steadfast love. *Hesed schmesed!* I knew you'd go soft. Don't you realize your mercy makes a mockery of your justice?!

Go ahead, God, and take my life," Jonah said. "I'd rather die than live in the kind of world you've set up."

He was one of the chorus of God's cranky people who through the years have said, "I hate God's enemies with perfect hatred. Why can't God do as much?"[5] Writer Anne Lamott's priest friend Tom says, "You can safely assume you've created God in your own image when it turns out that God hates all the same people you do."[6] And in his spiritual snit Jonah asks to make his own sweet exit from the world.

Like all of us, Jonah wants to write his own end to the story. But he can't and we can't. Only God can write the end of the story. We want to control the outcome, but we cannot—only God can do that. We're consumed with trying to write our own biography. God is the only true biographer. Spiritual sanity is giving the end of our story and everyone's story to God. It is a releasing of all outcomes and verdicts into God's hand.

Act 7: A Plant, a Worm, and a Question

There is one more scene, quite unanticipated, another unforeseeable turn. As Jonah sat there hoping to die, God "appointed" a plant, a green leafy plant, to grow up over him and become a shade against the blistering sun. For Jonah the plant was a sign of some goodness left in the world; it was a respite of joy, like the joy we take in the first green shoots of spring or in a shimmering rainbow against the darkened sky at the end of a storm.

But as the dawn came, God "appointed" a worm, and, in the muscular language of the King James Version, "it smote the gourd so that it withered" (4:7). The sun beat down even hotter and Jonah was cross-eyed with rage.

God asked a question: *"Do you do well to be angry? Is it right that you are angry?"* "Am I right?" Jonah answered. "I indeed do well to be angry; I'm so angry I could die." This man is angry unto death. God then asks one more question, the last words of the book:

> Jonah, you pity a little plant you did not make or tend or grow and which perished in the night. Can I not feel pity for a city of 120,000 people who cannot tell their right hand from their left, not to mention the animals? (Jonah 4:10-11)

The book of Jonah ends with that question, the only book in the Bible that ends with a question. Such an ending puts the final question back on us. When it gets down to the basics of basics, what do you want, God's justice or God's mercy?

Perhaps our very salvation consists of this, where we place ourselves. Do we place ourselves in the sinful circle of humanity who do not know their right hand from their left? . . . a people who some days cannot tell right from wrong? . . . who even when trying to do good do evil, and who therefore are a people totally dependent on God's mercy? Or do we place ourselves outside that city of humanity and blindly hope for God's justice?

Every one of us has deep within a zeal to see justice done *and* a longing for mercy. Both. Jonah is a stark portrait of humanity fixed on justice, oblivious of the need for mercy. Perhaps this is why the story of Jonah is read every year at dusk on the Jewish high holy day of Yom Kippur, the Day of Atonement. Every year it reminds the Jewish people of the power of repentance and the final need for mercy. So should we all be reminded. And those who have fixed a New Testament onto the Hebrew Bible read Jonah to be reminded as well of one "greater than Jonah" who preached repentance but also loved the mercy of God—one who said, "Blessed are the poor in spirit," and whose death on a tree was atonement for us all.

Notes

1. Frederick Buechner, *Telling the Truth: The Gospel as Tragedy, Comedy and Fairy Tale* (New York: Harper & Row, 1977), p. 57.
2. Leonard Michaels, "Jonah," in *Congregation: Contemporary Jewish Writers,* ed. David Rosenberg (New York: Harcourt Brace Jovanovich, 1989), p. 232.
3. Ibid., p. 234.
4. Herman Melville, *Moby Dick* (New York: Norton & Norton, 1976), pp. 261-63.
5. Thomas John Carlisle, *You! Jonah* (Grand Rapids, Mich.: Eerdmans, 1968), p. 43.
6. Anne Lamott, *Bird by Bird: Some Instructions on Writing and Life* (New York: Doubleday, 1994), p. 22.

14

Amos of Tekoa

If the prophetic vocation was born with Elijah, it came into particular power in the prophet Amos. Amos was the first of the "classical prophets" of Israel, the first of those we call the "writing prophets" because many of their oracles were preserved in full written form.

Many of their prophecies tragically came true, but their primary calling was to unveil not the future but the Absolute.[1] They were among the first to dream God's dream of a Messiah to come, but their major focus was on the urgent conditions of the nation in their own time and place. They have been called social reformers, but they were more than social reformers. They were, to use Samuel Terrien's words, "poets of divine presence."[2] They had received, to quote Longfellow,

> The prophet's vision
> The exultation, the divine
> Insanity of noble minds.[3]

But more even than poets of divine presence, the biblical prophets were poets of a better, truer world, a world ordered by the justice and peace of God. Their poetic speech, says Walter Brueggemann, was "a prophetic construal of a world beyond the one taken for granted."[4] They saw the irrationality of the present social order and envisioned in ecstatic speech an alternative reality shaped by God. It was a pronouncement of judgment on the present order in hopes that the nation would return to God and God's ways. A quintessential prophetic speech is this one by Amos (in 5:11):

> Therefore because you trample upon the poor
> and take from him exactions of wheat,
> you have built houses of hewn stone,
> but you shall not dwell in them;
> you have planted pleasant vineyards,
> but you shall not drink their wine.

The prophets appeared on the scene at critical junctures in the history of the northern and southern kingdoms, Israel and Judah. They preached hoping to avert the nation's downfall. As you can imagine, they were not welcomed with open arms. People called them insane, but their madness was "the insanity of noble minds."

I

Amos was the mouthpiece of God, "the Lion [who] roars from Zion." Describing and defending his call, Amos said, "[God] kidnapped me from behind my flock" (7:15).[5] "Like some lamb seized by a mountain lion, I was seized by God's word," said Amos. "The Lord God has spoken; *I* must prophesy" (3:8).

His first (and perhaps last) sermon was an unforgettable scene. It was the most high and holy day for the nation of Israel—the yearly celebration at Bethel. On this day the people worshiped at the shrine of civil religion, where patriotism and religion mixed. The state and church joined arms to sing "God bless our Israel, land that we love." They had good reason to be happy. It was eighth-century Israel, the highest pinnacle of military strength and economic prosperity that the Northern Kingdom would ever reach. King Jeroboam II was rating high marks in the polls, and Wall Street was happy.

This yearly celebration at Bethel was like Inauguration Day in America. The president was there and so were the priests and the poets. One thinks of John Kennedy's inauguration—the Catholic cardinal looking on as Robert Frost read his poem, the wind blowing his white hair, or of Maya Angelou reading her poem at Bill Clinton's inauguration, or Billy Graham representing the American religious community at others.

Suddenly into the middle of the ceremony at Bethel walked an unknown, poorly dressed migrant farmer. Part of the year he tended a peasant's variety of sheep on the fringe of the desert. Then he moved north, where he pinched back sycamore trees, and then headed south again to herd a scrawny type of oxen. Known only as "Amos of the shepherds of Tekoa," perhaps an orphan, in he walked, like Cesar Chavez crashing an inaugural celebration, and announced an unforgettable message from God.

The crowd was confused and nervous at first—what would this rude intruder say? But soon their anxiety gave way to approval and applause. For Amos began pronouncing God's judgment on the *enemies* of Israel. (That'll preach!) "Thus says the Lord," his voice rang out:

"For the sins of Damascus I will punish them," says the Lord.

Amen! said the senators.

"For the sins of Gaza I will destroy them."

Amen! said the judges.

"For the sins of Tyre I will send proper punishments."

Amen! cried the Religious Right armed with Bibles and polling results.

"For the sins of Edom and Ammon I will repay," says the Lord.

Amen! answered the whole crowd, breaking into spontaneous applause. "This preacher may be scruffy-looking, but he knows how to *preach!*"

Then as they leaned forward, licking their lips in anticipation of the next denunciation from the Lord, Amos let them have it between the eyes.

"For the sins of *Israel*, for *your* sins, God will punish *you*."

To stunned silence, Amos went on: "You sell your righteousness for cash. You buy and sell the needy for *a pair of sandals!* You trample the heads of the poor into the dust."

Then he looked over the sea of $10,000 gowns, top hats, and tuxedos and said: "You lie on ivory beds while people are cold and lonely." He looked out at the pampered rich ladies and said: "You cows of Bashan, you sit around and say 'Bring me more to drink,' while people starve."

He turned to the judges and said: "Your courts of law are a sham. The famous and rich get preferential treatment; the poor and forgotten get no justice at all."

He said: *"You've been crooked so long you don't know what straight is.* Let me show you a straight line. I saw the Lord in a dream. He was standing beside a wall with a plumb line in his hand and he said, Amos, what do you see? and I said, A plumb line, and he said, This plumb line I now set in the midst of my people." Only God's word can set us straight.

II

Then Amos turned to the religious folk in the crowd, the preachers and the churchgoers, and gave an even harder word. "This is what God has to say to you: 'You come to church and use my name, but you ignore the needs of your neighbor. You may have religion but you don't have love. For that reason I despise your covered-dish suppers and your fancy worship services. When you take up offerings, I turn my head; you sing hymns but they are like noise to my ears.

"'Here is what I want,' says God: *'Let justice roll down like waters and righteousness like an everflowing stream'"* (5:24).

God would say this again and again through his prophets: "I don't want your lavish ceremonies; I want lives that are in line with my righteousness and mercy."

Newspaper columnist Sydney Harris once wrote a comment that evoked bushels of negative mail: "God could do well with less praise from his children and more imitation." That word was no more popular than Amos's word. God wants more than orthodoxy—right praise; God wants orthopraxy—right practice.

"Let justice roll down like waters and righteousness like an everflowing stream."

III

"Like waters . . . like an everflowing stream." A remarkable image, placed in Israel's geology and climate. God's justice and righteousness are life-giving streams of society. They replenish the barren land. And like an *everflowing* stream they must come— not like the flood waters that periodically rush over the parched land, never soaking into the soil, washing and wasting, leaving only ruin. Like an everflowing stream God's justice and righteousness should flow.[6]

Implicit in the image is a warning of judgment. When we block the flowing waters of justice with the dam of our greed, prejudice, and selfishness, then the earth dries up and withers. The waters heap up dark and furious against the walls of the dam until finally they break through, the torrential waters pouring over the land, destroying everything in their path. When this happens, God's justice has become judgment and his righteousness has turned into wrath.

Like an everflowing stream. God needs from us more than ritualistic kindness—fruit baskets at Christmas, a check once a year to United Way. Along with charity God wants justice. A Christmas turkey does not substitute for a living wage.

"Let justice roll down like waters and righteousness like an everflowing stream."

Remember a while back when the media publicized the famine in Central Africa? Our compassion moved us to send thousands of tons of grain, such huge quantities in such a short span of time that the grain spoiled and rotted on the loading docks.

Justice: Like rolling waters it needs to be, like an everflowing stream.

"Justice" and "righteousness" are key words in the Hebrew Bible. Twin words, they are used interchangeably. They are two sides of the same coin. The Bible does not let us choose between personal righteousness and social justice. We are called to both. I like to put them together: justice/righteousness. It is personal righteousness—telling the truth, keeping commandments; and it is social righteousness—a society ordered by the justice and mercy of God. It is racial justice and economic justice and a judicial system that operates equally for all. It is equal rights for all, regardless of gender or sexual orientation, and protection for the weak, disabled, and despised. It is the opportunity for work to all who want to work. These matters need more than occasional guilt-ridden splurges of concern, an occasional benevolence, voting once every four years in a presidential election. Like waters they need to roll, like an everflowing stream.

Justice in the Bible is the "righteousing" power of God setting things right in our lives and in our world, creating healed relationships, healed communities, and a healed earth.

How do we picture a just society or find a measure for one?

In John Rawls's classic, *A Theory of Justice,* he gives us an intriguing measuring stick.[7] A just society is one that is a humane place to live, no matter *where* in that society you find yourself living.

Rawls invites us to pick a society and a century. If you had to pick a nation and a period of history in which to live, which nation would you pick, knowing you could not choose where in that society you lived? First-century Rome, sixth-century China, seventeenth-century France, nineteenth-century England, mid-twentieth-century United States? The more just a society is the better your chances of a good life, regardless of where you were born in it.

What is social justice? Michael Novak gives a good, if dispassionate, description:

> The essence of social justice is to look with the eyes of justice ("give to each his due") at the present condition of society; to reflect with others about what needs to be done to improve things; and to act with others in practical, effective ways to move toward that goal.[8]

Are there prophets in our land, in our time? Marian Wright Edelman is as much like Amos as anyone in America today. As founder and president of the Children's Defense Fund, she challenges a prosperous America to stop ignoring the needs of its children and families, especially those at the lower end of the economic spectrum. She uses prophetlike, highly charged language (for example,"BMW is not an advanced degree,"[9]) and wields statistics like the sword of the Lord:

> Does it make sense for our federal government to spend each hour this fiscal year $33.7 million on national defense, $23.6 million on the national debt, $8.7 million on the savings and loan bailout, $2.9 million on education, and $1.8 million on children's health?[10]

Edelman issues this direct challenge to move America off its disastrous course. When the new century dawns, America will only be ready to compete economically and lead morally if we:

> stop cheating and neglecting our children for selfish,
>   short-sighted, personal, and political gain;
> stop clinging to our racial past and recognize that America's

ideal, future, and fate are as inextricably intertwined with
the fate of its poor and nonwhite children as with its
privileged and white ones;

love our children more than we fear each other and our
perceived or real external enemies;

acquire the discipline to invest preventively and
systematically in all of our children *now* in order to reap a
better trained work force and more stable future tomorrow;

curb the desires of the overprivileged so that the survival
needs of the less privileged may be met, and spend less on
weapons of death and more on lifelines of constructive
development for our citizens;

set clear, national, state, city, community, and personal goals
for child survival and development, and invest whatever
leadership, commitment, time, money, and sustained effort
are needed to achieve them;

struggle to begin to live our lives in less selfish and more
purposeful ways, redefining success by national and
individual character and service rather than by national
consumption and the superficial barriers of race and class.[11]

We are moving toward a future where one out of four of our
children will live in poverty. "The mounting crisis of our children
and families is a rebuke to everything America professes to be,"[12]
the lioness roars. The nation sits in silence.

IV

*"Let justice roll down like waters and righteousness like an everflow-
ing stream."*

Amos's words from God were not easy words, and they got
even harder: You talk about the future Day of the Lord when
the Lord God will come to earth and fix things. You think God
will defend you and judge your enemies. Instead it will be a day
of darkness for you because you have ignored God's ethical
demands. Woe to you who desire the Day of the Lord. "You will
be like a man running from a lion and running headlong into a
bear" (5:19).

There are echoes here of modern Christians who talk glibly
about the "Rapture" and speak of how glorious it is that they
("true believer" Christians) will escape the "Tribulation" God has

planned for others, all the while ignoring God's justice and right-eousness in the here and now. "You may have a surprise in store," warns Amos.

Amos had still another vision: Israel is like a basket of overripe fruit. The spoilage has already begun. The end is near (8:1-3).

Then came the darkest prophecy of all from Amos: There is a famine coming that is much worse than a famine of wine and grain, much worse than a shortage of oil and gas. "Behold, the days are coming," says the Lord, "when I will send a famine over the land; not a famine of bread, nor a famine of water, but of hearing the words of the Lord." All of Amos's words were hard words, just as some of Jesus' words were hard. But there is something far worse than hearing the hard word of a just God. It is hearing nothing at all. The final price of disobedience is that God will make his word so scarce that no one will be able to find it, so scarce, in Buechner's words, "that the world won't even know what it is starving to death *for.*"[13]

V

As you can guess, Amos did not become the king's favorite prophet. He was not invited to the White House to preach. In the seventh chapter of Amos we have a comic confrontation between Amos and the king's priest Amaziah. Amaziah sent a message to King Jeroboam, saying, "Amos has started a conspiracy against you. The land is not able to bear all his words!" (Sometimes we cannot "bear" God's word; but neither can we afford to ignore it.)

Then Amaziah confronted Amos face-to-face and invited him to leave town: "O man of visions, go back to Judah and do your prophesying there." (Love thy neighbor—send him your prophets.) "Never again prophesy at Bethel. This is the king's sanctuary." Prophets rarely belong in a king's sanctuary. A book was published a few years ago that was entitled *Sermons Not Preached at the White House.* Amos's sermon belonged there.

Amos replied: I am no prophet or son of a prophet. I am not here by profession or by choice. I am a shepherd, a pincher of sycamore trees. I was minding my own business, tending my flock, when God Almighty kidnapped me from behind my flock. Like some sheep seized by a mountain lion, I was seized by the word of God. The lion roars and I can do no other than roar myself.

VI

With that, Amos was thrown out of Bethel. Most likely he then went underground back to the south where he wrote down his visions and spoke to a small group of followers, two of whom might well have been a man named Hosea and a younger fellow named Isaiah who also had their prophecies recorded. The prophetic tradition continues.

As far as we know, for the northern kingdom of Israel Amos was God's last call to repent. *"Seek the Lord and live!"* Amos pleaded. *"Let justice roll down like waters and righteousness like an everflowing stream."*

But the people did not repent and the waters of God's justice and righteousness heaped up dark and furious against the walls of their stubbornness. Finally the waters broke over the dam of their sins, justice turned to judgment, and the Northern Kingdom fell to the mighty Assyrians and vanished from the pages of history.

Eighth-century Israel fell as most nations have fallen, not from without but from within. The inner decay of a people who will not hear God's word is what actually destroys a nation. All an outside nation has to do is mop up what's left.

VII: Conclusion

The lion roars still. Jesus did not abolish the law and the prophets; he fulfilled them. The kingdom of God has to do not only with the finding and losing of souls but also the finding and losing of nations. As Walter Rauschenbusch, father of the social gospel movement in America, said, "Nations die of legalized injustice."[14] A nation's only hope is to live under the "righteousing" power of God.

God is not mocked. If justice does not flow like waters, it turns to judgment. If righteousness does not roll like an everflowing stream, it turns to wrath. *"Let justice roll down like waters and righteousness like an everflowing stream."*

So says the prophet to us and to our nation: "Seek the Lord and live!"

Notes

1. Samuel Terrien, *The Elusive Presence* (New York: Harper & Row, 1978), p. 227.
2. Ibid.
3. Cited in Terrien, p. 227.
4. Walter Brueggemann, *Finally Comes the Poet* (Minneapolis: Fortress, 1989), p. 4. See also his *The Prophetic Imagination* (Philadelphia: Fortress, 1978).
5. Terrien's translation, *Elusive Presence*, p. 236.
6. See Martin Buber, *The Prophetic Faith* (New York: Harper & Row, 1960), p. 102.
7. John Rawls, *A Theory of Justice* (Cambridge: Harvard University Press, 1971).
8. Michael Novak, *Business as a Calling: Work and the Examined Life* (New York: Free Press, 1996), p. 149.
9. Marian Wright Edelman, *The Measure of Success: A Letter to My Children and Yours* (Boston: Beacon, 1992), p. 69.
10. Ibid.
11. Ibid., pp. 93-4.
12. Ibid., p. 94.
13. Frederick Buechner, *Peculiar Treasures* (New York: Harper & Row, 1979), p. 11. Author's emphasis.
14. Walter Rauschenbusch, *Christianizing the Social Order* (New York: Macmillan, 1912), p. 333.

15

The Story of Esther

The story of Esther is one of the most popular in scripture. Call her the Jewish Scheherazade. Esther is one of the five scrolls of the Hebrew Bible read in their entirety at the five great Jewish festivals. Read at the feast of Purim, it celebrates God's deliverance of the Jewish people from a Persian holocaust through the courage of Esther and the wisdom of her foster father, Mordecai.

But Esther has not always been popular in scholarly circles, Christian or Jewish. It's the only Hebrew book not represented in the Dead Sea Scrolls. Martin Luther once said, "I'm so hostile to Esther that I could wish she did not exist at all." It has not always fit into the "politically correct" or "doctrinally pure" canons of thinking. It is a bit racy and more than a little bloodthirsty. Moreover, the name of God is not mentioned once in the story. The Persian king is mentioned 190 times—God zero. But this very absence cries out for attention. It's as if the writer and hearers of the story are winking at each other to say, "God is absent? Watch and see!"

Whatever the scholarly objections, people of faith have always loved this story. It is the story of God working through people like us to overcome the dark powers of the world.

Scene 1: Vashti Banished

The story of Esther begins with the words, "This happened in the days of Ahasuerus." He is most likely the Persian king historians call Xerxes I. The opening scene is a banquet. (This book is replete with banquets, and the king is pictured at almost every moment as heartily imbibing wine.)

King Ahasuerus threw a feast for his officials and ministers at the palace city of Susa, his winter home. This feast lasted half a year—180 days. Then he threw a follow-up feast for all the citizens of Susa "both great and small," which lasted for seven days. All the men were in one hall, in a kind of stag party; the women were in another hall with Queen Vashti. On the seventh day when the king was "merry with wine" (read: "sloshed"), he commanded Vashti his queen to come before him wearing her royal crown so he could show off her beauty. (It may well have been a command to wear *only* her crown.) Vashti refused and the king exploded in wrath. It's probably not too modern a projection to say that she refused to be exploited and he grew wrathful at her lack of submissiveness.

Furious and humiliated, the king sought the counsel of his advisers. The chamberlain suggested that since Vashti had set a bad example for the wives of the kingdom by not obeying her husband, she should be replaced as queen. After all, the social fabric of the kingdom might unravel if wives get the idea they don't have to obey their husbands. So banish her as queen; get another "better than she," (read: "more compliant"). Then all women throughout the kingdom will properly honor their husbands.

This advice "pleased" Ahasuerus, and he ordered it done. (All through the story the Persian king acts on the counsel of his advisers. He seems to be a puppet in their hands. In fact, one of the few unaided initiatives he takes in the entire story is here at the start, drunkenly asking for Vashti to come parade her beauty for all his friends at the party.)

The chamberlain also had another plan that pleased the king. A new queen would be selected by means of a "great queen hunt" held throughout all Persia. The king would appoint officials who would go throughout the land and bring the loveliest maidens to the palace. These "finalists" would each receive a year's beauty treatment and then be presented to the king. The king then would choose the fairest to be queen. The plan would have made Hugh Hefner green with envy. It "pleased" the king and so he ordered it begun.

Scene 2: The Great Queen Hunt

Enter Mordecai the Jew from the tribe of Benjamin. He had been carried away from Jerusalem along with other captives by King Nebuchadnezzar. He found himself in Susa, the Persian capital, and in the role of foster parent to a young Jewish girl named Esther. Esther was an orphan, the daughter of Mordecai's uncle. She was "fair and beautiful," the scriptures say, and Mordecai brought her up as he would have his own daughter.

When the maidens were gathered, Esther was among the finalists in the king's search for a queen. With all the others she was given twelve months' beauty treatment at the king's private spa: six months bathing and massage in oil, six months with balsam and other perfumes and beautifiers.

Uncle Mordecai went every day to see how she was doing. He carefully instructed her to keep her Jewish identity hidden for a while, and she followed his guidance. (This issue of not disclosing her Jewish identity is a small detail to most modern readers; it was a life-and-death detail to many early listeners.) Finally the list of maidens was whittled down to seven beauties, and each went before the king. The moment Esther appeared, the contest was over. Ahasuerus "loved Esther above all the other women," and he made her queen on the spot. He then threw another feast, "Esther's feast," to celebrate her becoming his queen. (There was apparently no occasion that didn't call for a feast.)

Mordecai meanwhile kept his post at the king's gate. He had become a shrewd observer of life in the capital. One day he overheard a plot to kill the king being arranged by two of the king's inner circle. He told Esther of the plot and gave her the names. She reported to the king, who mounted an investigation, arrested the leaders of the coup, and had them hanged. The plot was foiled, and it was noted in the king's chronicles that Mordecai was the source of the information.

Scene 3: An Obscene Decree

After this shake-up in the palace leadership, King Ahasuerus raised up a man named Haman to be his chief prince. It was a bad choice. (If this were a melodrama, Haman would enter wearing a black mustache and cape, the music would turn ominous, and the audience would boo and hiss. A tradition at Purim is that every time Haman's name is sounded in the community rereading, the children hiss his name: Ha-man, Ha-man!)

All the king's servants were required to bow down to Haman, but Mordecai refused to do so. Those hearing the story would understand at once: a pious Jew bends the knee to Yahweh alone. The king's servants observed Mordecai's refusal to give homage and reported it to Haman.

When Haman heard, he flew into a fury. He thought of killing Mordecai on the spot but decided instead to make Mordecai's death part of a larger plan to exterminate all the Jews in Persia. *Evil always overreaches*—and if unopposed ends in holocaust.

Haman cast *purim*, or lots, to fix his strategy. A day was set for a pogrom to exterminate the Jews. He then went to the king with his speech, a masterpiece of political paranoia and racist innuendo. "There is a certain people," he said with a slur in his voice, "scattered throughout the kingdom. Their laws and customs are different from everybody else's, and they do not keep the king's laws. They are dangerous to the kingdom. It does not profit the king to tolerate them. If it pleases the king, they should be destroyed. Let us issue the decree and pay ten thousand talents to the ones who will carry out the king's plan." The idea of course pleased the king, who was putty in the hands of anybody who flattered him or alarmed him sufficiently. He took his ring off his finger and gave it to Haman: "The job is yours. Do as you wish with these people."

The king wrote the decree and sealed it irrevocably with his royal seal. The letters were an authorization to "destroy, kill, and annihilate all Jews, young and old, women and children in one day, the thirteenth day of the twelfth month of Adar." The Hebrew text captures the horror and insanity in these terse phrases:

> As the couriers swiftly fanned out with the king's resolution and as the decree was proclaimed in Susa's citadel, the king and Haman settled down to drink [!] while Susa was struck dumb.[1]

The city was dumbstruck, or as it is variously translated: perplexed, disturbed, thrown into confusion. The people of Susa knew in their bones something was wrong, terribly wrong.

Scene IV: A Young Queen's Crisis

When Mordecai heard of the decree he tore his clothes, put on the sackcloth and ashes of public mourning, and went through the city crying out loudly and bitterly.

Esther's maid came and told her what Mordecai was doing. Esther had not heard of the decree. (We may think it odd that she had no knowledge of the decree, but not so. Though she was queen, she did not rule. She was more like the most favored of all the harem.) She sent Mordecai some new clothes and begged him to take off his sackcloth and ashes. But Mordecai refused the clothes.

Esther then sent a chamberlain to see what was so distressing her foster father. Mordecai sent back a copy of the decree and begged her to make intercession before the king on behalf of her people.

Esther received the message and sent this response: "All the king's servants know that whoever disturbs the king uninvited in his inner chamber will be killed unless the king holds out his golden scepter and spares that person's life in his mercy. I have not been called to go to the king for thirty days."

Mordecai read her words, then sent back this forceful answer: Do not think that you shall escape in the king's palace any better than the rest of the Jews. If you keep silence, help will come from somewhere else, but you and your father's house will perish (Esther 4:13). Then these immortal words: "Who knows? Perhaps you have come to the kingdom for such a time as this" (4:14).

To this point in the story Esther has been undistinguished except for her beauty. Beauty is a good thing in its own right, but it can work to one's disservice. In one of his novels Frederick Buechner tells of a certain character, Mrs. Schroeder. "The main trouble with Mrs. Schroeder," he writes, "was that she was so pretty." She was so pretty that she never had to be anything other than pretty to have friends or enjoy success. "She never learned to be kind and generous and unselfish because she never had to."[2] Physical beauty can be a handicap if it keeps a person from developing deeper personal virtues of character.

Up till now, Esther has sailed through life on her great beauty. Mordecai had taught her from childhood the great virtues of character valued by the Jewish faith, virtues like courage and faithfulness and compassion. Will these habits of character emerge in this time of crisis? Or will she only be beautiful?

Pop culture wizard Andy Warhol said in his now-famous line that everybody has "fifteen minutes of fame" in life, one short moment when the world is watching and the spotlight is on. I'm not sure about the "fame" part, but he identifies something real: we each have slender moments of opportunity, crisis moments, times of decision when something crucial in our lives and in the lives of those around us is at stake. In that moment will we respond with our best self? Will our truest character come forth? The stories of the faithful from scripture are meant to be a training in character so that in those fifteen minutes of fame, in those times of crisis, our best can come to the fore, our virtues of character will shine. Flannery O'Connor wrote that "the [one] in the violent situation reveals those qualities least dispensable in his personality, those qualities which are all he will have to take into eternity with him."[3]

It was such a time of crisis for Esther. Mordecai underscored the moment: *"Who knows? Perhaps you have come to the kingdom for such a time as this."*

Esther pondered and then acted. Taking a bold initiative, she sent this word to Mordecai: Go, gather all the Jews in Susa. Fast for me. Neither eat nor drink for three days. I and my maidens will fast alongside you. Then I will break the royal law and go uninvited to the king's inner chamber. "If I perish, I perish."

She *had* come to the kingdom for such a moment as this. Her character shone forth; she was more than beautiful. She seized the moment prepared by God, and she trusted in God and God's way regardless of what was to happen.

On the third day Esther put on her royal apparel and stood in the yard of the king's inner court. The king saw her, and she had favor in his sight. He held out the golden scepter and spared her life.

She drew near. The king was moved (was it her beauty, her startling courage?). He said, "What is it you desire, Queen Esther? Whatever you request I will give you, up to half my kingdom."

Esther asked the king to bring Haman with him that day to her place for a banquet, at which time she would make her request. (Clearly she knew how to get him in a good mood.) The king, always ready for a party, called Haman and the table was set. This was quite an auspicious moment for Haman to be invited to dine alone with the king and queen. The honor was not lost on Haman, we can be sure. While they were "drinking wine" (!) the king again made his offer to Esther. She again delayed her answer and asked that they come the next day for another banquet. Then she would reveal her wish.

Haman and the king left. Haman was no doubt ecstatic. He was sure Esther's request would bode well for him, else why was he invited? But when he walked through the king's gate, his countenance changed. There was Mordecai the Jew, again refusing to bow to him!

Haman filled up with anger. He went home and revealed his pathetic soul to his wife and friends. He recounted all his accomplishments: his riches, the number of his sons (not daughters), all his political promotions up to chief prince, and now the honor of dining with the queen. (His wife and friends' eyes probably glazed over; they'd heard this spiel before, ad nauseum; the daily hearing of one's resumé gets a bit old.) But then Haman concluded: All this does me no good so long as I see Mordecai sitting at the gate insolently refusing to bow to me! Haman finds it impossible to be happy with what he has; he is made unhappy by everything he doesn't have. He lets the recalcitrance of one man spoil his feast. The sidelong glance has ruined him. Haman looks ridiculous but his disease afflicts us all—brooding envy, the incessant unhappiness of comparisons, the manic desire to have it all.

His wife arrived at a solution for her pouting husband: build a gallows fifty cubits high, and in the morning ask the king's permission to hang Mordecai on it. The suggestion "pleased" him and he ordered it built.

Fifty cubits high! Noah's ark was only thirty cubits high! The size is preposterous, but so is the size of Haman's envy and anger and ego. A gallows the size of the ark. An electric chair atop the county courthouse. It would be as much fun as a nationally televised execution. Haman licked his lips. (The story's exaggerated details are a bit of "gallows humor" designed for the pleasure of the audience, who knew the outcome already.)

Haman's wife went on. "After you make all these arrangements, go on to the queen's banquet. You'll feel better then," she said, patting him.

Scene V: A Delicious Turn

Chapter 6 begins with the words, "that night the king could not sleep." If the first turning point came with Mordecai's challenge of "who knows . . ." and Esther's courageous action, the second one was when God disturbed the king's sleep. God does that sometimes. The king rose and asked the servants to bring him some insomniac's nighttime reading, the king's chronicles—as good as any sleeping pill. As they were read to him, he noticed for the first time the name of Mordecai as the one who had reported the plot to assassinate him.

The next morning he called his servants and asked, "What has been done to honor this man Mordecai?" "Nothing," they replied. The king noticed a stirring in the courtyard. "Who is in the courtyard?" he asked."Haman," they replied. "Good. Send him in." Haman had come, of course, to seek Mordecai's demise.

The king said, "Haman, what should be done for a man whom the king wishes to honor?" Haman, thinking the king was referring to him ("Who else would the king wish to honor more than me!?"), replied, beaming: "Why, put the king's robe on him and put him on the king's horse. Prepare a parade for him. Let him ride throughout the city with a spokesman proclaiming, 'This is done for the man whom the king wishes to honor.'" The king liked the idea. "Good," he said, "take the king's robe and horse as you've said and prepare it all for Mordecai the Jew, who sits at the king's gate."

Mordecai?! Haman was morti*fied*! Now he had to prepare a parade for the man he had prepared to hang! There Haman trudged through the streets ahead of Mordecai, proclaiming, "Thus shall it be done to the man whom the king delights to honor." (My guess is the look on his face didn't mirror the king's delight.) Haman returned to his house crestfallen. He told his wife what had "befallen him." Befallen *him*! Envy has an invincibly egocentric universe. As he was moaning to his wife, the king's eunuchs arrived to whisk him off to the queen's banquet.

Again at table, again "drinking wine," the king repeated his offer to Esther. Esther finally revealed her request. "If I have found favor in your sight, let my life be given to me and to the lives of my people." She now unveils for the first time her identity: "My people and I are sold to be destroyed, killed, annihilated" (7:4).

The king replied dim-wittedly (after all, he had signed the order) and indignantly, "Who is the one who would presume to do this? And where is he?" Esther replied, "A foe, an enemy, and now sitting with us. It is Haman!"

The king rose in fierce anger (and probably not a little bewilderment) and went to walk in the garden. Haman, terrified, rushed to the queen's couch to beg for his life. When the king returned and saw Haman fallen at the queen's couch, he exploded. "Would you even force the queen before me in my house?" The text says that the king's words "left the king's mouth and covered Haman's face." Like ashes.

Then one of the king's ubiquitous chamberlains said, "Your majesty, a gallows with scaffolding fifty cubits high is available. It was the one built by Haman for Mordecai, whose word saved your life." The king took the bait: "Hang Haman on these gallows!" So the ashen-faced Haman was taken away and hanged on the very gallows he had built for Mordecai. And all the city could see.

Scene 6: A Disposition Regarding the Jews

Then Esther came before the king, fell before him, and pleaded that the king put away the decree he had signed to kill the Jews: "How can I endure to see evil and destruction come among my people?"

Ahasuerus called the scribes. Under Persian law, even he could not undo the earlier decree, but he could counteract it. He signed another decree granting the Jews the right to self-defense. They were allowed to gather together on the stated day of extermination, the thirteenth day of Adar, and stand for their life and destroy those who came to destroy them. (The Jews could not be killed with impunity. The right to self-defense claimed by modern Israel finds deep reverberations in this story.)

The king's new decree was signed, sealed, and delivered throughout the kingdom. When the day of Pur came, the day

Haman had set for the massacre of the Jews, the Jews gathered and killed their attackers.

Scene 7: And the Story Goes On . . .

Some amazing turnabouts have happened: Haman hanged on the gallows he had built for Mordecai, the mercenaries seeking to kill and plunder the Jews themselves killed. The thirteenth day of Adar, instead of being a pogrom for Jewish destruction becomes a day of deliverance and victory.

And Mordecai is given royal robes to wear. The story tells us that he grew and grew in "greatness." He "sought the welfare of his people and spoke *shalom* to them." He demonstrated the victory of statesmanship over raw political power—to use the words of Brazilian archbishop Dom Helder Camara, "the might of right" over "the right of might." Esther and Mordecai become champions of virtue in difficult times as they exhibit the qualities of wisdom and courage and loyalty and compassion and justness. Sir Thomas More said, "The times are never so bad but that a good man can live in them."[4] Or a good woman.

Esther's story is told to remind us that even though God may seem to be absent, God is present. God is in the shadows, behind the curtain of history, but forever at work. Esther also teaches us that God needs *our* hands, *our* hearts and minds and bodies to do the work of deliverance, and if *we* do not, God will keep on searching until someone else answers. Redemption is urgent business, and God uses human hands to do the work. Hitler was finally defeated, for example, but what if earlier on more had stood against him and for the Jews and the other victims of Nazi madness? God is at work, but if we do not join God, insanity and violence will have a longer day.

God is calling us as well to the exercise of uncommon virtues in difficult times. Like Chinese students standing and dying for freedom in Tiananmen Square, like Russian citizens stopping tanks with their bodies, like Rosa Parks, who refused to move her body from a seat in a Birmingham bus and ignited a civil rights movement.

In her violent situation, her moment of truth, Esther revealed those qualities least dispensable to her: courage and wisdom and

loyalty and compassion and justness. And these she had to take
into eternity with her.

Notes

1. Translation by Jack M. Sasson, "Esther," in *The Literary Guide to the Bible,*
   ed. Robert Alter and Frank Karmade (Cambridge: Harvard University
   Press, 1987), p. 336.
2. Frederick Buechner, *The Wizard's Tide* (San Francisco: Harper & Row,
   1990), p. 4.
3. From "On Her Own Work," cited in frontispiece of André Dubus, *The
   Times Are Never So Bad* (Boston: David R. Godine, 1983).
4. Ibid.

16

God and Human Tragedy:
The Story of Job

The story of Job is concerned with the deepest of problems: the problem of suffering in a world that was created by a loving God. It's what philosophers call the problem of evil, or theodicy. It wrestles with the challenge raised by MacLeish's words in his play based on Job, *J.B.*: "If God is God He is not good, if God is good He is not God."[1]

What answer do we have for the suffering of the innocent? for bad things happening to good people in a world created by a good God? MacLeish's character suggests that either God is powerful and not loving, or loving and not powerful. Such are the deeps the story of Job seeks to traverse.

Job's story is not unfamiliar to us. Death strikes and wrenches our child from our arms. A plane goes down and with it a dear friend. An accident permanently disables a young person. Job's story is the story of Liberia or Bosnia, where civil war has unleashed horror upon horror. Job is the twentieth-century Jew watching newsreels of the Holocaust—six million children of Abraham exterminated by a so-called Christian regime. At some point Job's story touches ours, and the anguish of his heart becomes our anguish. Pat answers will not do; they stick in our throats. The book of Job is given us to help us through the terrible dark of our suffering until we find our way back to God.

Listen to the story of Job.

I

Once many years ago lived a man named Job. You could have searched the world over and not found a better man. The Bible says he was "*blameless and upright, one who feared God and turned away from evil*" (1:1). Job had it all. He was good-hearted and enormously successful in all his endeavors. He had seven sons and three daughters and more sheep, camels, oxen, and donkeys than you could count. The Midrash adds that everything he had acquired he had acquired honestly. His house was open on all four sides so that every beggar through town could sit and eat. He helped the sick, the widows and orphans—all who had need.[2]

The scene shifts to heaven, where a dialogue ensued between God and one the text calls "the satan": (*hassatan* in Hebrew). The word means "accuser." Stephen Mitchell has translated it well: "the Accusing Angel."[3] God bragged to *hassatan* about the blamelessness of Job, and *hassatan* raised the challenge: "Does Job serve God for nothing? Test him and see." Do any of us serve God for nothing, with no thought of return? The events that follow will test Job to his limits, as life sometimes tests us all. Up to this time Job had been a model of righteousness and faithfulness. How long will Job last?

What comes now is a series of calamities, awesome in their suddenness and savagery. A messenger came running in and said, "The Sabeans took your donkeys and killed your servants who were watching them." Before he had even finished speaking, another came and said, "Lightning struck your sheep barn, burned the whole flock. Even the shepherds were killed!" Then as he was finishing, another servant rushed in and cried, "The Chaldeans raided your camels, killed your camel drivers. I alone am left." And while these words still hung in the air, another messenger came and said, "Sir, your sons and daughters were at a party when a great windstorm came and flattened the house. Every one of them is dead."

In one day Job lost his children, his flocks, and his fortune. He tore his robe, shaved his head in grief, but refused to curse God. "The Lord gives, the Lord takes away. Blessed be the name of the Lord," he said. It's more than we could have said.

Then Job himself was struck with leprosy. Sores covered his

whole body from head to foot. He went and sat down on an ash heap and scraped his boils with a piece of broken pottery. Job's wife came to him and said, "How long will you go on clinging to your innocence? Curse God and die." Did she think if Job made an exit the calamities would be reversed? But Job would not curse God. He rebuked his wife and fell silent.

II

Enter Job's three friends—Eliphaz, Bildad, and Zophar. When they saw Job, they could hardly recognize him, so ravaged was he by his misfortune. And seeing him, they broke down and wept. For seven days, says the text, they did not open their mouths. They simply grieved with him. They were there in silent, empathic presence. The Midrash says that in deference to the mourner one imitates his behavior. When Job arose, they arose. When he ate, they ate. When he wept, they wept. We are moved by their compassion and good sense.

But after seven days they opened their mouths, and when they did, they turned into fools. Listening itself is an act of acceptance and understanding, but they couldn't help themselves—they started talking back.

Job, you see, finally began to speak, and what he said questioned all the basic tenets of the accepted dogma of the day. Conventional religion said life is easy to explain—good things happen to good people and bad things happen to bad people. God rewards the just and punishes the wicked. The good prosper; the evil perish. Simple. But Job began to question this theology, and when he did, his friends rushed in to defend it.

III

Job's raw anguish is captured in Stephen Mitchell's translation:

> God damn the day I was born
>> and the night that forced me from the womb.
> On that day—let there be darkness;
>> let it never have been created;
>> let it sink back into the void.

*   *   *

I sit and gnaw on my grief;

> my groans pour out like water.
> My worst fears have happened;
> my nightmares have come to life.
> Silence and peace have abandoned me,
> and anguish camps in my heart.[4]

Job's friends were scandalized by his brazen and angry words, and they began to speak. Eliphaz had his say first. "Job, you should not be so impatient. God is faithful and just. He will work things out, just have faith. You comforted others in their grief with the wisdom of God; now take your own advice. If you are innocent, my dear brother Job, you have nothing to worry about. In God's good plan the righteous win, so hang in there. I'm telling you this for your own good, Job. Sometimes you just have to wait on the Lord" (chaps. 4–5).

Bildad spoke next. "God doesn't make mistakes, Job. You reap what you sow. Your dead children must have been guilty of *something*. What you need to do is get right with God. Just look at the canvas of history: those who forget God wither and die. Don't you know, Job my friend, that bad things don't happen to good people? So don't look to God for the answer; go take a look in a mirror" (chap. 8).

Zophar then entered the conversation. "Job, you are obviously guilty. God is punishing you *less* than you deserve, and you just add to your guilt by your complaints. Don't forget that God's ways are beyond our comprehension. God is Mystery. Do not presume or demand to understand it all [not a bad theological point, but used like this it only brings anguish]. Get your heart right, Job, and God will bless you" (chap. 11).

IV

With three friends like these, the saying goes, who needs enemies? Job called them "worthless physicians" and added, "If you would be silent, that would be your wisdom." Paul Scherer once said, "When you meet trouble with a truism you make trouble." Not all that the friends said was false. Some of it was true, but they were fools to say it so glibly in the face of another's tragedy.

Job faced his accusers and defended himself, voice trembling: "You do not understand the depth of my grief. My burden is as heavy as all the sand of the sea to me. You tell me to be patient? How can I be patient? Am I made of stone or bronze? Cannot I have feelings?"

Then Job turned to God and challenged him: "You are responsible for my pain, but it makes no sense to me. I do not deserve what I have received. You use me for target practice. You laugh at my misery. You are like a tyrant, a wild beast, a ruthless warrior. I am torn apart by my grief, destroyed by disease." Job's scream filled the air: *"Earth, do not absorb my blood! Let the cry of it wander all over the earth"* (16:18). All Job had left was words, and he was using them for all they were worth.[5] (See chaps. 6-7, 9-10, 12-14, 16.)

Upon hearing Job's words, the three friends attack him with a greater ferocity, a ferocity only the "righteous" can have. Eliphaz accused: "Job, you have simply forgotten all those sins you have committed. Surely you robbed the clothes off the backs of brothers. You must have refused food to beggars. There must have been widows and orphans sent away with nothing. Does not God see everything? Search your heart, Job. Be honest, Job. Make peace with God. Stop making him your enemy." Then Eliphaz thrust the dagger of scripture in to make his point clear: "God brings down the proud and saves the humble!" (chap. 22).

Job, weary and worn out by his friends' theologizing, refuses to debate their arguments. Instead he speaks with new poignancy about his lost intimacy with God: "Once God and I were as close as two can be. There was a time when his lamp shone on my head and by his light I walked through darkness. The friendship of God was upon my tent; God was near and my friends were near and my children were all about me. But now my wealth is gone, my friends are gone, my children are gone. Even God is gone. I look for him in front of me and in the back, to the right and to the left, but God, my God, is nowhere to be found. I speak and God no longer answers. I stand and God merely looks at me" (see chaps. 23, 29–30).

Each of Job's earlier speeches ended with a prayer to God, but now he cannot even pray. What he does is to raise his final defense. Job had prayed for someone to come plead his case—a Mediator, an Advocate, a Redeemer. No one came to his side, so now he becomes his own defense attorney.

One by one he lists all the ways a person might sin, at each point declaring, "I am innocent." Then he closes his argument, puts his signature on his legal brief and says, "I rest my case. It is *your* turn, God, to answer *me*." The last verse of chapter 31 says, "The words of Job are ended."

V

At this point a new speaker arrives, a bright and brash young theologian named Elihu. He has been overhearing the debate, dying to break in (suffering what has been called the "pain of undelivered speech"). He began: "All of you are wrong, but I, though young, have God's Spirit in me, so I can bring wisdom to this discussion. My words are like wine in new wineskins with no vent. I must speak before I burst" (32:19-20).

Elihu proceeded to debate all that had been said, then concluded, "I have something to say on God's behalf. Let a man lose himself in adoration of God and he will have no room for self-pity. Be assured, Job, God strengthens and purifies you through adversity: 'He delivers the afflicted by their affliction and opens their ear by adversity.'" (Again, good enough theology but cruelly imposed on someone in the throes of great suffering.) Then Elihu closed his argument with a glorious description of God's grandeur and tied the bow with a theological flourish that is aimed at Job (but is in fact an unwitting self-condemnation): "God does not regard any who are wise in their own conceits" (37:24).

VI

When Elihu has finished his smug theologizing, God breaks his long silence. From out of a whirlwind God answers Job. Job has asked God to answer and answer God does. God's answer is in the form of a series of questions—impossible, outrageous rhetorical questions, questions with images so intense that Job does not just hear God's voice, he *sees* God's voice.[6]

> Where were you when I laid the foundation of the earth? . . .
> Who measured the earth and laid its cornerstone? . . .
> Have you entered into the springs of the sea
>   or walked in the recesses of the deep? . . .
> Where is the way to the dwelling place of light? . . .

> Have you entered into the storehouses of the snow? . . .
> Has the rain a father? . . .
> Who has begotten the drops of dew? . . .
> Can you bind the chains of the Pleiades
>   or loose the cords of Orion? . . .
> Do you tell the antelope to calve
>   or ease her when she is in labor? . . .
> Is the wild ox willing to serve you? . . .
> Do you deck the ostrich with wings? . . .
> Do you give the horse his might? . . .
> Is it by your wisdom that the hawk flies,
>   stretching his wings on the wind? . . .
> Is it by your command that the eagle soars?

God asks Job,

> Shall a faultfinder contend with the Almighty?
> Has my critic swallowed his tongue?

Job answers,

> I am speechless: what can I answer?
> I have said too much already;
>   now I will speak no more.

Still God keeps on:

> Am I wrong because you are right?
> Will you condemn me that you may be justified?
> Would you like to take my throne
>   and execute your own justice?

Then God speaks of the forces of evil and chaos, the monsters Behemoth and Leviathan:

> Can you corral these two?
> Can you catch the monster of the sea with a fishhook?
> Who then is he that can stand before me?

Job answers in a whisper:

> I have spoken what I did not understand.
> I had heard of you with my ears;
>   but now my eyes have seen you.
> Therefore I must be quiet,
>   comforted that I am dust.[7]

Job bows before the mystery of God. We strain after the meaning. Sometimes this need leads us to assign blame in the midst of tragedy and pain—blaming self, or God, or others. God's presence in the whirlwind reminds us that the mystery of suffering is deeper than our minds can comprehend.

Job stands in awe before God. His spirit is very much like that of the psalmist:

> O Lord, my heart is not lifted up,
>   my eyes are not raised too high;
> I do not occupy myself with things
>   too great and too marvelous for me.
> But I have calmed and quieted my soul;
> like a child quieted at its mother's breast,
>   like a child that is quieted is my soul.
>   —Psalm 131 RSV, adapted

VII

God then turns to the friends of Job. "I am angry with you," God said, "because you have spoken falsehood about me. Your answers were falser than Job's questions. His doubts were truer than your beliefs." We hope they got the point.

The final scene ensues. God blesses Job with new wealth and with new children, seven new sons and three new daughters, not to replace those lost but to bring new comfort and joy. In wonderful Hebrew detail the text highlights the giving of the daughters by telling us their names—the eldest daughter Job called "Dove," the second, "Cinnamon," and the third, "Eyeshadow."[8] And it says: "In all the world there were no women as beautiful as Job's daughters."

Job asked for a Mediator (9:33), an Advocate (16:19), a Redeemer (19:25), someone to plead his case, to stand by him and with him and for him. His boldness in the face of suffering was answered by God in the whirlwind.

And there have been answers for us as well. Jesus spoke of the Holy Spirit as Paraclete, literally, "one called alongside us," our comforter, counselor, and strength. People have been sent as paraclete alongside us in the darkest of hours. And so was Jesus, Paraclete from God, bone of our bone, flesh of our flesh who bore our sorrows and was acquainted with grief, who was executed on a Roman gallows and who quoted Job-like from that cross the psalmist's cry: "My God, my God, why hast thou forsaken me?" (Psalm 22:1 KJV).

So the New Testament book of Hebrews says,

> We have not a high priest who is unable to sympathize with us in our weakness, but one who in every respect has been tempted as we are, yet without sin. Therefore, let us come boldly before the throne of grace that we may receive mercy and find grace to help us in the hour of need. (Hebrews 4:15-16)

Job—and Jesus—lead us there.

Notes

1. Archibald MacLeish, *J.B.* (Cambridge, Mass.: Riverside, 1958), p. 14.
2. Elie Wiesel, *Messengers of God: Biblical Portraits and Legends* (New York: Random House, 1976), pp. 215-16.
3. Stephen Mitchell, *The Book of Job* (San Francisco: North Point, 1987), p. 8.
4. Ibid., pp. 13-14. Mitchell's translation of Job 3:1-4, 24-26.
5. Wiesel, *Messengers of God*, p. 229.
6. Mitchell, *Book of Job*, p. xx.
7. This excerpt from Job chapters 38-40 blends the RSV and Mitchell in its translations.
8. Mitchell, *Book of Job*, p. 91.

17

The Story of Tobias: A Young Man, His Dog, and an Angel—

Introduction to the Apocrypha and the Book of Tobit

When I was growing up a boy in the Protestant and Baptist South, I had never heard of the book of Tobit or the Apocrypha. I'd never opened a "Catholic" Bible, and the only thing I knew about Catholics came from watching the basketball players recruited from New York City by the University of North Carolina make the sign of the cross before free throws. Because they won the 1957 national championship, I was pretty impressed.

The "Apocrypha" is the name given to a set of writings that came into existence in the last few centuries before Christ. The word *apocrypha* in Greek means "hidden," and the term is used to refer to books not widely accepted or not to be read in public, books not included in the final canon of scripture or books with secret or hidden wisdom.

The Jewish community excluded the books in the Apocrypha for two reasons: (1) they were written in Greek, not Hebrew, and (2) they were written after the time of Ezra and Nehemiah, the time they considered the cutoff for true inspiration.

Through the centuries the Christian church has debated whether to keep the Apocrypha in its Bible. Today Roman Catholic, Greek, and Slavonic Orthodox Christians still include the

Apocrypha in their Bibles, which means more Christians around the world include it than exclude it. Protestants have not included it, following the same reasons advanced by the Jewish leaders but also because they thought there was some doctrinally dubious material in it. In his monumental 1534 translation of the Bible into German, Martin Luther placed the Apocrypha at the end of the Old Testament, asserting, "These books are not held equal to the sacred scriptures, and yet are useful and good for reading."

All English translations of the Bible before 1629, including both Wycliffe's first translation (1382) and the King James Version (1611), contained the Apocrypha. Today many modern translations include the Apocrypha in what are called "ecumenical editions" that can be used by all Christians.

The book of Tobit is part of the Apocrypha. Most scholars place its time of writing around 200 B.C.E. and its place of writing in Mesopotamia or Palestine. The only complete form of the book is in Greek, but Hebrew fragments of the book have been discovered among the Dead Sea Scrolls, which suggests that it may have had a Hebrew or Aramaic original.

The book of Tobit was written to stress the providential care of God in our daily lives and to illustrate the way obedience must be lived out in daily home and community life. But the message is not as bland as it might sound.

The context of the book is crisis—political, social, and spiritual. Its frame of reference is *exile*. The northern kingdom of Israel fell to Assyria in 734 B.C.E. and Hebrew people were taken captive to Nineveh. The southern kingdom of Judah fell to Babylonia in 587 B.C.E. and Hebrew people were taken into Babylonian captivity. "How can we sing the Lord's song in a strange land?" they cried. Postexilic Judaism grew up in the aftermath of these national and spiritual tragedies and in the centuries of reconstruction and political upheaval that followed as they returned to their homeland.

The book addresses three main questions: How do people stay faithful to God while living in captivity? How do exiles survive emotionally and spiritually? How do believers keep their faith when all tangible signs of God's providence are gone?

Can we believe that there is a goodness at the core of existence? New Testament scholar Oscar Cullmann says, in a wonderful phrase, "There is faithfulness at the heart of all things."[1] This is the message of Tobit.

And the book turns us to the ordinariness of our days and to our daily obligations as the sphere where we prove our faithfulness in the darkest of times. It is not unlike the message of the prophet of the exile named Jeremiah: What is the path of hope in time of exile? It is the way of everyday faithfulness and ordinary love lived out in family, friendship, and community. How were the exiles to live in Babylon? Jeremiah wrote:

> Build houses and live in them, plant gardens and eat what they produce. Take wives and have sons and daughters; take wives for your sons, and give your daughters in marriage, that they may have children so they . . . may multiply there, and do not decrease. But seek the welfare of the city where I have sent you into exile, and pray to the Lord on its behalf, for in its welfare you will find your welfare. (Jeremiah 29:5–7)

In other words, when the big picture is dark or obscure, pay attention to the little picture; take care of those persons and duties closest at hand.

The Story of Tobias:
A Young Man, His Dog, and an Angel

Here is the story of Tobias. It reads like the libretto of a great comic opera. It is a wild and entertaining tale. Many characters move in and out of an intricate plot. The most famous scene has been captured in paintings through the years: Tobias, a young man carrying a fish, accompanied by an angel and a dog.[2] You may have seen such a painting and wondered what was going on in the scene. The story that follows will explain.

Tobit's Character and Calamities

Tobit was as good a man as could be found. He devoted himself to truth, righteousness, and charity. He came from the tribe of Naphtali, one of the twelve tribes of Israel. Although the tribe of Naphtali broke away from the house of David and set up its own place of worship in the mountains of Galilee, Tobit still returned faithfully to Jerusalem during holy days to offer his sacrifices in the Temple. Here was a man of uncommon loyalty. He gave not one tithe but three. The first tithe of crops and herds he gave to the priests of the Temple. The second tithe he distributed in Jerusalem. The third tithe every third year he gave to widows and orphans. This was no ordinary man.

Tobit married a woman named Anna, and they had an only child named Tobias. Then came the Exile, however, when he and other Hebrews were deported to Nineveh. Because of his faithfulness to Jewish dietary restrictions, God rewarded him. He found favor in the eyes of the Babylonian king Shalmaneser and became a buyer of the king's supplies.

During this time he performed many acts of mercy. He gave bread to the hungry and he clothed the naked. If he saw the dead bodies of his kinspeople thrown over the walls of Nineveh, he would, like a Hebrew Antigone, go out and give them a decent burial. King Shalmaneser had died, you see, and had been succeeded by an evil king, Sennacherib, who was killing many Jews. Tobit would steal the dead bodies lying in public humiliation in the streets and bury them.

When the king heard what Tobit was doing, he ordered Tobit's execution. When his property was seized, Tobit fled Nineveh in fear. Sennacherib, however, was murdered soon after by one of his own sons, and Tobit was given the freedom to return. The new king restored his property, and Tobit was united with Anna and Tobias.

Then came the Jewish festival of Pentecost, a festival celebrated today by both Jews and Christians but for different reasons. For Jews it was the celebration of the harvest, and a festival meal was prepared.

Tobit sat down to the lavish meal, but before he ate he told his son, "Go seek out a poor loyal-hearted man from among our exiled kindred and bring him here to share this meal." The benevolence of Tobit was again at work. The boy went but returned with this message: one of our people has been murdered, strangled, and his body thrown down in the marketplace. Tobit jumped up and left, his meal untouched. He took the body from the square and hid it until sunset when he could bury it. When he returned to the feast, he washed, ate, and remembered the words of Amos, "Your festivals shall be turned into mourning and all your songs into lamentation."

Then Tobit wept for his people.

At sundown he dug the grave and buried the body. His neighbors watched and laughed: "He had to run away the last time when they hunted him down for doing this. Now he's doing it again." They thought him stupid; Tobit was simply trying to be faithful.

That night he bathed and went out in the courtyard to sleep. It was a hot night and so he left his face uncovered. He didn't know there were sparrows on the wall above him. Their droppings fell, still warm, into his eyes [I'm not making this up!] and caused white patches to form over them. The doctors tried various ointments to no avail: Tobit was blind. Misfortune had struck a good and righteous man. Such things happen. And we agonize over the absurdity. Black children killed by a bomb in a Birmingham Sunday school class. Tragedy that strikes the good and the bad without distinction. Here Tobit, a good and righteous man, suffers the ridiculous and absurd fate of blindness by way of bird droppings.

During the next four years Anna took up piecework to support the family. She spun wool and made cloth. One day when she delivered her cloth, the owners paid her in full and also gave her a kid from the goat herd. When she brought the kid home, it began to bleat. The blind Tobit heard it and asked, "Where did you get that kid? I hope you didn't steal it. Give it back! We have no right to anything stolen."

Apparently Tobit had more charity for other people than for his wife! She explained that it had been given to her as a present above her wages. Tobit refused to believe her and insisted she give it back. Anna retorted, "So much for all your good works and charity. Now we see what you are!" It wasn't the first time a speech like that has been heard in a home: To everyone outside the home you're a saint, but to us at home you're a jerk!

The exchange sent the blind Tobit into even greater agony. He wept and moaned and groaned and wept and finally prayed that God would end his life. "It is better for me to die than to bear so much misery."

Would God answer his prayer? We shall see.

Sarah's Tribulation

A new character is now introduced. At the very same moment that Tobit was praying, a young woman in another part of the country was praying a similar prayer. Her name was Sarah. Sarah had been given in marriage seven times, but on each wedding night before the marriage was consummated, the groom had been killed by the demon Asmodeus. After seven you begin to get concerned.

To add insult to mayhem, Sarah is reproached for her terrible misfortune. Her father's maidservant blamed Sarah for the deaths. "It is you who killed your husbands." Then she cursed Sarah: "Go and join them in death. May we never see one of your sons or daughters." It's terrible enough to suffer evil; it is even worse to be blamed for the evil that has occurred. In such a case we sometimes begin to take on that blame and believe our accusers.

Sarah was desolate; her heart was crushed. She went to her father's attic with the intent of hanging herself. But as she prepared to commit suicide, she had second thoughts, not for her sake but for her father's. "If I kill myself, they will blame my father. I cannot cause this sorrow to come upon him." So instead of hanging herself, she, like Tobit, begged God to let her die. She was dissuaded from suicide by a slender thread of faith and her love for her family.

Here then we have Tobit and Sarah, an older man in one place and a young woman many miles away, both in agony and both praying to die. The story says, "At that very time the prayers of both were heard in the glorious presence of God." God indeed heard their prayers and came to answer them, but not in any way they could have imagined.

In answer to their prayers God sent the angel Raphael, one of the seven great angels of God's throne. His name means "God heals," and we shall see why. Tobit ended his prayer and went back to his house; Sarah came down from the attic. Raphael was on his way.

Tobias's Journey

When Tobit got up from his prayer, he suddenly remembered some silver (worth about $20,000) he had left on deposit in Media with a kinsman named Gabael. Tobit thought, "I've asked to die.

I need to get my things in order. I should explain the money to my son Tobias and send him to get it."

Tobit did so, and gave Tobias a fatherly speech about how Tobias should conduct his life after Tobit's death, a noteworthy summary of Jewish wisdom:

Give your father a decent burial.
Show respect for your mother.
Revere God all your days.
Never deliberately do what is wrong or break God's
    commandments.
Do what is right.
Give to the poor.
Beware of immorality.
Marry one of your own people—take no foreign wife.
Pay fair wages to your workers on the day of their work.
What you hate do not do to anyone [a variation of the Golden
    Rule].
At all times bless the Lord and ask that your way may be straight.

Tobit then told his son to get the silver in Media at the home of his kinsmen Gabael. Tobias went out to find a man to accompany him to Media. He'd never been on such a journey and needed a guide and companion. Suddenly he found himself face-to-face with the angel Raphael, not knowing he was an angel, much less one of the seven great archangels of God.

Tobias proceeded to question the angel. "Where do you come from?" The angel told a fib. "I am an Israelite, one of your kin. I've come to find work." (Angels are allowed to fib occasionally, for good ends, of course!)

"Do you know the way to Media?" Tobias asked.

"Have I been to Media?" the angel exclaimed. "I know the way like the back of my hand, and when I go, I stay at the house of a fellow countryman named Gabael. You may know him." (!) Tobias's eyes got big. He couldn't believe his luck. He ran to tell his father about the good news.

Tobit called Raphael in for a job interview. When they met, Raphael offered a cheery greeting: "May all be well with you!"

Tobit, who had not been cheery for a long time, retorted grumpily, "What do you mean, Be well? I'm blind as a stump, can't see the light of day; as good as dead, wish I were."

Raphael answered, "Take heart; in God's design your cure is at hand."

Raphael introduced himself as "Azariah." Again he fibbed, but the fake name was a good one. It meant "God helps!" Raphael couldn't tell him his real name or the gig would be up. Tobit gave him the job and offered to pay him one drachma a day. I'm not sure what an angel can do with a drachma, but Raphael agreed. Tobit sent his son and the angel off on the trip with a blessing.

Now it was Mother Anna's time to fall apart. She broke into tears and accosted her husband. "Why have you sent my boy away? He was our only one. Money means nothing compared to my son." (I am reminded of the prayers of Augustine's mother, Monica, who begged God not to let her wayward son go to Italy, where he would surely be led further from God's way. But in Italy Augustine met Ambrose, who led him to faith.) Tobit tried to reassure her. "An angel will watch over them!" Little did he know!

Tobias and Raphael took off. Tobias's dog joined them. (This is the only place in scripture where a dog figures as pet, friend, and companion.) The three—a young man, his dog, and an angel—set off on their journey.

It was a wild adventure. First, Tobias decided to go swimming in the Tigris River. A huge fish leaped out of the water and tried to swallow the boy's foot. [The orchestra begins to play the ominous music from *Jaws*.] When Tobias cried out, Raphael said, "Seize the fish!" Tobias seized it and hauled it to the bank.

Then the angel said, "Split the fish open and clean out the guts but keep the gall, the heart, and the liver." Tobias cleaned the fish as instructed. They cooked some of the fish for supper, salted the rest for the journey, and made off for Media.

As they approached Media, Tobias asked Raphael, "My friend, you said these fish parts are for medicine. What kind of medicine?" Raphael said, "The heart and liver are to run demons off. Cook them on a charcoal fire and demons will run like the devil." [Now we hear the theme song from *Ghostbusters*.] "The gall," he added, "is for anointing blind eyes." [The reader is beginning to see how things might fit together.]

When they entered Media, Raphael said, "Tonight we must stay at the house of Raguel, one of your kinsmen. He has a daughter named Sarah, their only child. You are next of kin and have the right to marry her. She is thoughtful, courageous, and very beautiful. I'll introduce you and, if you agree, begin to make the marriage arrangements." [Raphael the matchmaker!]

Tobias wasn't persuaded by Raphael's Cupid act. "Whoa, wait a minute," he said. "I've heard she's already been given to seven husbands and they've all died on their wedding night. This is not a good sign. Some say it's a demon that kills them. I think I'll pass. Bachelor life—that's for me. Besides, I'm an only child and I need to be around to take care of my parents. 'Honor your father and mother'—isn't that what the Good Book says?!"

Raphael reminded him of his father's command to him to marry a kinswoman. "No more demon talk," the angel said. "Take her as your bride. Here's the plan. When you go into the bridal suite on your wedding night, put the liver and the heart of the fish on the incense burner in the room. [There's a romantic thought!] The smoke will take care of the demons. God has planned Sarah for you," Raphael reassured him. "She will bear you children. You will be her savior."

When Tobias heard these words, he fell in love with Sarah sight unseen—and with God's plan.

The Wedding

When they got to the house on the wedding day, the marriage contract was drawn up. Sarah's father was honest and told him about grooms one through seven, but Tobias forged fearlessly ahead.

Raguel sent for Sarah. He joined their hands and they made their marriage vows before God.

Then they sat down to eat the wedding feast. Raguel called to his wife Edna and asked her to prepare the bridal chamber. She did. Taking Sarah there to show her the room, she said to her, "Courage, daughter. May the Lord of heaven turn your grief to joy. Courage." Then Edna left Sarah alone.

When the feast was over, the groom joined his bride in the bridal chamber. [The orchestra now plays some scary music from a Stephen King movie.] Tobias took the fish liver and heart and put it on the incense burner. Sarah must have wondered at her groom's strange behavior!

What are you doing in there, dear?
Just getting freshened up.
No, what's that smell?
Uh, just a cheap cigar my best man gave me.

The smoke rose and drove off the demon Asmodeus—all the way to Upper Egypt, where the angel Raphael pursed him and bound him hand and foot.

When they got into bed, Tobias rose and said, "Get up, my sister. Let us pray to God to show us mercy and keep us safe." It was no idle prayer. The demon had been driven off, but Tobias did not know that. And for all Tobias knew, the chambermaid might have been right. Sarah might have killed her husbands herself!

Tobias stood and prayed. The prayer has been widely used in weddings throughout Christian tradition, most of its users oblivious to the story line:

We bless thee, O God of our fathers.
We praise your name for ever and ever.
You made Adam and for him you made Eve his wife as a helper.
From these two the human race has sprung.
You said, It is not good that the man should be alone;
let us make a helper for him like him.
And so I take thee my sister
not in lust
but in sincerity.[3]
Grant that she and I may find mercy and grow old together.

"Amen," they said and went to bed.

Meanwhile, out in the backyard the father-in-law, Raguel, had started digging a grave! [Again, I'm not making this up. I know—it looks like an episode from *The Addams Family*, with the music from Alfred Hitchcock's *Psycho* screeching in the background.] Raguel didn't *want* Tobias to die, but if the demon was going to do him in too, Raguel didn't want the neighborhood to know about it; so he got a grave ready for a quick nighttime burial, just in case.

You can imagine Tobias and Sarah in bed and Tobias catching the sound outside the window of a shovel striking the soil.

"What's that sound?" Tobias asks. Sarah answers, "Oh, it's nothing . . . Now, where were we?" she says, kissing him quickly on the mouth.

Later, after the grave was dug, Raguel called his wife to go check and see if Tobias was still alive. The wife sent the maid. The maid returned with the great news: He is not dead! All is well. Raguel blessed the Lord, then instructed his servants to hurry up and fill in the grave before dawn when everybody would wake up.

God indeed answered their wedding-night prayer. The story says that they not only made it through the night but grew old together, Tobias dying in peace at the age of 117.

The family decided to extend the marriage feast for fourteen days. There was plenty to celebrate. While they partied, Raphael slipped off to Gabael's house to get the money for Tobit. Everything was set for the journey home.

The Homecoming

The homecoming scene tells the rest of the story. Tobias, Raphael, and the dog returned home. What's a homecoming scene without a dog wagging its tail and barking happily as they come in sight of home? Tobit and Anna had been worried about their son, and now the air was filled with joy.

Then Tobias took the gall from the fish and anointed his dad's eyes, and his father could see again. Tobit cried out, "I can see you, my son, the light of my eyes."

When Tobit and Tobias went to pay "Azariah" (or Raphael) for his help, Raphael revealed his identity: not Azariah but Raphael, one of the seven great angels of God. It was he who tested Tobit at the Pentecost feast to see if Tobit would rise and take care of his kinsman's body. It was he whom God sent to answer the prayers of both Tobit and Sarah—though in much different ways than they envisioned.

When they learned who Raphael was, Tobit and Tobias fell flat on the earth trembling. The angel said, "Be not afraid. Bless God forevermore. I was only doing God's pleasure."

The End.

Conclusion

Why did the community want to keep this book? To teach some important truths about some of the things God calls us to do, as revealed through the rollicking turns in the story:

1. *The call to trust in the goodness of God and God's providential care even when things seem the darkest.* Tobit and Sarah prayed to die, as many are tempted to do, but God preserved them in their despair and answered their prayers in ways they could never have expected.

2. *The call to serve God in the ordinariness of our days and with the obligations of family and community life.*

3. *The intrepid call to face the darkness in yourself and in your mate or family or friend—not to flee it but to face it.* God is on our side and will help us face our darkness and redeem it. Tobias had the courage to face Sarah's demon and, with God's help, helped save Sarah from the demon.

4. *The call from Hebrews 13:2: "Do not neglect to show hospitality to strangers, for by doing that some have entertained angels without knowing it."*

Azariah turned out to be Raphael—the stranger, God's angel. Not only are the heavens populated by angels but the earth is also. All kinds of people—stranger and friend—can be God's angels, or messengers (the meaning of "angel"). And what these angels come to say is this:

Be not afraid

There is a faithfulness at the heart of things.

Bless God forevermore

God's good pleasure is at work.

Notes

1. Cited in David Steindle-Rast, *Gratefulness, the Heart of Prayer: An Approach to Life and Fullness* (New York: Paulist Press, 1984), p. 102.

2. For example, by Neri di Bicci, exhibited in the Metropolitan Museum of Art, New York City.

3. Marriage is for more than self-gratification; it is for sacrificial love and service to the world.

18

Introduction to the *Euangelion,* the Good News of Christ, and the Christian New Testament

The first "Bible" for the early Christian church was the Jewish scriptures, which included the Torah, Prophets, and Writings.* Jaroslav Pelikan, noted church historian, has said that the most important decision of the church in the second century C.E. was the decision to be a people of *two* books, not just one, that is, to keep the Hebrew Bible along with the emerging Christian scriptures.[1] In the mid-second century the church decided not to go the way of the influential gnostic, Marcion, who wanted to eliminate all of the Jewish scriptures from the Christian Bible, along with parts of the New Testament that didn't suit his theological program.

The Christian scriptures emerged as the writings and teachings of the apostles and their disciples were collected and became the foundation of what Christians now call the New Testament: four gospels, Matthew, Mark, Luke, and John; a sequel to Luke's gospel called the Acts of the Apostles; a set of letters or epistles, predominantly by the apostle Paul but also including writings of

---

*The early Christians used primarily what is called the Septuagint, the Greek translation of Jewish scriptures which came out of Egypt. A common Jewish name for these scriptures was Tanak, an acrostic made up of the tri-part division: Torah (Law), Nebi'im (Prophets), and Kethubim (Writings). At the time of Jesus, the Law and Prophets were well set, but the Writings and Psalms were in the process of being set as a unit of scripture.

different theological stripes (James, Peter, John, Hebrews); and the last book of the New Testament, the Apocalypse of John, often called "Revelation" because the word "apocalypse" means "an unveiling."

The gospels offer us the story of Jesus of Nazareth from the perspective of those who call him *Christos* (Messiah) and *Kyrios* (Lord). "Gospel" comes from the Greek word *euangelion*, which means "good tidings" or "good news." In the English language the word evolved from "god-spel," that is, good spiel, or story.

The gospel of Jesus brought with it a new kind of speech,[2] and the four gospels were a new genre of human literature. Amos Wilder, Thornton Wilder's theologian brother, wrote that "the new speech of the gospel was not a matter of words on a tablet but a word in the heart, not a copybook for recitation but winged words for life."[3] Ben F. Meyer says that Jesus' proclamation of the kingdom "kindled a blaze of new speech, much of it his own, but continuing far beyond him."[4]

The gospels are one part "travel narrative," telling Jesus' story from baptism until his final entrance into Jerusalem. They are another part "Passion narrative," which tells of his death— from his triumphal entry into Jerusalem through his crucifixion and burial. They are another part "Resurrection narrative," describing his resurrection appearances to followers. Two gospels include birth narratives (Matthew and Luke), and one gospel includes a theological prologue (John). The gospels brought together "sayings gospels," which compiled Jesus' sayings, with records of his life and deeds.

Matthew, Mark, and Luke are called "synoptic" gospels because they are very much alike, "synoptic" meaning "to look with a common eye." John's gospel is the most distinctive of the four, both in its theological presentation of Jesus and in its chronology of events. Most scholars agree that they were all written in the last three decades of the first century C.E.

How do we look at the relationship between what has gone before, the Hebrew scriptures, and what we now have as the Christian New Testament? In the introduction to this book I pictured the Hebrew and Christian scriptures as a series of concentric circles.

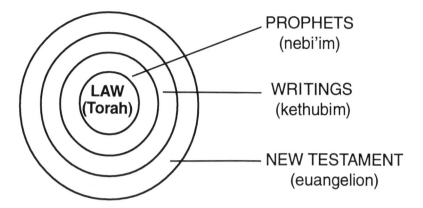

The innermost circle is the Torah, the five books of Moses; the next circle is the Prophets, which commented on, expanded, and applied the Torah; the third circle is the Writings, which commented on, expanded, and applied the first two circles. The fourth circle is the gospel, the Christian New Testament, which comments on, expands, and applies the first three circles. In Christian confession it is the fulfillment of all that has gone before. The risen Christ says in Luke, "These are my words which I spoke to you, . . . that everything written about me in the Law of Moses, and the Prophets and the Psalms must be fulfilled" (24:44).

Jesus said, "I have come not to abolish the Law and the Prophets, but to fulfill them" (see Matthew 5:17). He said this because that is exactly what he was accused of trying to do. Many of his contemporaries, especially in the religious establishment, took his mission to renew and fulfill his tradition as a program to abolish it. Such is the way of religious institutions— they call reformers "destroyers."

I offer the story of Jesus of Nazareth as in part the story of God's attempt to renew and reform religion so that its focus is on the love of God and neighbor—where God meant it to be all along.

Jesus' parable of the Last Judgment is a case in point. When the Son of man, the Messiah, comes and sits on the final throne, he will divide the sheep from the goats. The sheep, those who enter into the joy of the Lord, are those who fed Jesus when he was hungry and gave him water when he was thirsty and clothed him when he was naked and visited him when he was in prison. The sheep are pleased to be invited into the eternal joy but are curious:

"When did we see you hungry and feed you and thirsty and naked and in prison?" And the Messiah will answer, "Inasmuch as you have done it unto one of the least of these, you've done it unto me" (Matthew 25:31–46). This parable from the mouth of Jesus is a commentary on and fulfillment of Torah, Prophets, and Writings. Inevitably as we read the story of Jesus we face the agony of his rejection by the Jewish leadership and his crucifixion by Roman authorities with the consent of Jewish leaders. We should not focus on this tragic historical occurrence, however, as simply the opposition of Christianity and Judaism.

The New Testament was written during a period of intense antagonism between the church and the synagogue, but we need not freeze this frame of history and make it determinative of all the ways Christians and Jews relate to one another as they side by side worship the one God of us all.

Let's look at the gospel of John as a case study in this problem. New Testament scholarship is indebted to the seminal work of J. Louis Martyn for his reconstruction of the historical context of John's gospel[5]— the expulsion of Jewish followers of Jesus from synagogues between approximately 85 and 100 C.E.— and how this historical situation reveals itself in the text. In John 9, for example, a blind man is healed by Jesus and undergoes, along with his parents, intense interrogation by Jewish leaders. The parents are afraid to answer: "His parents said this because they feared the Jews, for the Jews had already agreed that if any one should confess him to be Christ, he was to be put out of the synagogue" (9:22).

John 16:2 is also reflective of the historical situation. "They will put you out of the synagogues; indeed, the hour is coming when whoever kills you will think he is offering service to God."

Martyn has assembled historical evidence of a practice the synagogue adopted in the late first century to expose secret believers in Jesus. Every service a lay reader would read the Eighteen Benedictions, and the congregation would answer each by saying "Amen." As the tension grew in the first century, the twelfth benediction was reformulated as a curse against Nazarenes (Christians) and other heretics. When a person was suspected of being a Christian, he would be asked to read the benedictions in worship.[6] If he faltered on the curse against Christians, he would be cast out of the synagogue, ostracized, maybe even killed. You can imagine as well that eyes would also be on the congregation to see if anyone failed to say the "Amen" to the curse.

The gospel of John was written to these persecuted Jewish Christians who faced the threat of being cast out of the synagogue. The term "the Jews" is a code word in John. It does not stand for the Jewish people or the Jewish faith, but for those Jewish authorities and their followers who participated in the execution of Jesus and were now persecuting his followers. So when you read "the Jews," do not hear it as anti-Semitic. Hear it out of the anguish of a bitter family quarrel.

It is a tragedy of immense proportion that the Christian church has taken the language of John's gospel, ripped it out of its historical situation, and made it normative for Christian attitudes toward the Jewish people.

In a breathtaking and dismaying reversal of religious violence Christians have perpetuated spiritual and physical violence against Jews, referring to them with epithets like "Christ killers." Anti-Semitism has gone on for two thousand years, often blessed by the church.

Marc Chagall has captured the horror and bitter irony of this reversal of sacred violence in his 1938 painting *White Crucifixion.* In the center of the white canvas is a figure of the crucified Jesus. Above his head is the Hebrew inscription "Jesus of Nazareth, King of the Jews." He is wearing not the nondescript loincloth of most paintings of the crucifixion but rather a Jewish prayer cloth, a *tallith*. Underneath the cross is a temple candelabra. Circling the cross is a series of scenes from the holocaust: a synagogue looted and burned, as in *Kristallnacht;* a Torah set on fire; an orthodox Jew fleeing for his life, the Torah in his arms; a boat carrying screaming women; storm troopers tramping through a village on fire, and so on. In horrifying irony John 16:2 is reenacted *against the Jews*: "They will put you out of the synagogues; indeed, the hour is coming when whoever kills you will think he is offering service to God."[7]

You will see in the story of Jesus a critique of the religious structures of Jesus' time, but these passages from the gospels should not be read as a condemnation of Jewish faith or Jewish people, but as the critique of the prophet of God against religion gone awry, in that time and in every time. I take the pains to set the teachings of Jesus and the language of the gospels in their specific historical context not just to qualify the nature of Jesus' attacks on Jewish religion but also to extend his critique of religious structures to include those of all times and places, including the contemporary menagerie of religions and spiritualities.

The stories of Jesus that follow will correspond to the general line of the gospel narratives: A son is born to Mary, a young Jewish maiden. She and her betrothed, a carpenter from Nazareth, are simple Galilean commoners.

At the age of thirty this man named Jesus begins his public ministry by being washed by John the Baptizer in the Jordan River. A one-man reform movement within Judaism, John offered a way of radical repentance and purification that didn't depend on the temple sacrifice system. You could be washed for free, the only requirement being a heart ready to turn and be changed by God. As Jesus rose from the Jordan's waters, the Spirit like a dove descended and a Voice from heaven said, "You are my son, the Beloved."

Full of the Spirit, anointed with sonship, Jesus set out on his own reform movement. He healed and taught. He preached the kingdom of God not as some distant hope but as a real, compelling, immediate, and gracious opportunity. His ministry challenged the religious structures, dominated as they were by holiness maps and purity codes, with his offer of the free grace of God and his call to live in the presence of the Spirit. His ready miracles and flowing forgiveness undermined an elaborate and increasingly oppressive system of temple sacrifice and purification. His table companionship embodied the graciousness of the kingdom he preached: he ate with saint and sinner, clean and unclean alike, with outcasts, prostitutes, tax collectors, and sinners. Women were included in his close circle of followers. Gentiles were healed; the kingdom was coming to all.

Opposition started early. His hometown congregation heard an early sermon and tried to throw him off a cliff. Official religious leaders were especially threatened, not only because he undermined the religious status quo but also because he threatened the fragile political peace. His growing following might smell of insurrection to the Roman overlords, and they might come in with full military fury and destroy the nation. Ironically, forty years later it happened anyway, both Jerusalem and its Temple being destroyed in a war with Rome.

At some point in his ministry Jesus knew his death was inevitable, not just because his people refused to accept his challenge and his reforms but also because he believed his death would be the salvation of all the world, his shed blood God's forgiveness of the sins of the world, including the sins of his Jewish nation. John the Baptist saw it early when Jesus came to be baptized: "Behold the Lamb of God who taketh away the sin of the world" (John 1:29). Jesus himself saw this approaching death as a kind of sacrifice for the sake of the world: "For the Son of man also came not to be served but to serve, and to give his life as a ransom for many" (Mark 10:45).

Jesus foretold his coming death three times to his disciples and "set his face" to go to Jerusalem, where he anticipated it would happen. An entrance into Jerusalem on a donkey and the prophetic act of cleansing the Temple brought things to a head. He was arrested, tried in both religious and political courts, and sentenced to death by crucifixion, the most humiliating of executions in the Roman world, reserved for the worst of offenders.[8]

This happened on a Friday. On the following Sunday morning an empty tomb was discovered and a risen Christ began to appear in a new "resurrection" body to his friends.

An Easter faith in a risen Lord was born in these appearances, and a scattered, demoralized, guilty, and grief-stricken company of disciples became the leaders of a new faith, at first a subgroup of Judaism but soon a missionary faith to Jews, Gentiles, and all the world. The early believers thought at first that Jesus' resurrection would be soon followed by the end of the world— the return of Jesus in power and glory and the "general resurrection" of all who had died (Daniel 12:2). This hope was disappointed, but what emerged was an utterly new faith based on the experience of the risen Lord in the community of faith and the promise of their Lord to be with them always to the close of the age, whenever that would come. Christ would live in them who followed him that they might be more like him. The kingdom he preached would be their mission. The earliest confession of faith was a baptismal confession, "Jesus Christ is Lord!" Jesus of Nazareth, they professed, has become Messiah (*Christos*) and Lord (*Kyrios*). And they themselves had become the messianic community living in the power of the risen Christ.

Jesus' mission was more than to reform his Hebrew tradition and to preach the inbreaking kingdom. It would also involve a sacrificial death that worked reconciliation between God and humankind. As the apostle Paul would later phrase it, "God was in Christ reconciling the world to himself, not counting their trespasses against them, and entrusting to us the message of reconciliation" (2 Corinthians 5:19).

Some historians and scholars make a radical separation between the "Jesus of history," prophet and sage, and the "Christ of faith," the divine son of God whose death was for the forgiveness of the sins of the world. But such a distinction makes the apostles and authors of the New Testament into inventors of an elaborate and audacious fiction. To be sure, these writers amplified and elaborated on the significance of the life and death of Jesus and searched the scriptures as well as the philosophies of their time for ways to understand and express the mystery of Jesus' birth, life, death, and resurrection. But the seeds of their theologizing were planted by the sayings of Jesus himself: "to give his life as a ransom" (Mark 10:45); "greater love has no man than this, that a man lay down his life for his friends" (John 15:13); "unless a grain of wheat falls into the earth and dies, it remains alone; but if it dies, it bears much fruit" (John 12:24); "this is my body which is for you . . . this cup is the new covenant in my blood" (1 Corinthians 11:23–25).

It can be argued that every saying of Jesus that reflects such a notion of a messiah's sacrificial death was invented by Jesus' followers and put into his mouth posthumously, but such a theological project cannot finally be proven or disproven, and its thesis seems more incredible than the received tradition of the church. Could the early church have survived against the extraordinary odds stacked against it had it been based on the self-conscious, if pious, fiction of its first leaders? I think it is better argued that Jesus knew his death was essential to his identity and mission and to God's own mission of redemption. James Hillman reflects on Socrates' *daimon*, who told him not to escape imprisonment and execution. "His death belonged to the integrity of his image, to his innate form." [9] The same could be said of Jesus' death, and more, that his death belonged to the integrity of God's way of redeeming the world. In one of the best reconstructions of the Jesus of history,

Ben F. Meyer concludes that Jesus' life was epitomized in his single act of going to his death and that the meaning of his death was properly realized in the tradition that was generated by his life, death, and resurrection— realized in such phrases as "he loved us and gave himself for us."[10] (See Galatians 2:20.)

I think we are left with a figure who made daring claims and asked us to follow him as the way to God. C. S. Lewis, one of our century's most dramatic converts to Christ, says to read the sayings of Jesus and conclude he was only a moral teacher is preposterous and patronizing. He was either a madman, a liar, or the Son of God.[11] One may be put off by Lewis's dramatic either/or, but it seems closer to the truth of Jesus than a dissected gospel that divides Jesus' sayings into the sayings of the human prophet and the back-loaded "Jesus the divine son of God" sayings. Reynolds Price voices a similar question as he speaks about the gospel of Mark: "Does it bring us a life-transforming truth; or is it one gifted lunatic's tale of another lunatic, wilder than he?"[12] And the claims of John's gospel may be more audacious than the other three, its message here gorgeously distilled by Price:

> The force that conceived and bore all things came here among us, proved his identity in visible human acts, was killed by men no worse than we, rose from death and walked again with his earthly believers, vowing eternal life beside him to those who also come to believe that he is God and loves us as his story shows.[13]

The stories of Jesus that follow will be taken from the four gospels. Then there will be a chapter called "The Acts of the Apostles," which retells the early history of the church through the eyes of the author of Luke's gospel. Finally will come the story of the Apocalypse, the vision of the end of all things as given to John on the Isle of Patmos near the close of the first century. An epilogue will re-present the life of Christ using the governing metaphor of Loren Eiseley's famous essay, "The Star Thrower."

Notes

1. Jaroslav Pelikan, *The Emergence of the Catholic Tradition, 100-600* (Chicago: University of Chicago Press, 1971), pp. 71-80.
2. Amos Wilder, *Early Christian Rhetoric* (Cambridge: Harvard University Press, 1971).
3. Ibid., p. 15.
4. Ben F. Meyer, "Jesus Christ" in *Anchor Dictionary of the Bible*, vol. 3, ed. David N. Freedman (New York: Doubleday, 1992), p. 779.
5. See J. Louis Martyn, *History and Theology in the Fourth Gospel*, 2d ed. (Nashville: Abingdon, 1979).
6. Ibid., pp. 58-60.
7. I am indebted to Jaroslav Pelikan for his introduction of Chagall's painting in *Jesus through the Centuries* (New Haven: Yale University Press, 1985), p. 20.
8. See Martin Hengel, *Crucifixion* (Philadelphia: Fortress, 1977), for a historical study of crucifixion as a form of execution.
9. James Hillman, *The Soul's Code: In Search of Character and Calling* (New York: Random House, 1996), p. 203.
10. Ben F. Meyer, *The Aims of Jesus* (London: SCM Press, 1979), pp. 252-3.
11. C. S. Lewis, *Mere Christianity* (New York: Macmillan, 1952), pp. 55-56. The passage in its entirety is as follows:

> I am trying here to prevent anyone saying the really foolish thing that people say about Him: "I'm ready to accept Jesus as a great moral teacher, but I don't accept his claim to be God." That is the one thing we must not say. A man who was merely a man and said the sort of things Jesus said would not be a great moral teacher. He would either be a lunatic—on a level with the man who says he is a poached egg—or else he would be the Devil of Hell. You must make your choice. Either this man was, and is, the Son of God: or else a madman or something worse. You can shut Him up for a fool, you can spit at Him and kill Him as a demon; or you can fall at His feet and call Him Lord and God. But let us not come with any patronizing nonsense about His being a great human teacher. He has not left that open to us. He did not intend to.

12. Reynolds Price, *Three Gospels* (New York: Scribner's, 1996), p. 128.
13. Ibid., p. 166.

A Brief Excursus on the Third Quest for the Historical Jesus

The Jewish and Christian faiths are historical faiths, that is, they are based on God's acts in history, not merely on myths that tell a great truth. Therefore the search for an accurate picture of the historical Jesus is important to people of Christian faith. There is among New Testament scholars today what is being called "the third quest for the historical Jesus."

The first quest happened primarily among scholars in Europe in the late nineteenth and early twentieth centuries. It was both summarized and brought to a close by Albert Schweitzer's monumental work, *The Quest of the Historical Jesus* in 1906.

A "new" quest was begun by students of Rudolf Bultmann in the 1950s. James M. Robinson's *A New Quest of the Historical Jesus* (1959) is as good a landmark as any for this "second quest."

A "third" quest for the historical Jesus is now in full swing. Begun in the 1970s, it has gained great public attention because of the work of a group of New Testament scholars called the "Jesus Seminar." Robert Funk, its leader, prefers to call this third quest a "reNewed quest" because it is in strong continuity with the "second quest." The Jesus Seminar is seeking to reconstruct the most historically probable picture of the historical Jesus. Because seminar members have judged that most of Jesus' sayings are not his words but words put into his mouth by those who came after, the Jesus Seminar has become the object of much public debate.

They have in their hands the results of an immense body of scholarship that has grown up around the two major archeological discoveries of our century—the Dead Sea Scrolls, discovered in 1947, a collection of Hebrew texts that belonged to an ascetic community called the Essenes who lived around the time of Jesus; and the Nag Hammadi Library, a set of early Coptic and gnostic Christian texts discovered in Egypt in 1945.

The work of the Jesus Seminar can be examined in *The Five Gospels*[1] and in *Honest to Jesus*[2] by Robert Funk. I would also recommend Marcus Borg's *Meeting Jesus Again for the First Time*[3] and Russell Shorto's journalistic account of the new scholarship, *Gospel Truth*.[4] For a contemporary approach from the evangelical perspective I would recommend Philip Yancey, *The Jesus I Never Knew*.[5] I would also highly recommend the work of Ben F. Meyer and N.T. Wright for rigorous scholarship that takes different courses than the Jesus Seminar.[6]

But there has developed in our spiritually pregnant age another tributary in the river as spiritually interested writers outside the New Testament scholars' guild and outside orthodox Christian faith are taking a look at Jesus of Nazareth. I recommend Reynolds Price's *Three Gospels*,[7] a new translation of Mark and John plus his own apocryphal gospel, all with extended introductions. Stephen Mitchell, a noted translator, has written *The Gospel According to Jesus*.[8] It is analogous to Thomas Jefferson's "Bible." While president of the United States, Jefferson edited the gospels in light of eighteenth-century Enlightenment canons of truth. Mitchell edits the gospels from the perspective of a broader, eastern spirituality. I mention one more: Guy Davenport and Benjamin Urrutia have published *The Logia of Yeshua: The Sayings of Jesus*.[9] Here a noted author and essayist, Davenport, and Urrutia, a Basque-Jewish Christian born in South America, join to present a set of sayings of Jesus, newly translated, from canonical and noncanonical sources. This collection of "logia" gives us a glimpse of what the "sayings gospels" looked like which were floating around in the first and second centuries, for example, the hypothetical "Q," which may have been a source for the New Testament gospel writers, or the gospel of Thomas, a "sayings gospel" unearthed at Nag Hammadi that probably circulated independently of the four New Testament gospels.

The various questers have all sought a clearer and more accurate picture of the historical Jesus, one less distorted by layers of cultural transmission. The enterprise is important, and it is fraught with dangers.

It is impossible to tell the story of Jesus without shaping him to some degree in our image. The very language and thought patterns we use color the story. Our telling of the story of Jesus reveals something of our theology, psychology, and biography. As the apostle Paul said, "We have this treasure in earthen vessels" (2 Corinthians 4:7). To "translate" Jesus to our time by way of our modes of thinking is inevitably an interpretation, as all translation is. The reader will no doubt see a generous amount of mud from my earthen vessel spattering the story of Jesus I tell, but I hope that Paul is right that God has placed the treasure of the gospel in our cracked earthen vessels so that the transcendent light will shine through. I pray you will see the light amid the clay.

Albert Schweitzer concluded his monumental *Quest of the Historical Jesus* with the observation that all "lives of Christ" reflect as much about their authors as about Jesus. He also observed that most had ignored the "eschatological" dimension of his message. Schweitzer himself believed that Jesus thought his death would set in motion the final "end time," and therefore died mistaken about what was to come. In Schweitzer's thought Jesus' ethic was an "interim ethic" designed for the brief time between his teaching and the final end of history. Such a conclusion gives us pause. Did Jesus die a fanatic deluded about the end time, like Marshall Applewhite or David Koresh?

Interestingly, for Schweitzer the mistaken eschatological vision of Jesus does not diminish his spiritual significance for us. We know Jesus not by reading books about him but by following him. Schweitzer himself followed Jesus even to Africa, where he set up a hospital in Lambarene, far from the comforts of his life in Europe as a physician, theologian, Bach scholar, and organist. The last paragraph of his *Quest* offers this mystical and elegiac conclusion:

> He comes to us as One unknown, without a name, as of old, by the lakeside. He came to those who knew Him not. He speaks to us the same word, "Follow thou me!" And sets us to the tasks which He has to fulfil for our time. He commands. And to those who obey Him, whether they be wise or simple, He will reveal Himself in the toils, the conflicts, the sufferings which they shall pass through in His fellowship, and, as an ineffable mystery, they shall learn in their own experience Who He is.[10]

The question still hangs in the air: Can we incorporate Jesus' eschatological teachings without turning him into a deluded fanatic?

Perhaps we can in this way: Jesus lived and died to inaugurate the coming of the kingdom of God. He died believing that his sacrificial death would be an essential part of the coming of that kingdom and the salvation of the world. He did not have knowledge of the timetable, by his own admission: "No one knows but the Father."

The resurrection of Jesus Christ on the third day after his death vindicated his message and his mission. There would rise from the ashes of his death a community of God's kingdom, itself heralding the presence of the kingdom. This messianic community would embody forgiveness, righteousness, mercy, peace, and grace as a foretaste of what God is bringing. And the power of their mission would come from the presence of the living Christ in their midst, present to them in "common *worship*, present in kingdom *work* and disciple *witness* to friend and stranger, and present in hearing the biblical *word* itself."[11] Such is the way of the servant people of God who follow Jesus and call him Christ and Lord.

Jesus lived and died to bring into our existence the kingdom of God. Those who follow him embody the presence of that kingdom in history until God chooses to complete history with the full dawning of the kingdom.

Notes

1. Robert Funk, Roy Hoover, and the Jesus Seminar, *Five Gospels* (New York: Macmillan, 1993).
2. Robert Funk, *Honest to Jesus: Jesus for a New Millennium* (San Francisco: HarperSanFrancisco, 1996).
3. Marcus J. Borg, *Meeting Jesus Again for the First Time* (San Francisco: HarperSanFrancisco, 1994); see also his *Jesus: A New Vision* (San Francisco: HarperSanFrancisco, 1996).
4. Russell Shorto, *Gospel Truth: The New Image of Jesus Emerging from Science and History, and Why It Matters* (New York: Riverhead Books, 1997).
5. Philip Yancey, *The Jesus I Never Knew* (Grand Rapids, Mich.: Zondervan, 1995).
6. See Ben F. Meyer, "Jesus Christ" and *The Aims of Jesus*; also N. T. Wright, "The Quest for the Historical Jesus," in *Anchor Dictionary of the Bible*, vol. 3, ed. David N. Freedman (New York: Doubleday, 1992), pp. 796-802.
7. Reynolds Price, *Three Gospels* (New York: Scribner's, 1996).
8. Stephen Mitchell, *The Gospel According to Jesus: A New Translation and Guide to His Essential Teachings for Believers and Unbelievers* (San Francisco: HarperCollins, 1991).
9. Guy Davenport and Benjamin Urrutia, trans., *The Logia of Yeshua: The Sayings of Jesus* (Washington, D.C.: Counterpoint, 1996).
10. Albert Schweitzer, *The Quest of the Historical Jesus* (London: A. & C. Black, 1922), p. 401.
11. James Wm. McClendon Jr., *Systematic Theology, Volume II: Doctrine* (Nashville: Abingdon, 1994), p. 240.

19

Nativity

Where does the story of Jesus begin? Jesus of Nazareth, the one who would be called the Christ (*Christos*—Messiah, the "anointed" of God) and Lord (*Kyrios*—the master of all life and of those lives who kneel before him and follow him).

John's gospel begins Jesus' story at the dawn of creation:

> In the beginning was the Word;
> And the Word was with God and was God . . .
> And the Word became flesh and dwelt among us,
> full of grace and truth. (John 1:1, 14)

Mark's gospel begins the story in the wilderness waters of the Jordan River, where another man named John, called the Baptizer, was baptizing for the repentance and forgiveness of sins. Jesus was washed by John, anointed by the Spirit, and called God's own son by heaven's voice. But Matthew and Luke give us what we most hunger for: stories of Jesus' birth.

Matthew's gospel begins with a Hebrew genealogy from Abraham to David to Christ, for the scriptures said the Christ would be of David's lineage, the promised "son of David" who would be called "Jeshua," or "Jesus," whose Hebrew name means "God saves."

Luke begins his gospel on the stage of world history: "In the days of Herod, King of Judea," who served at the pleasure of Caesar Augustus. God was changing the face of history, Luke is suggesting, not from the precincts of human power but from the small, occupied country of Judea and out of a small group within that country who were called the *"Anawim,"* or "the poor," because they had little of this world's goods and trusted only in God. Luke describes them as those "waiting for the consolation of Israel."

Perhaps you have heard the names of two such *Anawim*: Zechariah, a countryside priest, and his childless wife, Elizabeth. The miracle happened on the one day in Zechariah's life when he was chosen to go into the Temple and offer incense on the altar, that one day when he would be the priest of God for all the people of Israel. When he approached the altar, he saw an unexpected figure. It was an angel, and Zechariah fell on his face in fear. The angel announced that their long years of prayer would be answered: Elizabeth would conceive and bear a son. They should name him "John."

Another of the *Anawim* was a fourteen-year-old teenager named Mary, or Miriam. She was betrothed to a man named Joseph, a carpenter from Nazareth who was much older than she—a detail later stories love to explore.[1]

One day as Mary was doing her chores, a stranger suddenly appeared. "Hail, favored one of God," the angel said, "the Lord is with you." And that was only the beginning of wonders. Did Gabriel's wings unfold in gleaming green and copper, purple and gold? Did they beat slowly, casting rainbows like a prism around the room? Did Mary feel the soft breeze move across her face like a benediction? The Lord is with you, with you, with you.

"You will conceive in your womb and bear a son and call his name 'Jesus,'" was what the angel said next. Mary asked, "How can this be, since I have no husband?" The angel explained, "The Holy Spirit will come upon you and the power of the Most High will overshadow you. The child will be called holy, the son of God."

If you say yes, Mary, if you say yes. W. H. Auden puts these words in Gabriel's mouth: " . . . child, it lies / Within your power of choosing to / Conceive the child who chooses you."[2] Mary answered *yes*. "Behold, I am the handmaid of the Lord, the servant of the Lord. Let it be to me according to your word."

And the Spirit that once moved across the face of the deep and created the heavens and the earth overshadowed Mary's flesh and created a child of spirit and flesh named Jesus, which means *God will save us from our sins*. Christian theology calls this miracle the Incarnation: the grace and truth of God made flesh, the embodiment of *hesed,* the humanity of God.

Augustine said that Mary conceived Christ first in her heart before conceiving him in her womb. Such is the invitation of the Nativity to us all: to choose the Child who chooses us and to receive him in whose image we and all the world were made (Colossians 1:15-20).

Enter Joseph. The betrothal to Mary was an oddity from the beginning. He looked old enough to be her father, on some tired days even her grandfather. He never expected her to say yes to him when he proposed, but she did, and he found a new spring in his step. Old familiar aches and pains seemed momentarily to disappear. The neighbors chuckled at the sight of them: Hey Joe, you're supposed to be *building* cradles, not robbing them!

Luke's gospel highlights the role of Mary, but Matthew's gospel wants us to see the pivotal role of Joseph in the Incarnation. "She was found to be with child," is how Matthew begins the story.

"Found to be with child by the Holy Spirit," the gospel writer says, but that's more than Joseph knew or could comprehend. You might imagine the dismay of Joseph when Mary told him she was with child. He was not the father. He had feared she would not be content to stick with his old heap of bones with all the younger boys running around. Were his fears justified?

Her talk of angels and Holy Spirit conceptions and the son of God was not reassuring. He was a common man, not given to mystic visions and poetic flights of words or miracles that made no sense.

He could only suspect the obvious, and that was almost too painful even to think about. But Matthew says "he was a just man," and "just" in the Bible means more than simply following the rules. It is one part righteousness and one part mercy. By Jewish law Joseph could have had her publicly charged with adultery and stoned to death along with her unborn child. Instead he decided to divorce her quietly without public charges and go on with whatever life he had left.

But one night as he lay in bed, sick of heart, he fell asleep, and as he slept God sent a dream. In the dream an angel appeared and said:

"Joseph, son of David, do not be afraid to take Mary as your wife, for the child conceived in her is from the Holy Spirit. She will bear a son and you are to name him Jesus." . . . All this took place to fulfill what had been spoken by the Lord through the prophet: "Look, the virgin shall conceive and bear a son, and they shall name him Emmanuel," which means, "God is with us." (Matthew 1:20-23)

When Joseph awoke, he remembered the dream and "did as the Lord commanded him." Swallowing his male pride, he took Mary's word and the dream's words as the truth. He gave up his plan to divorce her and be done with all this oddness. He did what was right—one part justice, one part mercy, and no little courage—and took Mary as his wife.

Can you see how fragile were the conditions surrounding the Incarnation? God trusting his son's life and the world's salvation into our human hands and fugitive hearts? The Incarnation would not have happened apart from the trustful submission of a teenaged girl to the Mystery of God and the bodily processes of gestation and birth; or apart from the trustful obedience of a man named Joseph who turned aside from obvious conclusions and the letter of the law to obey the dream and join with Mary to love, cherish, and protect this life inside her womb that was not only life of their life but God's life as well—and the life of the world. "The world is with child" is how Buechner puts it.[3]

Nine months later we return to the familiar cadences of Luke's nativity story: "And it came to pass in those days that there went out a decree from Caesar Augustus that all the world should be taxed."

Caesar Augustus had become the official object of worship as he ruled the world from Rome. He was called the "savior of the world." The poet Virgil had prophesied an age of peace ruled by an emperor of divine virtue. The rule of Augustus and the Pax Romana were seen as a fulfillment. Augustus closed the Temple of War in Rome and consecrated the Altar of Peace which, rebuilt, stands even today. His birthday, September 23, was celebrated in some parts of the empire as New Year's Day, and an ancient inscription called the "Priene inscription" reads, "The birthday of the god has marked the beginning of the good news for the world."[4]

Luke was well aware of what the emperor worship cultus was all about, and we can see his birth story as a kind of "counter-propaganda." Luke is the only gospel to use the title "savior" for Jesus, a title that had taken on political as well as religious overtones in that day. He was saying, "The real savior of the world is Jesus. The true prince of peace does not sit upon a throne in Rome, but is a tiny child born to a Palestinian girl in Bethlehem."

Caesar Augustus's tax decree imposed a bitter double taxation on the Hebrew people. It was this occasion that brought Mary and Joseph to Bethlehem. She was heavy with child. While they were there, the baby decided to be born, and babies ready to be born do not wait, not even for taxes.

The next words of Luke's we've memorized from a hundred and one Christmas pageants: "And she brought forth her firstborn son, wrapped him in swaddling clothes, and laid him in a manger, for there was no room for them in the inn."

No room in the inn. The gospel doesn't offer details, though our story-hungry hearts press to fill in between the lines. All the rooms filled up as the town swelled with people arriving, as Mary and Joseph did, to enroll for Caesar's taxes. An innkeeper was too preoccupied or too dull to see what was unfolding before his weary eyes as he turned the couple away.

According to early tradition the place Mary and Joseph found as shelter for the night was a shepherd's cave. The image is as captivating and transformative as any in all our human history: God's son born in a stable. Not in a palace, not even in a Holiday Inn, but in a simple "lean-to" shepherds used to protect their animals and themselves from the elements. The Son of man, God's Christ, who later as an itinerant preacher would have no place to lay his head, would first lay his head in a manger, a rough feeding trough for animals—"a makeshift crib for a makeshift night." He lay on straw from which animals fed and was wrapped in "swaddling clothes," strips of clean cloth parents used to wrap their newborn child.

The scene now shifts to the countryside where shepherds were keeping their flocks in the night. In the period of late Judaism leading to Jesus' day rabbis compiled lists of thieving and cheating professions. Shepherds always made the lists. Shepherds could not hold office or be admitted to courts of law as witnesses. Luke's shepherds were not rosy-cheeked choirboys with treble voices, fake beards, and papier-mâché crooks. They were more like guys with a week's stubble of beard who paint houses by day and drink their way from bar to bar by night. Their music was more Merle Haggard than J. S. Bach. In our day think of migrant farmers or truck drivers, or the guys who line up on the street looking for day work. Instead of the boys on *My Three Sons*, think of Larry, Darrell, and Darrell on the old *Bob Newhart Show*.

Still, the earliest accounts of the birth stories agree: the first people to whom the angels appeared and told the good news of Jesus' birth were *shepherds*. And the first witnesses to the Incarnation were shepherds, people the law of the land would not allow to be witnesses in courts of law.

When the angel of the Lord appeared to them, the text says, they were "sore afraid." (Despite romantic notions to the contrary, who of us is ever ready to meet an angel of the Lord?) *Be not afraid,* the angel blessedly said. They had survived at least the first words of the angel, and now they began to peek from between their fingers.

"For behold, I bring you good news of great joy which shall be to all people," said the angel. This group was not used to any good news, much less what they were about to hear. "For unto you is born this day in the city of David a savior, who is Christ the Lord."

Then the angel gave them a sign: there is a babe wrapped in swaddling clothes and lying in a manger. They ran to find the child. Perhaps they knew the shepherd who had loaned his cave. As they ran, the whole night sky vibrated with light and the sounds of angels singing:

> Glory to God in the highest
> And on earth, peace
> God's favor upon all.

God's favor was on *them*, them of all people, and the prince of peace was not a Caesar in Rome but a child in a manger.

The "child in the manger" was an echo of the words of Isaiah: "The ox knows its owner; the donkey knows its lord, but Israel has not known me" (1:3).

The manger thereby becomes a sign of joy and of the miracle of *recognition*: God's people have begun to know the manger of the Lord. And who led the way of the new recognition but this humble collection of people—a country priest and his wife, a teenaged girl and her carpenter husband, and shepherds.

Martin Luther spoke of the irony of Christmas: God did not appear to the daughter of high priest Caiaphas, but to an unknown maiden of modest station. We could add, not to the tenured professors in the Temple but to simple believers in the countryside, not to the landed gentry but to their paid "hands."

The great reversal from Mary's song, the Magnificat, was happening: "My soul magnifies the Lord, for he has regarded the low estate of his handmaiden. . . . He has put down the mighty from their thrones and exalted those of low degree."

Even animals get in the act. What would a manger scene be without animals? So to a baby's sweet breath add a cow's. And to the smell of frankincense and myrrh, which would soon be brought by mysterious wise men from the east, add the smell of a livestock exhibit at the State Fair.

When the shepherds found the cave and saw the child, they knelt and adored him. Then they scattered to the hills to tell the good news to everyone they met.

The parts of us that can hear this story with quiet yet overwhelming joy are the smaller, hidden-away parts of ourselves, the forgotten priest in the little town, the childless woman, the scared but trusting teenaged girl, the bewildered fiancé, the cast-out, or outcast, or castaway parts of ourselves that live on the edge of life one step from oblivion, the parts of us that are not sure good news should ever or will ever come to us, the parts of ourselves, to use the words of a cowboy poet, "just before beyond redemption."

If you visit the Church of the Nativity in Bethlehem (still a small town today, now predominantly Muslim), you have to bow low to enter the place where they say Jesus was born. As you enter the tiny room, it looks for all the world like a cave. Candles are lit to break through the darkness, and if you bend low enough you can almost see a child there and almost hear a young woman offer, "Here, would you like to hold him?"

That God would bend so low that we could take into our arms and cradle our Creator, that we might be touched by his holy light and follow it and bear it to the world, the light that all the darkness in the world will never be able to put out—this is the wonder of all wonders called "Christmas." This is the Nativity of Jesus.

Notes

1. Apocryphal gospels, old and new, love to fill in the lives of the gospels with their own imaginative scenes. These are folk gospels, and they play on the humanity of Christ too often obscured by official religion's focus on his divinity. For modern apocryphal stories, see Romulus Linney, *Jesus Tales* (San Francisco: North Point, 1980).

2. W. H. Auden, "For the Time Being: A Christmas Oratorio," in *Collected Poems* (New York: Random House, 1976), p. 279.

3. Frederick Buechner, *The Life of Jesus* (New York: Weathervane Books, 1974), p. 30.

4. Raymond E. Brown, *The Birth of the Messiah* (New York: Doubleday, 1977), pp. 415-16.

20

Jesus: From Boyhood to Baptism

One of the most essential details about Jesus, a detail largely lost in a tradition of blue-eyed portraits of Jesus, is his Jewishness. The cultural attempts to "de-Judaize" Jesus have been all too successful, so that the earliest image of Jesus, Jesus the rabbi, is all but unrecognizable. Historian Jaroslav Pelikan wonders aloud if there would have been such anti-Semitism in the West, and the horrors of pogroms and concentration camps, had Christian churches recognized the Jewishness of Jesus and pictured him as "Rabbi Jesus of Nazareth, son of David, in the context of a suffering Israel and suffering humanity."[1]

I

Jesus was born into the home of a devout and poor Jewish family in Galilee. Mary and Joseph raised their child as deeply observant Jews doing "everything," the text says, "according to the Law of Moses" (Luke 2:22, 39). When he was eight days old, they took the infant Jesus to the temple to be circumcised. When he was forty days old, they brought him for the rite of purification. They could offer only two pigeons for sacrifice, a provision made for the poor who could not afford the usual offering of a lamb. As they followed the law of the Lord in rearing Jesus, "the child grew and became strong, filled with wisdom; and the favor [*charis* in Greek, or "grace"] of God was upon him" (Luke 2:40).

There are two hints that this young Jewish boy will have a reach that extends far beyond Jewish soil. The first hint comes from Matthew's nativity narrative. Three wise men (philosophers/astronomers/physicians) from Persia had studied the stars and the prophecies of Hebrew and Persian religions, and they followed a strange new star to find a child who, according to their reading of the signs, was born to be king. Matthew's description of their pilgrimage is itself a prophecy: Here is a child who will be king not only of the Jews but of the whole world. In this child east and west, north and south will meet (Matthew 2:1-12).

The second hint comes from recent historical research by New Testament scholars: Only four miles from Nazareth, where Jesus grew up, was located the Roman-controlled capital city of the province of Galilee, Sepphoris, a cosmopolitan, burgeoning commercial center of forty thousand people. It had an acropolis, a bank, and a trade center that linked different parts of the Mediterranean world.[2] It was totally rebuilt between 4 B.C.E. and 26 C.E.

A young Jesus could well have traveled to Sepphoris with his carpenter father Joseph to work on the many building projects of that growing city. And this boy would have been exposed to a new world of Greek and Roman culture, language, literature, and philosophy. This precocious child may have had many more cosmopolitan experiences than has been supposed until now.

After the birth stories the gospel accounts skip twelve years in the story of Jesus. Our story-hungry hearts want more stories about Jesus' growing-up years, but the four gospels supply only this one. At the age of twelve, we're told, Jesus was taken by his parents to Jerusalem, a sixty-five-mile pilgrimage each way, to celebrate Passover.

Mary, Joseph, and Jesus traveled with many others from their hometown in a kind of village caravan. When Passover was over and they set out to return home, Mary and Joseph did not realize that Jesus was not with them. They thought he was playing with some of the other children. It takes a village to raise a child—and to lose one! It was nightfall before they discovered that Jesus was missing. The next day they returned to Jerusalem and searched frantically until they found him in the Temple, talking with the scholars and amazing them with his knowledge and insight into the scriptures.

When they found him, they said, "Why have you treated us like this? We were worried sick!" Jesus replied, "Did you not know I must be about my Father's business?" It was the first hint that Jesus early on knew the primacy of God's calling and that his relationship with God would surpass all others.

The text from Luke underlines again that Jesus was brought up in the most devout of Jewish homes, and it says he "grew in wisdom and in stature, and in favor with God and man" (2:52 RSV). He did not spring fully formed from the head of God, as Athena from Zeus, but "grew up" physically, mentally, spiritually, and socially—as we all have to do.

There are other gospels that didn't make it into the New Testament. We call them "apocryphal" gospels (meaning "hidden," not read in public or widely accepted).[3] They have filled in the silence of these years of Jesus' youth with wild, fanciful tales that more resemble Superboy comic books than the New Testament gospels. Jesus is pictured as a supernatural child wizard who combined magical powers with boyhood mischief. In one story, Jesus' friends refuse to play with him. In a fit of disappointment Jesus turns them into sheep! The horrified parents go screaming to Mary, who insists that Jesus turn them back into children, which Jesus does. The last scene of the episode shows the parents lecturing their children: The next time Jesus wants you to play with him, you play!

You can see why such stories didn't make it into the Bible. All through the New Testament accounts of his life on earth, Jesus' divinity is cloaked in humility. His humanity was no sham—it was a real humanity subject to all our human conditions.

His divinity was not demonstrated by capricious use of supernatural power, but by these two characteristics: first, the intimacy of his relationship with his heavenly Father, whom he called Abba (the Hebrew child's first word for daddy or papa), and second, his willingness to do whatever God wished him to do. In both these examples Jesus modeled for us the way to live fully human yet deeply God-filled lives as inhabitants both of this world and the kingdom of God which was his mission to proclaim.

II

The gospel accounts now jump eighteen years to the baptism of Jesus by John in the Jordan River. Jesus was thirty years old now, the accustomed age of spiritual leadership in that culture, and John was preaching radical spiritual renewal and baptizing for the repentance and forgiveness of sins to all who asked for this symbolic act of renewal.

When John saw Jesus coming for baptism, he said, "Behold, the Lamb of God, who takes away the sin of the world!" (John 1:29). When Jesus asked to be baptized himself, John was reluctant. Why should he baptize for the forgiveness of sins the one who *was* the forgiveness of sins? But Jesus insisted on its rightness, and John obliged. When Jesus came up out of the water, the sky was "torn open," the Spirit descended like a dove, and a Voice from heaven said, "You are my Son, the Beloved, in whom I am well pleased." The gospel accounts are not clear if anyone but Jesus saw the dove or heard the Voice, but Jesus did.

Immediately, the text says, the Spirit "drove" Jesus into the wilderness to be tested. This was a kind of "vision quest" like those found in many cultures where the person is tested to prove his or her character and strength. Jesus fasted for forty days. Then, the text says, the "devil" appeared to offer a series of temptations.

The famished Jesus had eaten nothing for forty days. The devil appeared with the first temptation: "If you are the Son of God, command this stone to become bread." It was the temptation for Jesus to use his miracle-working powers to serve his physical needs. In regard to his mission, it was the temptation to be the messiah of our physical needs alone—the one who would gain followers by filling their empty stomachs instead of their empty hearts.

It's the temptation all of us have: to make this material world with its wants and needs the final, ultimate realm of life. Do we live by what we can see, taste, and touch alone, or by values we cannot see, such as truth, loyalty, love, justice, promise keeping, and compassion? We can use our human powers to serve our material needs and wants only, or we can use them to serve God's kingdom. Andy Warhol, icon of pop culture and its material values, is reported to have said that if reincarnated, he'd like to come back in his next life as a ring on Elizabeth Taylor's finger. An interesting thought, but is that all there is? That's as good an example as any of the material world taken as the final realm. It is the devil's first temptation for Jesus and for us.

Jesus answered this temptation with scripture taught him by his parents: "It is written, one does not live by bread alone but by every word that proceeds from the mouth of God" (Deuteronomy 8:3). He knew where his true nourishment came from, which offered eternal, not just temporal, sustenance.

Then came the second temptation. The devil led him up to a high place and showed him all the kingdoms of the world. The devil then said, "I'll give you all this, all their glory and power, if you will but fall down and worship me." Jesus again quoted scripture: "It is written, worship the Lord God and serve only him" (Deuteronomy 10:12).

This second test is the temptation of power, glory, fame. It's heady stuff. It can give you a rush as addictive as any drug. History is full of people who have sold their souls to attain their goals, people who have lusted after thrones and high places, to be heads of nations, CEOs of corporations, and ecclesiastical leaders. We will do anything and everything necessary to get what we want, only to discover that the judgment of God may sometimes be to let us have what we want.

Jesus, once again, answered the devil's test with words memorized from childhood: "There is only one true God; him only will you serve."

Then the final test, the third temptation, perhaps the most dangerous and most subtle of all. The devil took Jesus to the top of the Jerusalem temple and said, "If you are the Son of God, throw yourself down from here, for it is written, 'He will command his angels concerning you, to protect you. On their hands they will bear you up so that you will not even dash your foot against a stone'" (Psalm 91:11, 12). The tempter was a wily creature. Twice Jesus had answered him by quoting scripture. Now the devil was quoting scripture back to him. (As Shakespeare shrewdly observed in *The Merchant of Venice*, "The devil can cite scripture for his purpose" [act 1, scene 3, line 99].)

This third temptation was for Jesus to make himself immune from human suffering and to escape having to face death as the way of bringing God's redemption to the world. For us it is the temptation to magical thinking—pretending that reality doesn't apply to us—and the temptation to reject the understanding that our suffering can be part of God's redemption. In effect, the devil came to Jesus and said, "Haven't you read the 'Son of God Immunity Clause'? You need not die. The angels will protect you, as God's holy word says."

The temptation plays on our dearest spiritual hopes that God and God's angels will watch over us and protect us. This is real in the truest sense, that our lives are in God's hands. But we must remind ourselves that God's "providence" is not a magic blanket that protects us from all of life's onslaughts. There is mystery here—the mystery of the interworking of God's providence and our freedom, the interworking of the mystery of evil and the mystery of goodness.

In the midst of this mystery we can be tempted to magical thinking. Magical thinking says, "I can control things if I do the right thing or pray the right prayer." We say to ourselves, "If I love my children deeply enough, no harm will come to them and everything will turn out okay." Or "if I have enough (or the right kind of) faith, God will take my cancer away." It is the illusion that if we're good enough or spiritual enough or smart enough, life will go as we wish.

Another form of magical thinking says, "If I'm good or spiritual or smart enough I can live apart from the normal limits of human existence." But this is an illusion. If you jump out of a third-story window, gravity works 100 percent of the time. If you drink a quart of alcohol and take cocaine, you may well not survive. If you work to exhaustion over a long period of time, your body will eventually break down. If you injure a person deeply by your actions and words, the relationship will take a long time to heal, or it may never heal. The third temptation of the devil to us is the subtle and powerful lie: Reality doesn't apply to *me*.

Jesus answered the temptation by again quoting scripture: "Do not put the Lord your God to the test" (Deuteronomy 6:16). We could summarize the wisdom of scripture in the face of this temptation with these words: Happy is the one who knows what is real.

Jesus proved his identity and his worthiness for his mission, to himself as well as to his heavenly Father. Having conquered the temptations, he set off on his mission as the Christ of God. Luke ends the temptation account with this sobering verse: "When the devil had finished every test, he departed from him *until an opportune time*" (Luke 4:13, emphasis added).

The testing of his mission and identity would recur, and the temptations reappeared at every vulnerable, decisive moment in Jesus' life—from the time he fed five thousand and the crowd cried, "Make him king!" to the taunt of the crowd in his ears as he hung on the cross: "If you are the Son of God, call on the angels to come and take you down from there!"

The forty days stand in Jesus' life, and in our lives, as the time of testing, proving who we are and whose we are and how we will spend our lives. When the forty days come—and they will come—remember Jesus in the wilderness and how he answered. And remember the whole life of Christ and how it continued to prove his identity and his mission.

Notes

1. Jaroslav Pelikan, *Jesus through the Centuries* (New Haven: Yale University Press, 1985), p. 20.
2. Russell Shorto reports this research in *Gospel Truth: The New Image of Jesus Emerging from Science and History, and Why It Matters* (New York: Riverhead Books, 1997), pp. 43-47.
3. Reynolds Price, *Three Gospels* (New York: Scribner's, 1996), p. 239.

21

The Miracle at Cana:
The Kingdom as Joy

The first miracle Jesus performed, so says the gospel of John, was turning the water into wine at the wedding feast at Cana. Nothing remotely similar happens in any of the other gospels.

John's gospel is different from the other three gospels in a number of ways: in chronology, in an early Judean ministry of Jesus, in its long spiritual/philosophical discourses, and in Jesus' astounding claims for himself: "Truly, truly I say to you, before Abraham was, I am"; "I am the way, the truth, and the life"; "I and the Father are one." Only John has Jesus and his disciples baptizing others; only in John does Jesus observe three Passovers, which gives the clue that his ministry lasted approximately three years.

This chapter represents remembrances of Jesus' early ministry captured only in John, and it centers on a miracle at a wedding feast in Cana. It was the first of the six great miracles (John calls them "signs") that Jesus performed in John's gospel. These signs pointed to a deep spiritual truth at work in Jesus.

Are we surprised that a miracle such as turning water into wine should happen at all, much less inaugurate Jesus' ministry in John? Jesus often told parables that compared the kingdom of God to the joy of a wedding feast. The miracle of Cana is an acted-out parable of this great and high truth: the kingdom of God is joy!

From the start Jesus wanted us to know that God comes to visit us not only in our griefs but also in our joys. Dostoevsky said of this episode at Cana: "Ah, that sweet miracle! . . . He worked his first miracle to help men's gladness. . . . He who loves men, loves their joy. . . ."[1]

I

Soon after Jesus arrived at the wedding feast, a problem arose. To the hosts' great embarrassment, the wine ran out. Mary, Jesus' mother, went to him and told him about the social calamity. "They have no wine."

Some have suggested that Jesus' disciples were responsible for the supply of wine going dry and that Mary was scolding Jesus. This is doubtful. But we must not forget that Jesus was accused of being "a glutton and drunkard who eats with tax collectors and sinners." Jesus loved our joy and so opened himself to such criticism. Once in the gospels critics went to Jesus and said: "John's disciples are much given to fasting and the practice of prayer, and so are the disciples of the Pharisees; but yours eat and drink" (Luke 5:33 REB).

Jesus said, "While the bridegroom is here, should the wedding guests fast?" Jesus was not oblivious to our need for joy; there is always plenty of opportunity for sorrow.

When Mary told him the wine had run out Jesus replied, "O woman, what is that to you and me?" The address, "O woman," sounds a bit impolite to us, but it was the usual address of respect for that time. Still, it seems a bit formal for a son to his mother. The moment calls to mind an event in Matthew's gospel (12:46-50) when someone in the crowd told Jesus his mother and brothers were outside asking for him. Jesus replied, "Who is my mother, and who are my brothers?" Then he turned to his followers and said, "Here are my mother and my brothers. Whoever does the will of God is my brother, my sister, my mother."

We can sense some distance here, of a son who sees his allegiance to God and God's mission as superseding all allegiances, even to his family. Here in Cana, when Mary came to Jesus concerned about the wine, Jesus replied, "Woman, what has this to do with you and me?"

This reply is typical of conversations all through the gospel of John. Other characters always dealt with surfaces; Jesus dealt with the depths. Nicodemus thought Jesus was talking about being reborn physically; Jesus was talking about spiritual rebirth "from above." The woman at the well was talking about water drawn from Jacob's well, but Jesus was talking about a living water welling up from within, welling up to eternal life. Mary was concerned about the shortage of wine at a party (no small worry if you've ever been in charge of a wedding party), and Jesus was thinking of a deeper wine, the wine of the new covenant, a dearer wine, the wine poured out in his blood. In the midst of this scene with people scurrying around looking for more wine, Jesus peered into the future and saw the shadow of a cross and said something that no one could possibly have understood then, but which we, with hindsight, cannot fail to understand. "My hour is not yet come," he said, meaning the coming hour of the cross, the terrible glory.

II

Despite his words to his mother, Jesus performed the miracle. Although the hour of final glorification—the cross and resurrection—had not yet come, this was a fitting time for Jesus to give a glimpse of God's glory, the first glimpse, or "sign," displayed in his ministry.

John's gospel began with the words that in Jesus' human form we behold God's glory. Up until then, God had showed the world a bit of glory here and there, but in Jesus the glory was more fully revealed than ever before or since.

In a wonderful fantasy called The Christmas Mystery, by Jostein Gaarder, a little girl, Elisabet, is talking to an angel. They come to a field of wildflowers and Elisabet points and exclaims, "Look at the lovely wildflowers!" The angel nods and says, "They are part of the glory of heaven that has strayed down to earth. . . . You see, there's so much glory in heaven that it's very easy for it to spill over."[2] John's gospel says that Jesus is the glory of God revealed in human flesh. And his miracles were some of the glory of heaven spilling over.

Mary instructed the servants to do what Jesus said; Jesus told them to fill up some jars with water. These jars were not little Mason canning jars. Each of the six stone jars contained twenty gallons of water, all together 120 gallons. No stingy God here.

Then Jesus told them to dip some out and take it back to the steward of the feast. When he tasted it, what he drank was not water but wine, and not just any wine but like the choicest of aged wines. The steward broke out in a grin, slapped the bridegroom on the back, and joked: Most people serve the choice wine first and then later, when taste buds are dulled, serve the cheap stuff. "But you have kept the good wine until now."

That was the first miracle, the first of the signs performed by Jesus. We need not scramble to try to rationalize this miracle away. Some modern critics argue that the guests were so dazzled by Jesus' appearance that they only *thought* they tasted wine! Here is the only place I know where liberal Unitarians and conservative Baptists agree on how to interpret a miracle. Unitarians (generally speaking) don't believe in the supernatural miracles, so they say the people only *thought* they were tasting wine. Conservative Baptist teetotalers don't believe in *wine*—the Son of God would never make wine! So, again, the guests only *thought* they were tasting wine.

I like better the words of seventeenth-century mystical poet Richard Crashaw who wrote, "The conscious water saw / Its God and blushed."[3]

The Bible doesn't want us arguing over the details of miracles but wants us to see their meaning. Signs and miracles *always* point beyond themselves to say something about the kingdom of God and about Jesus, the one who brought the kingdom near.

III

So now we move in more deeply to see the meaning of this miracle. On the surface the steward is cracking jokes about the quality of the wine (he's probably also giddy with relief, having escaped the calamity of running out of drink for the guests). On a deeper level the miracle symbolizes the whole drama of salvation.

The 120 gallons of water turned to wine is an extravagant symbol of the superabundance and joy of God's kingdom. The

disciples should have grasped this. The Old Testament prophesied
that the latter days would see a superabundance of wine. Indeed
the book of Baruch prophesied that the earth would yield its fruit
a thousandfold, so that each vine would have a thousand branches
and each branch a thousand clusters and each cluster a thousand
grapes and each grape *120* gallons of new wine (24:5)! Was Jesus
saying that all this wine is but one grape of one cluster of one
branch of one vine in the vineyard of the kingdom of God?
     Still the symbols reach deeper. The six jars were Jewish puri-
fication jars. They were used for ritual cleansing before each
meal and between courses. Did the jars stand for the old order
of things, the Jewish purification laws as the only way to make
oneself clean before God? And did the new wine stand for the
new covenant of grace where God in God's love and forgiveness
does the cleansing?
     In the old order of things we try to purify ourselves by
washing the outside. There is no end of things to do, rules to
follow, penance to make. That "old-order" religion is still with us.
Flannery O'Connor wrote that the religion of the South is a "do-
it-yourself religion."[4] Self-help religion dominates the spiritual life
of people ancient and modern.
     That old order is gone, Jesus' miracle was saying. You can't
cleanse yourself from the outside in. You can't cleanse yourself at
all. Only God can make you clean. And God is doing it from the
inside out.
     The old order is being replaced by a new order; grace is
superseding our attempts at self-salvation.
     Mary doesn't know it, but she judges the old order when she
says, "They have no wine." In the old order the wine always runs
out. And the steward doesn't know it, but he is praising the new
order when he says, "You've kept the choice wine until now." Jesus
comes with a joy no earthly wine can touch.
     The fermented fruit of the vine can bring a few hours of cheer,
but it is short-lived joy and soon disappoints. C. S. Lewis says he
searched all his life for joy—in vain—until he was met by joy in
Jesus Christ. "I sometimes wonder," he wrote, "whether all pleas-
ures are not substitutes for joy."[5]
     "You've saved the best till last," the steward cracked. He
didn't know how right he was.

IV

In Dostoevsky's novel *The Brothers Karamazov,* Father Zossima, an old priest who has lived in the incredible joy of the kingdom, dies. His body lies in a coffin in a monastery. Alyosha, a young man who loved Father Zossima, comes into the room and hears a priest reading scripture over the coffin. He is reading John 2:1-11, about the wedding feast at Cana. Alyosha kneels to pray, and as he hears the scripture, he falls asleep and begins to dream. He dreams of a wedding feast. The couple, the guests, Jesus—they are all there. As the dream goes on, the room where the feast is happening begins to grow wider and wider until Alyosha himself is there. Then an old man gets up from the table and comes toward him. It is Father Zossima himself. He is no longer in the coffin—he is there with the wedding party. The old man calls to Alyosha and says, "Why have you hidden yourself here, out of sight? You come and join us too. . . . We are making merry," he says, "we are drinking the new wine, the wine of [a] new and great joy."

Then he calls him to look at Jesus. "He is changing the water into wine. . . . He is expecting new guests, He is calling new ones unceasingly for ever and ever."[6]

So the same room of Cana's wedding feast expands wider and wider and wider until it includes us today two thousand years and more thousands of miles away. And John, the teller of the story, looks at us and says, Why are you hidden away? You can join us too!

V

Rilke wrote in his *Sonnets to Orpheus:*

> Praising, that's it! He was as one appointed to praise,
> and he came the way ore comes, from silent
> rock. His heart, a wine press that couldn't last
> made us an endless supply of wine.[7]

Those lines are as perfect a commentary of this miracle at Cana as any I could imagine, of the day Jesus turned water into wine and pointed obliquely to the day his own heart would become a winepress for our joy. "He is changing the water into wine. . . . He is expecting new guests, He is calling new ones unceasingly for ever and ever."

Notes

1. Fyodor Dostoevsky, *The Brothers Karamazov*, trans. C. Garnett (New York: Heritage, 1949), p. 277.

2. Jostein Gaarder, *The Christmas Mystery* (New York: Farrar, Straus & Giroux, 1996), p. 69.

3. Richard Crashaw, "Aquae in Vinum Versae," in *Epigrammata Sacra* (1634), as quoted in *Bartlett's Familiar Quotations*, by John Bartlett, 15th ed. (Boston: Little, Brown, 1980), p. 292.

4. Flannery O'Connor, *The Habit of Being*, ed. Sally Fitzgerald (New York: Farrar, Straus & Giroux, 1979), p. 350.

5. C. S. Lewis, *Surprised by Joy* (New York: Harcourt Brace, 1955), p. 170.

6. Dostoevsky, pp. 278-79.

7. Rainer Maria Rilke, *Sonnets to Orpheus*, 1.7, trans. David Young (Hanover, N.H.: Wesleyan University Press, 1987), p. 15. First line altered by H.S.S.

22

The Galilean Ministry and Early Opposition

"Jesus came . . . preaching" is how Mark's gospel begins the Galilean ministry of Jesus (Mark 1:14). And the message of his preaching was this: "The time is ripe, the Kingdom of God draws near; turn and believe the good news" (Mark 1:15).

There are two kinds of time: The first goes by the Greek word *chronos*, clock and calendar time. Then there is *kairos* time, "fullness of time" time, moments of special opportunity and significance.

Jesus announced the fullness of time, the ripeness of time, a *kairos*. The kingdom of God draws near. The kingdom of God, or reign of God, is at hand, he said. The kingdom of God is *entos* you, he said, among you, inside you (Luke 17:21). In other words, the kingdom is *here*, not there, *close*, not far, as close as your own breath. The kingdom is not some far distant hope of a cosmic intervention of God. The kingdom is nearer and more subtle than that. "The kingdom comes not with observation," said Jesus. (You must have "eyes to see" and "ears to hear," eyes and ears of faith, that is, eyes and ears opened by God.) The kingdom is coming *now* in gracious invitation. But you must hear and believe and enter.

What is the response the kingdom demands of us? "Repent and believe the gospel." Literally, "turn" and trust the good news, the *euangelion*. Turn and believe it as a child would, trusting in the goodness of God.

I

Jesus came preaching in Galilee. He preached first in his home country, setting up headquarters in the seaside city of Capernaum where his first disciples, Peter and Andrew, lived.

Not only did Jesus preach the kingdom; it came near in miracles that he, full of the Spirit, was able to perform. "Every kind of disease and sickness" was healed and evil spirits were cast out. One of his first miracles was the healing of Peter's mother-in-law, who had a high fever. He made her well—which probably helped ease the pain of losing the daily presence of her son-in-law, who "left everything" to traipse with Jesus all over the countryside.

Large crowds began to follow Jesus, crowds from Galilee, the Decapolis, Jerusalem, and Judea. But early interest in Jesus was mixed with opposition, even in his own hometown; Jesus' preaching of the kingdom of God did not sound like good news to everybody.

After early success in Capernaum Jesus came to his hometown, Nazareth, and went to the local synagogue on the sabbath. He rose and read from the prophet Isaiah and then began to teach. From the sixty-first chapter of Isaiah he read:

> The spirit of the Lord is upon me,
> because he has anointed me
> to preach good news to the poor,
> to proclaim release to the captives
> and the recovering of sight to the blind;
> to set at liberty those who are oppressed,
> to proclaim the year of God's favor.
> —Isaiah 61:1-2, author's translation

Then he put down the scroll and said, "*Today* this scripture has been fulfilled in your hearing." That sounded good to their ears, and people punched each other and winked and nodded in appreciation and approval. "That's Joe's boy preaching!" they said, grinning. Then Jesus turned the text in an unexpected way and as he did, they turned on him.

"You will no doubt quote to me the proverb, 'Physician, heal thyself' and say, 'Do here in your hometown what we've heard you've done in Capernaum'" (that is, the miracles, exorcisms, and other gracious acts of God's mercy). "But I tell you," Jesus said, "there were many widows in Israel in Elijah's time, but God sent Elijah to a Gentile widow in Sidon. And there were many lepers in Israel at the time of Elisha, but none of them were cleansed except Naaman, general of the Syrian army." His illustrations about Elijah and Elisha were not tame ones. It was like his saying to us today, "There were a lot of poor Christian widows in America, but God's prophet blessed the home of a black Muslim widow on the southside of Chicago. And there were many lepers in America, but God's prophet healed the generalissimo of Fidel Castro's army in Cuba."

The congregation grew furious. The kingdom is dawning, the year of God's favor is dawning, but this man is saying *they* may not be in on it! And Jesus' hometown congregation turned into a lynch mob. They hauled him out of the synagogue and carried him to a cliff where they planned to throw him to his death. Miraculously Jesus escaped.

Surely this is an unexpected turn. Jesus has moved from "Home Town Boy Makes Good" to the "Most Wanted" list. How do we interpret this? Perhaps the message is this: We want God's favor and blessing on *us*, but not necessarily on *all*, and especially not on our enemies. But the way of the kingdom is clear: If you want an exclusive hold on God's favor, you find yourself outside God's favor.

The kingdom, Jesus said, is where the poor get good news, the captives find release, the blind see, and the oppressed go free. In any given moment of time you and I are

poor or rich,
bruised or healed,
blind or sighted,
captive or free.

There are only two ways you can enter the kingdom and experience its joy. One is to be *among* the poor, oppressed, bruised, blind, and brokenhearted; those to whom God comes as healing, comfort, justice, and freedom. The other way is to be among God's people who are *going to* the poor, oppressed, bruised, blind, and brokenhearted and bringing God's healing, comfort, justice, and freedom.

If you are neither of these, you are in a third group. These are the bored of the earth. We don't know for sure where the word "boredom" comes from. Walker Percy suggests it comes from the French word meaning "to stuff."[1] The bored of the world are those stuffed with the good things of life who refuse to share those good things. They sit as spectators of life, judgers and keepers rather than givers and receivers. They grow cynical, jaded, angry, and *bored*. Instead of entering into the activity of the kingdom, freely giving and receiving God's mercy, they sit coolly at a distance. The judgment of the Nazareth episode is on this third group. Jesus' hometown congregation have become the judgers, and instead of entering into the gracious activity of the kingdom, they react with rage and try to kill Jesus.

II

We have the comforting illusion that *we* would react differently if Jesus appeared in our churches—our liberal "cause of the day" churches or our conservative "sinner of the day" churches. What Carlyle Marney said of his own Southern Baptist people could be said of all denominations that are more culturally conditioned than Christ-conditioned: "We're more Southern than Baptist and more Baptist than Christian."

What if Jesus, today, took hold of all our religious institutions? How different might they look? Would they fall in such lockstep with nationalist, racial, and cultural interests?

What if Jesus took hold of our religious attitudes? Would we change from being a judging people trying to hold up the moral order of the universe by our own human, righteous hands and learn to trust in God?

What if Jesus took hold of our spiritual lives, looked into the ways we care for our own souls? Do you think he'd want us first to experience God's compassion for ourselves, our own sinning and judging selves? So that we might rise and live in the joy and power of the kingdom?

Do you think we would begin to go "under the mercy," to use Charles Williams's phrase? And *in* the mercy and *with* the mercy so the world might hear the good news and believe it?

This is the patch from the new garment that cannot be sewn onto the old one, to use one of Jesus' images. This is the new wine that cannot be placed in old wineskins. Knowing our human nature better than we, Jesus said, "No one after drinking the old wine wants the new, for they say, the old is better."

But the old is *not* better. It is a slow death. Come then and taste the new wine, he said.

> The time is ripe,
> the kingdom of God draws near;
> turn and believe the good news.

III

As emissary of the kingdom, Jesus came preaching and healing. He also gathered a circle of "disciples" (literally, "learners"). The first two were common fishermen, Simon Peter and his brother Andrew, then two more fishermen, James and John. "Follow me," Jesus said to them, "and I'll teach you how to catch people." The image of fishing for people called to mind an image from the Hebrew Bible of God saving people by catching them in his net, the way fishermen catch fish. Jesus was saying: My mission is to save people from destruction. If you follow me, you can help. The text says that "immediately they left everything and followed" (Luke 5:11).

Next Jesus called Levi, or Matthew, the tax collector. Tax collectors were, in the minds of the rest of the Jewish people, pond scum. As collaborators with Rome, they were traitors to their own people. Because they could extort as much money as they wanted from the citizens and pocket the excess, they were seen as thieves as well. Jesus called Matthew to leave the tax office and follow, and he did.

Jesus filled out the circle of twelve with men who could not be more different: one who had collaborated with Rome and one who aimed to start an insurrection against Rome (Simon the Zealot), activists and quietists, common noneducated men and at least one (if the younger, beloved disciple is the one who wrote the gospel of John) who had prodigious intellectual and poetic gifts. Jesus also called women to join a larger circle of disciples that accompanied him (Luke 8). His chosen group of companions was itself a sign of the kingdom of God rearranging everything.

And so were his dinner parties. Jesus broke the cultural and religious purity codes by eating with tax collectors, sinners, and women. "Look," said his growing ranks of opponents, "a friend of tax collectors and sinners." They meant it as condemnation. Jesus took it as commendation. When Jesus overheard, he said, "It is not the well who need a doctor, but the sick. I do not come to call the righteous [to make the respectable more respectable] but to call sinners to repentance" (Luke 5:31-2). Something new is afoot with Jesus, and the new has to do with the inbreaking of the kingdom.

Jesus' social and dinner companionship was a gauntlet thrown down before the religious establishment and its way of life. The "sinners" he ate with were not timid churchgoing sinners but notorious breakers of the commandments of God. The tax collectors and prostitutes Jesus befriended belonged to the universally despised professions.

Jesus believed in repentance, but the kingdom he preached reversed the old order of salvation; grace *preceded* repentance, communion came first, and conversion followed on its healing wings.

The eating and drinking with sinners and outcasts signaled another dimension of Jesus' mission of the kingdom, one with larger social and political implications. Against the "politics of holiness" that helped support the economic, political, and religious status quo, Jesus brought a "politics of compassion" that challenged it to its very roots. It is to this dimension of Jesus' mission we now turn.

Note

1. Walker Percy, *Lost in the Cosmos: The Last Self-Help Book* (New York: Farrar, Straus & Giroux, 1983), p. 70.

23

The Way of Compassion

As soon as she entered the room and saw him, the tears began to fall. He looked at her, and it was as if his face were saying, "It's okay."

She was on a mission of wholeness—to be herself made whole. He was on a mission of wholeness—to bring wholeness to God's people. God's people were well practiced in "holiness," but wholeness was a long way off.

Simon the Pharisee, Jesus' host that day (Jesus ate with Pharisees too!) was as good a representative as any of Israel's plight: the grandeur and the failure of well-scrubbed religiosity.

The nation was in crisis—social, political, and spiritual crisis. A foreign power was occupying the country and a foreign culture was tempting the people to accommodate. There was double taxation: the temple tithes to keep the religious structures going and the Roman taxes to keep Caesar's empire going. It was a grievous load.

In answer to this crisis, as a way of spiritual survival, the Pharisees led a way of renewal. This way redoubled the efforts at following the laws of God. (We know this story as our own: when in trouble, work twice as hard; if you've been praying twice a day, pray four times.) Their way could be called, to use the phrase of Marcus Borg, "the politics of holiness."[1] By politics we mean the whole way the culture organized and arranged its life. Their banner was the phrase, "Be holy as your God is holy" (Leviticus 19:2).

I

How did one get to be holy? By strictly observing the purity laws pertaining to cleanness and uncleanness. By being born in the right race, the right tribe, the right sex, the right religion, and in the right body.

Israel had a carefully drawn purity map—or set of maps. It was like those sets of transparent maps laid on top of one another. One map shows borders, towns, cities, counties, states. The next map shows topography: mountains, hills, and low places. The next map shows population concentration, and so on.

Israel's purity map had many layers. On one surface you saw geographical borders, kosher and nonkosher zones— kosher as in Judah, nonkosher as in Samaria or Sidon.

Another dimension of the map had to do with behavior. Did you follow all 613 laws of Moses? Did you observe all the rites of purification, all the codes of conduct, make all the proper sacrifices in the Temple? On this map were contrasted the righteous and sinners, the observant and nonobservant, the pure and impure. The category of "sinners" included all the nontithers and nonobservant, the immoral, and those in the wrong professions— tax collectors, swineherds, and prostitutes, to name a few.

One's purity also depended on the circumstances of one's birth. Another map. In these purity zones were priests, Levites, and Israelites. In the impurity zones were those of illegitimate birth and those born with various physical problems. Some by birth could be holy; others couldn't. Holiness here had to do with physical wholeness. Among the "impure" were the maimed, the hunchback, the chronically ill, the lepers, the eunuchs (those neither sexually intact nor "correct").

The purity map also had to do with gender. Women may have been anatomically intact, but they were not anatomically "correct." Their very femaleness rendered them impure during the most female of their days: childbirth and monthly flow. They could not be priests or rabbis. They could not even sit with their husbands in church. Parts of the Temple were closed off to them.

Wealth and poverty marked another dimension of the map. The conventional wisdom and practical theology of the day taught that wealth was a sign of righteousness and poverty was a sign of sinfulness. Thus the poor were "unclean." In ancient Israel the poor couldn't afford to observe all the laws of temple taxation and sacrifice. Their poverty forced them to be nonobservant Jews. There are many people today who do not go to church because they feel too economically different from the congregations situated around them.

The purity map had to do with race, Jew and Gentile: the circumcised (a rather male mark of distinction) and everybody else. Maybe the ones considered most unclean of all were the Samaritans, a half-breed, half-observant people, because at one time in their history they "knew better."

This was Israel's purity map in Jesus' time. It governed every aspect of their lives.

But Jesus, filled with the Spirit, came to challenge this map. Your map is not God's map, he said.

Instead of the banner "Be holy as your God is holy," Jesus brought a new way: Be merciful as your God is merciful, be compassionate as your Father is compassionate. (The Old Testament word for mercy comes from *rachem* or womb. It pointed to the deepest possible motherly, womb-like love for a child.) In a wonderful play on images Jesus said, "Be womb-like in your love, as your Father is womb-like."

Jesus' politics of compassion redrew the city maps. "Have you not heard God's word through the prophets?" he said to the politicians of holiness. "Go and learn what this means: 'I desire mercy, not sacrifice.'" Jesus was challenging the whole way the Temple and sacrificial system governed people's lives. You don't have to jump through all these religious hoops for God to love you and to be saved. No wonder the religious leaders wanted to get rid of him. What if your whole way of life was based on the buying and selling of God's grace and Jesus says, "It's no longer for sale. It's free. Only receive it and live it."

Jesus did not abolish the goal of holiness: that we be more like God. To be holy requires of us at times and places in our lives to be separate from the world and to be different. But the holiness Jesus brings is mingled with compassion, God's compassion for our imperfect girl, boy, human person selves, and our own compassion toward ourselves and for others. God's holiness is righteousness and compassion joined. Holiness without compassion does not lead to wholeness but to hatefulness and self-righteousness. It baptizes our bigotries, circumcises our fears, and demonizes our enemies. It creates scapegoats to preserve the illusion of our purity. The politics of holiness leads to inquisitions and crusades and holocausts and witch hunts and Klan rallies and hate crimes and murder for righteousness' sake. Quoting Pascal again, "Men never do evil so completely and cheerfully as when they do it from religious conviction."[2]

Jesus was for holiness, not for the external kind but for the kind that flows from a new heart (Mark 7:14-23). His politics of compassion began with compassion for our own selves. Purity maps not only divide our community; we have purity maps *inside* us dividing our souls. So the gospel's mission of compassion starts first with the inner self. Be compassionate as God is compassionate—to *yourself* and then with others. *Wholeness through compassion* was the way of Jesus. He embodied it in healing words and healing acts. Forgiveness and healing flowed together. His healing acts and free-flowing forgiveness upset the holiness codes: He healed the wrong people on the wrong day of the week in the wrong part of town. This politics of compassion he acted out by eating and drinking with sinners and outcasts, untouchables. These meals were an affront to a culture based on purity maps. Perhaps more than in any other way, Jesus' socializing with sinners demonstrated the collision course between the Jewish leaders' "politics of holiness" and Jesus' "politics of compassion." The leaders thought uncleanness was contagious, hence the life of separation from sinners. Jesus thought cleanness was contagious, hence the mission of the kingdom to all.

The story from Luke of the woman of the city who broke into a dinner party where Jesus was eating is as good an example as any in the gospels.

II

She came from the "wrong side of the tracks" according to the purity map—in almost every way. She was a woman and a sinner.

She was described as "a woman of the city," which probably meant what it sounds like. I would not doubt she also had some physical infirmity.

Everything she had been taught by her culture and religion told her she was not welcome in the presence of a holy man, a prophet, a teacher like this Jesus sent from God. But everything she had experienced about this man, as she hung back around the fringes of the crowds when he spoke and healed, gave her a hope that there was a way of wholeness that didn't have to go through the "politics of holiness."

"No one is good but God," she heard him say when someone called him good, which gave her the hope that she didn't have to be perfect to be whole. It was as if he were saying, "You don't have to *make* yourself holy by following all these rules; you *are* holy, God made you that way. Live from the inside out of that core of holiness." And like a wound healing from the inside out, that seemed to be what was happening to her as she listened to him.

So this day she decided to come near to him and do something for him. She heard he was in town eating at the house of Simon the Pharisee. Hillary Clinton could not be more unwelcome in the house of Rush Limbaugh—or Madonna in Jerry Falwell's house—than this woman was in Simon's house. Everything about the place screamed Not Welcome!—except that Jesus was there, and he made her feel like the guest of honor at any banquet life could give, the first time she'd ever felt like that. So she bolstered up her courage and entered.

As soon as she walked into the room and saw his face, she knew she would start crying. She didn't intend to but there they were, falling down her cheeks, a river of tears. She had wept the first time she heard him, his words coming like the first daybreak, words about the mercy of God flowing free, as free as the sun that shines and the rain that falls, freer. She felt healing happening.

So when she entered the room holding the carved alabaster box of perfume to anoint his feet, the tears began to fall. Because her hands held the box, she could not wipe them away. They just fell. Undeterred by her tears and the stares of the guests, she moved to where Jesus was reclining and knelt. The tears spilled down her cheeks and onto Jesus' feet until they were wet with her tears.

What was she to do? She let down her hair—another scandalous act for a woman to do in public—and dried his feet with her hair. Then she kissed his feet and anointed them with the perfume. This scene can be told overheated with romanticism. We should remember that here was a poor woman, an outcast. Her hard life and at-risk profession had probably taken its toll on her body and her health. One Scandinavian novelist has pictured Mary Magdalene with a cleft palate. Here is no cheap romance novel—Julia Roberts coming to see Kevin Costner. It is the romance of the *gospel:* God comes to love not our perfect skin or chiseled features but our cleft palate.

The focus now turns to the host of the meal, Simon the Pharisee. Jesus loved Pharisees too. His mission of wholeness was for them as well—and for the inevitable Pharisee lurking somewhere in us.

By entering the dining room and anointing Jesus, the woman had crossed all the boundaries on the purity map, and it was Simon's duty as a Pharisee to enforce the lines. He couldn't believe Jesus had let her do this. He thought to himself, If this man were a prophet, he would know what sort of woman this is who is touching him. She's a sinner.

But Jesus read Simon's thoughts (proving he was a prophet) and turned to Simon and said, "Simon, I have something to say to you." Simon said, "Speak," and Jesus told him this parable. A creditor had two debtors. One owed five hundred denarii (about $50,000) and the other owed fifty denarii (about $5,000). When they could not pay, the creditor freely forgave them both. Both debts forgiven, the $50,000 and the $5,000.

Then Jesus asked: "Now which of them will love him more?" Simon answered, "The one, I suppose, who was forgiven the greater debt." Jesus then moved in for the clincher:

Do you see this woman? I entered your house; you gave me no water for my feet, but she has bathed my feet with her tears and wiped them with her hair. You gave me no kiss of greeting, but she has not stopped kissing my feet. You did not anoint my head with oil, but she has anointed my feet with this perfume. Therefore, I tell you, her many sins are forgiven for she loved much; but one who is forgiven little, loves little. (Luke 7:44-47, author's translation)

Simon may well have had a servant perform all those duties of hospitality—the washing, the anointing, the kiss—or his wife. But not Simon himself. This woman had done what he had not done. Simon had manners (Pharisees are good at manners), but he didn't have love.

All love has manners but not all manners have love. You can tell the difference. It's the difference between going to church to do something nice for Jesus (Sunday as "Be Nice To God" Day), or loving him with all your heart, mind, soul, and strength. It's the difference between mumbling some hymn or dancing before the Lord with all your might. True religion is not set up to make the respectable more respectable and to hell with the rest, but to turn us passionately alive to go into the world with God's love.

The woman's act and Jesus' parable probably ruined Simon's dinner. He needed wholeness as much as she. The sadness is, he didn't know it. He thought his "politics of holiness" would get him there. It can't.

Jesus then turned to the woman and said the words she'd already heard, words that had brought her there and had brought her tears. Words that had let down her hair and kissed his feet and anointed them, words that were *life* to her.

"Your sins are forgiven," was what he said. Then he said, "Your faith has saved you, made you whole, and made you well. Go in peace."

III

I think there's some Simon in all of us, trying valiantly to manufacture holiness with a kind of self-help religion, what Flannery O'Connor saw in southern religion. "The religion of the South," she wrote, "is a do-it-yourself religion, something I as a Catholic find painful and touching and grimly comic."[3]

I've seen people scourge themselves with the Bible, turning its word into a leather whip imbedded with stones. I've seen them sing "Amazing Grace" but be practicing a religion of works; grace seems a lost, foreign word, and there's no music in their voice. I've seen people hate themselves and hate others with the hate they think God has for them. I've seen the purity maps drawn on their souls dividing them up, alienating them from their own selves, propelling them to self-destructive acts and contradictory lives and everyday misery. I've seen that in them and I've seen it in me and, in some measure, in every human soul.

But Jesus wants to come into every part of our souls, come down every street, into every ghetto and hidden part, clean and unclean, public and private, bringing the healing balm of compassion. This is the gracious act of God in Christ. It is God's *eudokia*— God's good pleasure and will—for us, God's beloved children.

Notes

1. Marcus J. Borg, *Jesus: A New Vision* (San Francisco: HarperSanFrancisco, 1987); *Meeting Jesus Again for the First Time* (San Francisco: HarperSanFrancisco, 1994).

2. Blaise Pascal, *Penseés*, 895, trans. W. F. Trotter, *Great Books*, vol. 33 (Chicago: Encyclopaedia Britannica, 1952), p. 347.

3. Flannery O'Connor, *The Habit of Being*, ed. Sally Fitzgerald (New York: Farrar, Straus & Giroux, 1979), p. 350.

24

One: The Healing of the Demoniac

The mission of Jesus in announcing the coming near of the kingdom involved miracles, exorcisms, and healings, especially in the Galilean phase of his ministry. As Jesus exorcised demons, he claimed he had bound the strong man (Matthew 12:29) and so could enter his house. "I saw Satan fall like lightning from heaven," he said (Luke 10:18). The kingdom of God was taking over the kingdom of evil. One evidence of this was one of the most dramatic healings—that of a demoniac living in a graveyard.

Jesus had come to the other side of the Sea of Galilee to the area of the Gerasenes, which was Gentile, not Jewish, territory. There he met a man who was a terror to himself and others. He had an "unclean spirit" and lived in a graveyard. Graveyards were themselves considered places of uncleanness, with corpses and burial caves and the like. The townspeople had banished the man there. We have banished the psychotic to similar graveyards in our century.

For a while they had tried to keep him tied with chains. No more. He'd break them. Day and night he wandered among the graves and through the hills screaming and slashing himself with stones.

I

It is a disquieting picture, and more a picture of our lives than we'd want to admit, even to ourselves. Decades ago Dr. Karl Menninger called it "man against himself." We are filled with self-hatred, and the self-hatred has taken the form of self-abuse and self-destructive behavior. "Self-care" is impossible when we no longer care what happens to us. We, like this man, feel unclean and alone, living in the isolation of a graveyard.

She came into my office, dear child of God, and showed me her arms: hundreds of tiny scars where she had cut herself over the years, not to kill herself but to hurt herself. And I've seen others who have done the same thing to themselves emotionally, scars not on their arms but on their minds. Lacerations of the soul. Drugs, alcohol, professional suicide, flunking out—all can be ways of punishing the self out of self-loathing. And there are more. We are endlessly inventive in finding ways to hurt or punish the self. For example, to hurt those close to us is to hurt the self. If we cannot love, cherish, and protect the self, we cannot love, cherish and protect our families, the first extensions of the self.

The evil spirits that had inhabited the man Jesus encountered are in the text of the story literally called "unclean spirits." Other places in the Bible they are called "demons" or "demonic spirits." The connection is suggestive. In the Bible "satan" means "accuser." Satan is the one who mounts the charges against us, indicts, convicts, sentences, and if we let him, he will execute us too. The spirit of uncleanness is the spirit of self-accusation and self-hatred. Sometimes it is the culture around us or people around us who have named us unclean, and we have believed them.

Self-hatred can intensify to the point of mental illness, but this is only a difference of degree from what all of us suffer at our own hands. We find ourselves living in dark burial caves, slashing ourselves with one kind of stone or another. We feel unclean and maybe, just maybe, our own blood will be our cleansing. Unable to accept the atonement, we are bent on repeating it.

Sometimes our self-hatred is severe because we haven't done our "hate work." When we've been deeply injured, deeply hurt, there is no other natural response than hate. It's a way of restoring boundaries and self-respect. It is the rage that comes with being hurt or humiliated.

In situations like these God calls us to love steadfastly and to hate expeditiously. I heard the phrase "hate expeditiously" from Carlyle Marney. To hate expeditiously is to do our hating cleanly, responsibly, completely, then be done with it. If it gets lodged in us, it can kill us. We can get stuck in our hatred for another, or we can turn the hate inward. It is a deadly path in either case.

Marney reports from his pastor's study what I have found to be true: that the only hate most Christians will let themselves feel is *self*-hatred. That's the only kind we'll admit because we think that's the only kind of hate God allows. It's unthinkable to hate others; it's okay to hate ourselves. We don't know how to hate expeditiously, so we turn hate inward toward ourselves.

"Hate" is another word for rage, and rage is the appropriate response of the injured or violated self, the energy that restores ego boundaries and self-respect. It only becomes sin when it is expressed in violence or vindictiveness, when it turns into intractable bitterness or unrelenting self-hatred. God calls us to responsible hate work: to do our hating and get it over with and get on with life.

II

The man in the story is overwhelmed by the spirit of uncleanness. He is shamed, out of control, scary and scared, barely clothed, his skin slashed and bleeding, and alone.

As you might imagine, no one else will come near him. But Jesus comes near. The man falls at his feet and says, "Jesus, Son of the Most High, don't punish me!" The spirit of accusation and uncleanness has so permeated this man that the only thing he can imagine God doing to him is punishing him. He doesn't fall down before Jesus asking for, hoping for, healing but expecting punishment and begging to be spared. Is that how we come before God and live our lives, expecting punishment? Do you live your life that way?

Jesus is here for deliverance and for healing. He orders the unclean spirit out of the man: Leave him alone! Begone! Scram! And he comes to banish the spirit of uncleanness from our lives.

Jesus asks the evil spirit's name. The answer comes from the man's lips. "My name is *Legion!* For we are many." A legion of soldiers was numbered a couple of thousand. So some translate this, "My name is *Mob*." Ever felt like you had a mob inside? A crowd of people, not just one? Or that your inner self was a contest of forces vying for control? Like you had this "evil twin" inside and you didn't know who'd win?

When C. S. Lewis was on the road of conversion to Christ, the Spirit of God confronted him with the real but not so pretty truth about himself. He thought he was a happy, reasonably decent pagan, but now this is what he saw:

> For the first time I examined myself with a seriously practical purpose. And there I found what appalled me: a zoo of lusts, a bedlam of ambitions, a nursery of fears, a harem of fondled hatreds. My name was Legion.[1]

The Spirit's revelation about his true condition was a step on the road to salvation for Lewis. It is our true condition too. We live with a split self or divided self and need the healing of Jesus, who makes us *one.*

Think of yourself as three selves. The first self is the *ideal self:* an illusionary perfect self, the grandiose picture of ourselves as being without fault, better than and different from others.

The second self is the *false self.* It is the disinherited self. It becomes the compulsive self that acts out all the parts of the self the ideal self won't allow. It is the part most shaped by our world, most vulnerable to the distortions of sin: pride, sloth, envy, anger, greed, gluttony, and lust. You could call it the flip side of the ideal self. But neither self is your real self.

The third self is the *real self,* the *true self.* This is the self created by God, blessed by God with original blessing and called good. This is a self vulnerable to sin and possessing ordinary human weakness. To recognize this real self is to join the human race. Such is the beginning of wisdom. This is the self that can grow spiritually toward wholeness and conquer the control of sin. It is a self characterized by both humility and hope. Humility comes from the word "humus," or soil. To be humble is to recognize that we are from the earth, finite and fallible creatures. It is to acknowledge and accept our human weakness, take responsibility for it, and live responsibly within it. The real self also has hope, the power that sustains us in our journey toward wholeness when we cannot see or feel the possibility for wholeness.

Jesus freed the demoniac from the unclean spirits that divided him and restored him to his "right mind," to his *real self*. Artist Adrian Martinez has painted the scene in a way that moves me deeply.[2] In his painting Martinez has captured the demoniac in the instant of being healed, in midhealing, as it were. One hand is grasping for Christ's cloak to cover himself in his shame. It is as if he is saying, "My name is Legion, don't look at me." The other hand is reaching for the face of Christ, as if the very presence of Christ has moved him from shame to hope. He now sees what would have seemed impossible moments before—the blessing of God on the face of Christ—and he reaches to receive it, the reaching itself evidence of power of salvation at work within him.

III

The story now takes a comic turn. It is as if God knew we needed some comic relief at this moment. The unclean spirits beg Jesus not to send them out of the territory. You see, this was Gentile territory, "unclean" Gentile territory, and the unclean spirits knew they had it made here. It was like their saying, "Jesus, cast us out of this man, okay, okay, okay, okay, but don't drive us out of Las Vegas. This is our kind of place!" You can almost picture them lining up to do a soft-shoe number for Jesus and singing, "My kind of town, Gergasa is!" (Gergasa is scholars' best guess as to the name of this area.)

It's clear we're meant to laugh at this part of the story. As C. S. Lewis reminded us (following Martin Luther), the devil cannot stand laughter.[3]

The mob of demonic spirits beg Jesus not to cast them out of Gentile territory. "*Please* let us stay here in Las Vegas! If you send us to Salt Lake City with all those righteous Mormons, we'll starve to death!"

Then the unclean spirits spy a herd of pigs nearby. They get a great idea. Unclean pigs are a great temporary holding area for unclean spirits. "Hey!" they beg Jesus. "Why not send us into those pigs over there!"

The story becomes the reverse of Brer Rabbit in the briar patch. Remember how Brer Rabbit tricked Brer Bear and Brer Fox when they caught him? *"Please* don't throw me in that briar patch," he begs. "Do anything, but don't throw me in the briar patch!" They toss him in and he scampers merrily away. Brer Rabbit looks back grinning as he hops along: "I was born and bred in a briar patch!" In this story, Jesus tricks the unclean spirits—or lets them outsmart themselves! (That's how it usually works.) He gives them their wish, lets them go into the pigs, but at once the pigs rush headlong into the sea and drown.

Now the townspeople are upset. Two thousand pigs—that's a significant economic loss. Now *they* beg Jesus to leave. (Of course, with a little more resourcefulness they could have hauled the pigs out of the sea, slaughtered them, cooked and chopped the meat, added a little pickle and spices and oil, and voila! Deviled ham!)

But the scene Jesus leaves is vastly different from the one with which he began. The demoniac now sits by Jesus' feet, "clothed and in his right mind," in John Greenleaf Whittier's phrasing,

> Reclothe us in our rightful mind;
> In purer lives thy service find,
> In deeper reverence, praise.[4]

It is a beautiful and astonishing picture—this man sitting at Jesus' feet, brought from bondage to freedom, from divided self to one true self.

The townspeople are a different story. They don't care about who's been healed; they care only about the two thousand pigs that just went over the cliff into the sea. That's a lot of bacon, as they say. Jesus' way often upsets the equilibrium of unjust economic systems: cotton farming based on slavery; tobacco farms subsidized despite widespread lung disease; prostitution and pornography; corporate exploitation of third-world workers; profit-driven destruction of the environment; underground drug trafficking that destroys the lives of thousands of young people. We politely ask Jesus not to interfere with our economic arrangements. We counsel Christ's minister to keep his or her mouth shut. People getting free and getting healthy sometimes disturb the equilibrium of the family system or the economic equilibrium of a community. (Later, in the book of Acts, as we shall see, Paul delivers a slave girl from the evil spirit that gave her fortune-telling powers. Her owners get upset because Paul has ruined their little business, so they have him thrown in prison.)

Why has Jesus' healing caused such upset? We like it better when we've got the demoniac identified as the one over *there* in the graveyard. What do we do when he's now sitting among us, harmless and sane? Now we've got to deal with the evil in us! Now we've got to let Jesus reveal our own divided selves, our own secret uncleanness. So the townspeople draw back from the healing Jesus would bring them all, and run him out of town.

Sounds like the United States of recent years. What happens when we can't hate the Russians and blame them, when the "Evil Empire" is no longer evil? Whom can we hate now—Japanese, Arabs, gays and lesbians, liberals, fundamentalists, feminists? What if we can't blame it on Reagan or Bush or Bill or Hillary Clinton? Maybe then we have to look at ourselves and examine our own hearts of darkness.

Conclusion

If we do, we will find ourselves moving, as the demoniac moved, from shame to hope, from a life divided, compulsive, torn, to a life made whole and made one.

Look at this man. No longer naked, clothed; no longer bruised and bleeding, he has learned self-care; no longer crazy, sane; no longer many, one.

Christ's healing comes to us, too—to make us *one*, to help us discard the ideal and false selves characterized by grandiosity, compulsiveness, and despair and to come home to the one real self, the one that is fallible and yet utterly loved by God, and the one called out of its sinfulness and incompleteness to holiness and wholeness.

Do you want to be *one*, not ruled one minute by the grandiosity of the ideal self, the next minute by the futility and self-hatred of the false self, but as one who fully inhabits the real self, originally blessed by God, a flawed human person saved by grace, a responsible self growing toward God-likeness?

One, that is what Jesus wants us to be, one. What if we could find our center, our one unfragmented self? That center is Christ, and to know him is to know your own true self. He is our center and in him the center holds. He is the simplicity on the yonder side of complexity. When Jesus is not Lord, anything or anyone can be. When Jesus is not Lord, we have a legion of forces vying for control. But when Jesus is Lord, when he is our center, our "great dignity," to use a woman mystic's phrase, lover of our soul, friend, savior, then we become one.

There is something healing to me when I say the "Hear O Israel" from Deuteronomy 6, the confession of faith that begins every Jewish synagogue service: *Shema Y'Israel*, Hear O Israel; *Adonai Eloheinu*, The Lord is our God; *Adonai Echad*, the Lord is *One*. If God is one, maybe I can be too.

Notes

1. C. S. Lewis, *Surprised by Joy* (New York: Harcourt, Brace, 1955), p. 226.
2. The painting of the demoniac by Adrian Martinez was commissioned by University Christian Church, Fort Worth, Texas.
3. C. S. Lewis cites Martin Luther in the frontispiece of his classic, *The Screwtape Letters* (New York: Macmillan., 1960): "The best way to drive out the devil, if he will not yield to texts of Scripture, is to jeer and flout him, for he cannot bear scorn."
4. John Greenleaf Whittier, "Dear Lord and Father of Mankind," stanza 1; hymn text written in 1872.

25

Parables of the Reign of God

The main subject of Jesus' teaching was the kingdom of God, or reign of God. And the main way he taught about it was in parables.

Think of our world as one circle and the kingdom of God as another circle. Jesus said by the grace of God the circles had overlapped. Part of our life had entered the kingdom's circle and part of the kingdom's circle had entered ours. Parables picture the area where the circles overlap: that region partaking of both. The mission and purpose of Jesus' parables is to move more and more of our lives and the life of our world into the realm of God's reign.

Parable literally means "to throw alongside." Parables are therefore *metaphors of the kingdom,* that is, they bring together things not usually brought together in order to give us a startling new vision of what the kingdom of God is like.

Jesus told hundreds of them, of a father prodigal in his love for both of his sons; of a Samaritan risking life and limb to save the life of a Jew; of priceless treasure found in your own backyard; of the first becoming last and the last first; of mustard seeds growing into great trees; of surprised workmen, lost coins, good neighbors, foolish virgins, and joyous wedding feasts. In this new world we see, to use the words of Welsh poet R. S. Thomas,

> Festivals at which the poor man
> Is king and the consumptive is
> Healed; mirrors at which the blind look
> At themselves and love looks at them

Back; and industry is for mending
The bent bones and the minds fractured
By life.[1]

To hear a parable is like entering the magic wardrobe in C. S. Lewis's fantasy tale, *The Lion, the Witch and the Wardrobe*.[2] In the story the children spy a door in the back of the closet, open it, and go through to find themselves in a whole new world called Narnia, a land both strange and familiar. In Jesus' parables we are invited to enter a familiar world, but before we leave it that world has been turned upside down or inside out—or right side up!

For instance, there was this shepherd who had a hundred sheep. One wandered off and got lost. The shepherd left the ninety-nine and went after the one that was lost until he found it. The shepherd is God and we are the sheep, either one of the ninety-nine or the one who got lost. Are you glad the lost one is found? Or are you perturbed about the stupid sheep who wandered off and caused the shepherd all that trouble? Parables have a way of getting under our skin and holding a mirror to our faces.

And again, there were these guys who got hired at the customary pickup time for day workers, 6 A.M. More were hired at 9 A.M. and 12 noon and 3 P.M. Then the owner went out and hired a final crew at 5 P.M., one hour before sundown. When the workday ended and the owner came to pay the wages, he started with the ones hired last and paid them what he'd promised to pay the others, a full day's pay. For just one hour's work. The ones who'd worked all day were pretty upset (even though they got what they'd agreed to). No fair! Obviously we should get more than they do! Henry Ford is quoted as saying, "What's good for business is good for religion." Well, this doesn't seem like very good business—and not very good religion either. The parable turns our assumed values of work and reward upside down. And I think by the time it's over, Jesus is saying, "Do you really want God to be fair with you? Really?" Grace isn't fair. Grace is generous! When you meet God at the end of life, would you rather God be just or be generous?

Parables bring us to a crisis of identity. We begin by identifying with one character; then we're not so sure. Maybe we're the other one. Parables force us to choose which character we are—or most want to be—and that choice determines whether or not we dwell in the kingdom of God.

Are you the tax collector or the Pharisee? The younger brother or the older? The Samaritan or the priest and Levite, or maybe the one lying bleeding in the ditch?

In the parable of the weeds a farmer has planted good seed but someone has crept in and planted weeds. (Sounds like every garden I've planted.) The garden is my life and yours, and the church's, and the world's. Should we go in and rip out all the weeds? No, said Jesus, if you do you'll pull up the good plants along with them. Wait till the harvest; then you can separate the good from the bad without harming the good plants. It is a parable of profound moral, psychological, and social truth. Too aggressive a weed-control program can destroy the good plants. Let God be the weeder, the parable suggests.

In another parable Jesus said that the kingdom is like a farmer who plants seed and goes home to bed. During the night the seed sprouts and grows, though he knows not how. His crop grows even while he sleeps! This parable tells us that we're not the ones who bring in God's kingdom. *God* is. Sometimes we think God's kingdom is all *our* work and its success is all up to us. Jesus says, "It grows while you sleep; it grows in ways beyond your comprehension." Martin Luther caught this truth when he said, "As I sit here drinking my pot of Wittenberg beer, the kingdom of God goes marching on!"

The kingdom of God is the kingdom of *God.* It's okay to take a nap, or a vacation, or a sabbath.

The kingdom of God is like, is like, is like . . . Jesus said, spinning parable after parable. They help open our eyes to see the kingdom at work and they invite us to join. "Blessed are your eyes because they see and your ears because they hear," he said (Matthew 13:16). They provoke and tease us into awareness, and they ask us to change our lives. "I will open my mouth in parables, I will utter things hidden since the creation of the world" (Matthew 13:35).

Jesus' parables reveal something new, and something as old as the wisdom of God that created the world. Mark's gospel says, "He did not speak to them without a parable" (4:34).

Notes

1. R. S. Thomas, "The Kingdom," in *Later Poems* (London: Macmillan, 1984).
2. C. S. Lewis, *The Lion, the Witch and the Wardrobe* (New York: Macmillan, 1950).

26

"A Certain Man Had Two Sons"

We have tended to name parables according to the "main point" of the story: the *good* Samaritan, the *prodigal* son. Such a process not only narrows the possible meanings of the story, it announces the punch line of the story and ruins the surprise. It is like introducing a joke and spilling the punch line before you start. "Say, did you hear the one about the golfer who dragged his dead golf partner from the fifth hole to the eighteenth?"

The early church was wise to name parables by their first line. The parable of the good Samaritan was called "From Jerusalem to Jericho," for example; the parable of the prodigal son was named "A Certain Man Had Two Sons." We now turn to the parable of Jesus that has the greatest universal reach. There may not be a better story ever told. A certain man had two sons . . .

> Again he said: "[A certain] man . . . had two sons. The younger of them said to his father, "Father, give me the share of the property that will belong to me." So he divided his property between them. A few days later the younger son gathered all he had and traveled to a distant country, and there he squandered his property in dissolute living. When he had spent everything, a severe famine took place throughout that country, and he began to be in need. So he went and hired himself out to one of the citizens of that country, who sent him to his fields to feed the pigs. He would gladly have filled himself with the pods that the pigs were

eating, but no one gave him anything. But when he came to himself he said, "How many of my father's hired hands have bread enough and to spare, but here I am dying of hunger! I will get up and go to my father, and I will say to him, 'Father, I have sinned against heaven and before you; I am no longer worthy to be called your son; treat me like one of your hired hands.'" So he set out and went to his father. But while he was still far off, his father saw him and was filled with compassion; he ran and put his arms around him, and kissed him. Then the son said to him, "Father, I have sinned against heaven and before you; I am no longer worthy to be called your son." But the father said to his slaves, "Quickly, bring out a robe—the best one—and put it on him; put a ring on his finger and sandals on his feet. And get the fatted calf and kill it, and let us eat and celebrate; for this son of mine was dead and is alive again; he was lost and is found!" And they began to celebrate.

Now his elder son was in the field; and when he came and approached the house, he heard music and dancing. He called one of the slaves and asked what was going on. He replied, "Your brother has come, and your father has killed the fatted calf, because he has got him back safe and sound." Then he became angry and refused to go in. His father came out and began to plead with him. But he answered his father, "Listen! For all these years I have been working like a slave for you, and I have never disobeyed your command; yet you have never given me even a young goat so that I might celebrate with my friends. But when this son of yours came back, who has devoured your property with prostitutes, you killed the fatted calf for him!" Then the father said to him, "Son, you are always with me, and all that is mine is yours. But we had to celebrate and rejoice because this brother of yours was dead and has come to life; he was lost and has been found." (Luke 15:11-32)

I

He went to his father and asked for his share of the inheritance. He was the younger of two sons, and so his share was one-third of the estate; the firstborn son would get the other two-thirds.[1] The request was a shocking insolence. It was like his saying to his father, "I wish you were dead." Inheritances were not to be dispersed for spending until the father's death. If it was the supreme insult for the son to ask for his inheritance, it was a fool's gesture for the father to give it to him. What if the son squandered it or died? The old man might not have anyone to take care of him in his old age. He was giving up his Social Security.

Why are hurts and conflicts so deep when it comes to dividing up inheritance? It's the money, but it's more than the money. "Who loved who most" and "who deserves what" get all tangled up with the disbursing of possessions.

When the younger son asked for his inheritance, his older brother had all kinds of reasons to be upset. It was unheard of for the old man to give a son his inheritance before his death. The elder son saw the hurt this request caused his father. It's likely he also saw how this situation might affect him: if his brother lost all his money and came crawling home, his soft-hearted dad would probably receive him back, and then his good-for-nothing brother would be living off *his* two-thirds. The rest of the family resources were supposed to be his.

So the story is already off to a shaky start, full of unsettling emotions: the younger son's insulting request, the father's foolish acquiescence, the elder son's brooding anger.

II

The younger son went into the "far country"—Gentile territory— with his one-third. He promptly squandered it away in wild living, no details given. Add to his sin, bad luck. A famine arose and magnified his plight. In his desperation he sold himself to a pig farmer to work as a swineherd. For an upstanding Jewish family this would be the picture of utter degradation. He has reduced himself to human slavery; moreover, he is feeding pigs, which makes him spiritually unclean and unfit. He has cut himself off from family, community, and faith. He has degraded himself by his actions. He is lost.

What today would bring more horror and heartbreak to a parent's heart than watching one's child descend into shameful and degrading behavior? Imagine that, and you get a picture of the father's pain.

Then comes the moment of turning. The younger son "came to himself" (Luke 15:17). This is no small miracle. We can be lost, any of us. It is as if the cord is cut from God and self and family, and we are in free fall, untethered, "lost in space." Destructive behavior, shame, and guilt can drive us so far from our true self that we cannot get ourselves back there again.

Picture the self as a set of concentric circles. At the core, innermost circle is your true self created by God in God's image. This is you in your elemental goodness, where you dwell in the original blessing of God as God's beloved.

Around that circle draw another circle, the circle of wounds. Here reside early pain and trauma. It is encircled by a layer of shame, because for an infant or child any pain or trauma is experienced as shame: If something wrong or painful happens, it must be my fault; I must have caused it.

Around these circles of shame and pain draw another circle of compensating behaviors: things we do to cope with the pain, to try to erase it or escape it. We create imaginary, secret places where we go to escape the pain. Any momentary ecstasy, physical or mental, brings relief from the pain, and escape from shame and anxiety. Compulsive and addictive behaviors become a way of self-medicating the pain. Food, drink, work, love, most any created thing can be used to escape. But these behaviors, which are supposed to erase the pain, in fact generate more pain, and a vicious cycle is set up. Add another circle of shame.

Around this circle draw a circle of defenses. Here are the ways we defend and explain ourselves both to ourselves and to others, ways we defend ourselves against the layers of guilt and shame. In this circle reside denial, anger, and versions of the truth we tell ourselves. We believe that without this circle of defense we will not make it, we cannot survive. But this is an illusion, a tragic one, for the walls we erect to protect ourselves keep us from penetrating the circles in a healing journey back to our true self.

We live on the outer edge of these concentric circles. We're like a walled city against ourselves. The journey of wholeness and healing is the journey all the way down and all the way back to our own true self, all the way back through the circles of defense and self-defeating behaviors and shame and pain until we "come to ourselves." How do we get there?

It is the Spirit of God who is our companion on this journey of truth and wholeness, guiding us down through the circles of personal hell until we connect with our true self and experience our original blessing and belovedness. The Spirit is your non-shaming guide who helps you traverse the painful terrain until you reach the primal place of peace—where God holds you and nourishes you and binds your wounds. The Spirit sometimes enlists human helpers as spiritual companions. Jesus calls these spiritual helpers "paracletes" in the literal meaning of the word, those "called alongside" us by the Spirit to be our helpers.

Coming to oneself is a miracle of grace. The younger son has hit bottom, and when he does, he discovers *God is already there*. Christ has come to the far country of earth to meet us in the most hellish of places we find ourselves. Peter Kreeft describes Christ's journey:

> He came. He entered space and time and suffering. He came, like a lover. . . . He sits beside us in the lowest places of our lives, like water. Are we broken? He is broken with us. Are we rejected? . . . He was "despised and rejected of men." . . . Do we weep? . . . He was "a man of sorrow and acquainted with grief." . . . Does he descend into all our hells? Yes. In the unforgettable line of Corrie ten Boom from the depths of a Nazi death camp, "No matter how deep our darkness, he is deeper still."[2]

God's Spirit met the younger son in hell and carried him back to his own true self. The son's speech is sober and truthful:

> My father's hired hands abound in food, but I in famine perish. I will arise and go to my father and say, Father, I have sinned against heaven and before you. I'm not worthy to be called your son; make me as one of your hired servants. (Luke 15:17-19)

It was not a speech conjured up for quick forgiveness or to escape the consequences of his deeds. He had spent his inheritance. To be taken care of again as a son would presume upon his brother's share of his father's wealth. So instead he would go back and work and earn wages and room and board like all his father's other hired hands. This speech is honest confession. It acknowledges his real debt.

He had come to his true self, acknowledged his real condition and the consequences of his behavior. It is a miracle of grace.

III

So he arose and went home to his father. The homecoming scene is one of the most purely joyful in all human storytelling: "While he was afar off, his father saw him and had compassion and running, running fell on his neck and kissed him with great affection" (15:20).

The running and the kissing are all out of kilter, culturally speaking. A dignified oriental gentleman did not run. Ben Sirach said, "A man's manner of walking tells you what he is." Aristotle said, "Great men never run in public." But in this scene the father sprints down the road to meet his son; he wraps himself around his son's neck and kisses and kisses him. The Greek verb here describes affectionate, repeated kissing. This too is against cultural form. This is not a father's dignified kiss of greeting. This is a mother's kissing a long-lost child.[3] Where is the mother in this parable? The father—he is mother too.

Middle Eastern scholar Kenneth Bailey has given me new eyes to see this homecoming scene.[4] For seventeen years he lived and taught among Middle Eastern peasants who live today much as they did two thousand years ago. As he studied their lives and told them Jesus' parables, he heard their responses, which were quite unlike ours. This helped him recapture how these parables would have been heard by Jesus' contemporaries and opens a whole new level of meaning for us. Here is how he recreates the homecoming scene.

A wealthy Middle Eastern farmer did not live way out of town on a big ranch like J. R. Ewing, but rather in the village itself. This is not, then, a pastoral scene of a son running up the long entrance road to the house and the father running to meet him, the two solitary figures the only figures in the scene. Instead, it is a *village* scene. The father's house is on the edge of the village; you have to walk down the main street to get there. The son must go through the village, which now probably despises him, in order to reach the father's house.

The younger son's behavior has not only been an offense

to the family, it has also been an offense to the village. He has broken rules that keep a community intact. The whole town would have condemned the boy. If he came back, he would come back as a beggar.

Imagine it. As the son approached town, no doubt a crowd began to gather along the street, forming a kind of gauntlet of songs and jeers and abuse, verbal and maybe even physical, that he would have to run in order to reach his father's house. The father is fully aware of what the village thinks. They think the boy no good, no count, and they think him an old fool.

When the father sees the son, his son is beginning to make his way through the gauntlet of scorn formed there along the main road. The father has compassion, the parable says, like God has compassion. All the way through the gospel of Luke, compassion is God's other name, and Jesus' main command is to "be compassionate as your Father is compassionate." The boy's father has that kind of compassion and begins running down the street toward his son, running like an old fool through the gauntlet of hostile villagers. Do you see it? He runs the gauntlet *for* his son, taking on himself the son's humiliation. He meets him there and kisses and kisses him and takes him home in his arms.

The father is setting the tone for the village as well as for his home. What he says is, "This is my son. This is my son. The time of humiliation is over." The only tears he has rolling down his cheeks are tears of joy. No room for anything else. It's time to celebrate. "My son, he was dead, now he is alive. He was lost, now he's found. Come to my party. Everyone come!"

He calls his servants to put his best robe on him. "Give him my tux! Put a ring on his finger." It is the family signet ring. He's a son again, and it's like giving him the family credit card. "And put shoes on his feet." Sons wore shoes; servants went barefoot. The black spiritual captures the meaning: "All God's children have shoes."

A great feast is prepared, fatted calf and all. The village is stunned. The father has run the gauntlet of public shame for his boy and welcomed him home. Who would have, could have thought? This is the gospel Jesus preached. This is what God has done for all in Christ.

Jesus didn't end the story here, and what happens next is just

as surprising and just as much a part of the gospel Jesus wants
to convey.

IV

Suddenly the son we've forgotten all about, the elder brother,
enters the scene. He is predictably upset. His father's pet has come
home after disgracing the father's good name and squandering
his whole share of the inheritance. For Father to receive him back
home as a son is not fair! Does his brother expect to live off *his*
two-thirds?

He refuses to come to the party. This too is a public disgrace
for the father, just as much a disgrace as the younger son's behavior. But look what happens. The father does the same for the elder
son as for the younger. He does not wait; he *goes out* to meet him.
Divine Love always takes the first step, and every necessary step,
to bring us back home.

The father leaves the party and goes out into the field to meet
his son. The elder son's speech is full of venom. He has exited the
family as surely as the younger son did. He spews forth his
resentment:

> I've worked like a slave for you and never did you give me so
> much as a goat for a party. This son of yours ate up his
> inheritance with harlots and you killed for him the fatted calf.

Isn't it interesting that the parable has not told us how the
prodigal squandered his money, but the elder son has eagerly
filled in all the details. How we love to fill in the details of
another's sins—often with our own secretly imagined ones.

The elder son is in a fit of righteous rage. Notice how he
says "*this son of yours.*" Clearly he's cut himself off from brother
and father.

The father's answering speech is, however, one of the most
magnificent ever heard. "My dear child," he began, with the most
affectionate of address. The father has every reason to be hurt and
angry over this son's disrespectful and humiliating behavior, but
his address is not cold and formal. He speaks to his angry elder
son with the same compassion he showed for the younger son, in
words that are the tenderest imaginable: "My dear child, you are
always with me and everything I have is yours." The father is

reassuring him that he will still get his two-thirds of the inheritance. (The son may argue, "Yes, but my two-thirds will be less because he's back mooching off you!" But Jesus is clear that such calculations have nothing to do with the kingdom of God. In another place in Luke two brothers came to Jesus and asked him to settle an inheritance dispute. And Jesus said, "Who made me that kind of divider?" Then he told them the parable of the rich fool [Luke 12:13-21].)

"All that I have is yours," the father says here. That should be enough. "Your brother [note again the language—he was not going to let the elder son exit the family too easily] was dead, now is alive, was lost, now is found." There is only one right and necessary thing now and that is *joy!* There's nothing left but to put everything down and celebrate. Put *everything* down and celebrate.

We may not realize it, but the parable has ended with the most surprising of twists.[5] Everything has been set up for us to love the prodigal and receive him back with joy and to hate the elder brother and enjoy his getting booted out of the family. "You don't want to come to your brother's party? Fine! Suit yourself!"

It's fun to hate pharisees. The elder son has acted like the south end of a northbound mule. Let him have what's coming to him. The parable could well have ended with the elder brother's being cast out of the family, left to suffer the consequences of his self-righteousness and envy. Other parables in the gospels have ended this way. And I could cite scripture after Old Testament scripture where younger sons get the blessing over older sons. Isaac in, Ishmael out; Jacob over Esau; Joseph over his brothers; David over his brothers.

But not in this parable. The father loves both sons, prodigal and pharisee, and will do all he can do to bring both back into the family. Thank God, God loves both prodigal and pharisee, for there's a generous amount of both inside each of us as well. We're the prodigal whose behavior has injured self and others; and we're the pharisee who's been injured by our brother or seen him injure the family, and we'll be damned if we'll welcome him home.

Sin causes a debt, often a debt that cannot be repaid. It can only be forgiven. We can hold that debt over someone forever. Or we can forgive. It is for our sake that we forgive, not just for the sake of the one who has sinned against us. Anger and vengeance may be a delicious feast, but the carcass on the platter is *us*.[6] It's like a starving man devouring his own hand. There's a certain nourishment there, but it follows the law of diminishing returns. How does God deal with the pharisee in us? With the same patient love and deep compassion that God shows the prodigal.

Some people are running from God and self, their wills enslaved by twirling circles of pain, shame, and compulsive behaviors. Others are enslaved by righteousness and anger—they've got to be right! God comes to deliver us from both kinds of slavery.

What do you think would happen if you didn't have to be right, if you didn't have to be God and mete out all life's rewards and punishments? I think what would happen is that you'd give God a chance to be merciful to you. As Jesus said, God is merciful to the selfish and the ungrateful (Luke 6:35). Maybe there's a chance for us elder brothers and sisters too.

What God wants most is to put his arms around you and take you home to the party, for you to meet your brother and welcome him home. To do so would be *your* welcome home too. There are many sad things in this world: to live your lives in repetitive, self-defeating behaviors, running from God and from self and from anybody who might know you, living in hiding, never coming home. But perhaps this is the saddest: to try to buy what can only be given, to try to earn what is yours already, to search the world over for a treasure buried in your own backyard, to live forever trying to earn God's love and never discover that it is a gift as free as the sun that shines and the rain that falls from the skies.[7]

Notes

1. Fred Craddock, *Luke*, Interpretation (Louisville: John Knox, 1990), p. 187.

2. Peter Kreeft, *Making Sense Out of Suffering* (Ann Arbor, Mich.: Servant Books, 1986), pp. 133-34.

3. Bernard Brandon Scott, *Hear Then the Parable* (Minneapolis: Fortress, 1989), p. 117.

4. Kenneth Bailey, *Poet and Peasant and Through Peasant's Eyes* (Grand Rapids, Mich.: Eerdmans, 1980), pp. 180ff.

5. Again, I am indebted to Brandon Scott, *Hear Then the Parable.*

6. The image is Frederick Buechner's. See "Anger" in *Wishful Thinking* (New York: Harper & Row, 1973).

7. I have been helped by Marsha Witten's probing rhetorical study of how this parable has been preached in *All Is Forgiven: The Secular Message of American Protestantism* (Princeton: Princeton University Press, 1993). I hope that this chapter is more an example of "reframing" than of "accommodation" or "resistance."

27

Jesus and Prayer: The Wild Gratitude

Prayer is the basic theology. So to see how Jesus prayed and to hear what Jesus said about prayer teaches us a foundational theology and shows us his.

Jesus' prayer life was regular in its daily, weekly, yearly rhythm according to the custom of traditional Jewish piety. It was also at times an intense regimen that included detaching himself from all others and going off by himself for a period of time, at times praying all night long. "Come away by yourselves to a lonely place," he urged his disciples, "and rest for a while" (Mark 6:31). He needed the alternation of activism and contemplation. And it was characterized by what we could call the *Abba* experience, the extraordinary intimacy and trust he felt in the presence of God, whom he called *Abba*, a Hebrew child's affectionate name for "Father."

When he taught about prayer, he would say things like: no show-off prayers, those performed in public for purpose of gathering the admiration of those within earshot. And no long-winded prayers. We need not strain to get God's ear. God already wants to hear every word. We don't need to wear God down by our long praying. And when you fast, don't go around with a long martyr's face. Wash your face and comb your hair and look for all the world like you're going to a party (Matthew 6:1-18).

Pray like this, Jesus said, and gave us a model prayer:

Our Father who art in heaven,
Hallowed be your name.
Your kingdom come
Your will be done
On earth as it is in heaven.
Give us this day our daily bread
And forgive us our debts
As we also forgive our debtors;
And lead us not into temptation
But deliver us from the evil one.

The most important word of the prayer is "Father," or *Abba* in Jesus' Aramaic tongue.

I

Jesus was not the first to picture God as father. Homer and Plato did in Greek religion. The Old Testament has fourteen or fifteen references to God as the "father" of Israel, often in the context of saving acts. And there are maternal pictures of God as well:

When Israel was a child I loved him. . . . It was I who taught Ephraim to walk. I took them up in my arms . . . I bent down to them and fed them. (Hosea 11:1-4)
Can a woman forget her nursing child, or show no compassion for the child of her womb? Even these may forget, yet I will not forget you. (Isaiah 49:15)
As a mother comforts her child, so I will comfort you. (Isaiah 66:13)

As mentioned in a previous chapter, one of the key words for God's love/mercy/compassion in the Old Testament comes from the Hebrew word *rachem*, "womb."

So God partakes of motherly and fatherly characteristics—and Jesus made use of both—even as God, the Holy One, is beyond male and female and all our human analogies.

Jesus was the first, however, to call God *Abba*. *Abba* was the first babbling word the Hebrew child learned for father: *abba*, dadda, papa, daddy. In Jesus' day *Abba* was used by children and adults as a form of address for their parents. I still call my father "Dad."

The New Testament scholar Joachim Jeremias was first to

document a startling truth.[1] After studying every ancient Jewish document and every word of the New Testament, he concluded that (1) we do not have a single example of God being addressed as *Abba* in Judaism and (2) in startling contrast, the gospels record that Jesus addressed God as *Abba* in *all* his prayers. The only exception is in the prayer on the cross, "My God, my God, why hast thou forsaken me," and that is a quotation from Psalm 22.

No doubt as Jesus observed the regular Jewish routine of daily prayers and synagogue prayers, he addressed God in many traditional ways. But in his own personal prayers, as the New Testament has preserved them for us, he *always* prayed *Abba*.

There may be no speech form in the gospels as characteristic of the original voice of Jesus as this. The word used in the gospels is either the Greek *pater* or the Aramaic *abba*, but I think Jeremias is right in asserting that behind every *pater* is the echo of Jesus' own voice speaking in his common tongue, *Abba*.

Abba expressed the heart of Jesus' own experience with God. The *Abba* experience was the heart of Jesus' spirituality. It was the expression of trust, joy, intimacy, confidence, and reverence in the presence of God. Jesus thanked *Abba* for bread, for the sun and the rain and every good gift. He praised *Abba* for the beauty of the Galilean countryside, for the jewel-like surface of the Sea of Galilee sparkling in the sun, the meadows strewn with a gorgeous array of wildflowers.

But interestingly, the *Abba* prayers preserved in the gospels are mostly set in the face of adversity—when it would seem *hardest* to pray *Abba*. When it became obvious that the leaders of the Jewish people had rejected him and that, quite unexpectedly, his followers included sinners, simple folk, outcasts, women, and children, Jesus prayed the astonishing prayer amid the ruins:

> I thank thee, Father [*Abba*], Lord of heaven and earth, that thou hast hidden these things from the wise and understanding and revealed them to babes; yea, Father, for such was thy gracious will [*eudokia*, good pleasure]. (Matthew 11:25 RSV)

And in the garden of Gethsemane Jesus said to his disciples, "My soul is sorrowful unto death," and he fell on the ground and prayed, "*Abba*, Father, for you all things are possible; remove this cup from me; yet, not what I want but what you want" (Mark 14:36).

And on the cross he prayed for his killers, "Father, forgive them for they know not what they do."

And his last prayer was, "*Abba;* Father, into thy hands I commit my spirit." This was the nighttime prayer of every Hebrew boy and girl: "Now I lay me down to sleep."

Every time Jesus prayed a personal prayer in the gospels he used the word "father" and behind the word "father" (*pater* in Greek) lay Jesus' own Aramaic word *Abba.* No one had ever prayed like that before.

II

No wonder, then, that when Jesus taught us how to pray with the model prayer, he began it with his unique address, our Father, *Abba.*

The experience of God as *Abba* was the heart of Jesus' own experience of God, the heart of his faith.

To pray to God, or *Abba,* is to pray to God confidently, securely, intimately, trustingly. And, we should add, reverently; Jesus' *Abba* prayers included the yielding words, " Thy will be done." In other words, they didn't assume that our will and God's will were identical. *Abba* prayers play on the banisters of God's house. They are the sounds of children unself-consciously humming. *Abba* prayers know that God will hear our prayers. *Abba* prayers abide in the awareness of God's presence and of God's love for us.

This means that we do not need to strain to get God's ear. There are no magic words or formulas God needs to hear. All God needs to hear is the sound of our voice! We need not heap up empty phrases and go on and on thinking the more we pray the more likely God will answer—as if he will be worn down by our requests or won over by our praying. God already knows your needs before you ask, Jesus said, so you need not go on and on. Our prayers do not inform God or sway God; they open our hands to God.

God is at every point ready to give you what you need. Jesus uses a parental analogy: "What one of you if your child asks for bread will give him a stone, or if she asks for fish will give her a scorpion? If you, who are evil, know how to give good gifts to your children, how much more will your Father in heaven give good gifts to those who ask" (Matthew 7:9-10).

It is a profound analogy. As strong as the natural bond of love between parent and child is, *how much more* it is that God loves us.

III

The life of Jesus at prayer could be characterized as one of "wild gratitude," wild in its flights of exultation and wild in its fierce constancy in all seasons of life. There was an ecstatic experience of the goodness of God and the goodness of God's world that characterized Jesus' spiritual life: Look at the birds; look at the wildflowers! How extravagantly God cares for them; how much more extravagantly God cares for you. He taught a life of trust in the "faithfulness at the heart of things" (Matthew 6:25-34).

There is a poetry of anguish in scripture that accompanies the poetry of praise. Our age seems perversely to exult in the former. As William Morris wrote, "I am tired of the fine art of unhappiness." Poet Denise Levertov writes of the importance of praise:

> A passionate love of life must be quickened if we are to find the energy to stop the accelerating tumble . . . towards annihilation. To sing awe—to breathe out praise and celebration—is as fundamental an impulse as to lament.[2]

Jesus knew the poetry of lament, but he never forgot the poetry of praise, even in difficult circumstances.

There is a sculpture in Santa Fe that leaves me stunned with gladness every time I see it. The first time I saw it I thought I was looking at a wild, angular Saint Francis. Its long, long arms and hands are extended and birds are flying all around him. It is in fact a sculpture of Elijah being fed by the birds in the wilderness. But it also calls to mind Francis of Assisi rapt in his ecstatic praise:

> All creatures of our God and King
> Lift up your voice and with us sing
> Alleluia, Alleluia!

And it calls to mind Jesus praising the God of the birds and the wildflowers and the Galilean Sea, the *Abba* of all life.

It also reminds me of a poem by Edward Hirsch that pictured

the ecstatic gratitude of a British poet named Christopher Smart, who was locked up as one insane, but who wrote joyously beautiful poetry to God, "who," in Hirsch's words,

> . . . wanted to kneel down and pray without ceasing
> In every one of the splintered London streets,
>
> And was locked away in the madhouse at St. Luke's
> With his sad religious mania, and his wild gratitude,
> And his grave prayers for the other lunatics,
> And his great love for his speckled cat, Jeoffry.[3]

Christopher Smart's poem of August 13, 1759, blessed the postmaster general "and all conveyancers of letters" for their "warm humanity," and blessed gardeners "for their private benevolence / And intricate knowledge of the language of flowers," and milkmen for their "universal human kindness." How he loved to hear the "soft clink of milk bottles" as they were delivered outside the front door; the sound was clear in his memory even while he was locked away in the hospital. And he called his cat, Jeoffry, "the servant of the Living God duly and daily serving Him."

Jesus must have had such as Christopher Smart in mind when he prayed to *Abba*, and when he gave these beatitudes:

> You that are destitute, rejoice: our father's kingdom shall be
>   yours.
> Rejoice, you that are hungry: you shall feast.
> You that weep: you shall laugh with joy.
> Rejoice, you who are persecuted: our father knows you and
>   you will know him.[4]

Such was the gratitude of Jesus of Nazareth. Maybe this uncommon gratitude is one reason that when Jesus appeared in his resurrection body to two disciples along the road to Emmaus, they did not recognize him by his appearance or his explanation of scripture. But later that night when he broke bread and blessed it, they knew who he was. He was known by his gratitude. They'd never heard anyone give thanks to God like that.

Notes

1. Joachim Jeremias, *New Testament Theology: The Proclamation of Jesus* (New York: Scribner's, 1971), pp. 61-67; 178-202.

2. Denise Levertov, "Poetry, Prophecy, Survival," in *New and Selected Essays* (New York: New Directions, 1992), p. 144.

3. Edward Hirsch, "Wild Gratitude," in *Wild Gratitude* (New York: Knopf, 1990), p. 17.

4. Translation by Guy Davenport and Benjamin Urrutia, *The Logia of Yeshua* (Washington, D.C.: Counterpoint, 1996), p. 4. Saying 4 is a translation and compilation of Luke 6:20-21, Matthew 5:3-6, and Gospel of Thomas 54 and 69.

28

Prayer in the Last Days:
Thy Will Be Done

The phrase "Thy Will Be Done" in Jesus' model prayer joins with Jesus' Gethsemane prayer, "Not My Will But Thine Be Done," to cause us to ponder the mystery of prayer as it yields to the will of God. Jesus was facing his own imminent death and asked God to deliver him from this terrible end: "Father, if it be possible, remove this cup." But having made this honest cry, he yielded to the Mystery: "But nevertheless, not my will but thine be done." How do we begin to traverse this terrain?

I

"Lord, teach us how to pray." "Pray this way," he answered. "Thy will be done on earth as it is in heaven."

Thy will be done. How do we pray this prayer? Here is the phrase of the Lord's Prayer we know all too well. It is our song of triumph, our agony, a bitter cry, our peace. It marks the heart of our faith; it is also vulnerable to great misunderstanding.

First we ask, What is the will of God? We want to do God's will, more than anything. Down deep we know it is true: "God's will is our peace." Only sometimes we don't know what God's will is and other times we just don't have it in us to do it.

Moreover, sick religion and bad theology have made a mess of how we think and feel about the will of God. They turn whatever happens in life into a fate called God's will, and tell us to submit to it in pious resignation. Or they glorify "surrender" itself—turning faith into an unconditional surrender to anything or anyone. In that sense they manipulate our truest spiritual yearning—to give ourselves completely to our Maker—and turn it into an unhealthy giving up of the self, so that afterward we feel cheapened, diminished in the giving. When that happens, what can be the most sublime moment in our faith is twisted and misshaped into something quite the opposite.

So, *Thy will be done*—where do we begin?

II

Let's start with the two New Testament words for God's will. One is the word *thelema*, and it is always translated "will." The second is a beautiful word, *eudokia* (or the verb form *eudokeo*). It means literally "good pleasure," or to have good pleasure in or take delight in.

Oftentimes God's will is pictured as a dark line across God's face; "frowning providence" is a phrase in a hymn. Just as the phrase "act of God" usually refers to a natural catastrophe in idiomatic speech and insurance policies, "will of God" often refers to something terrible that has happened. Or to the iron command of God that seems formidable, dark, impossible, or to some fixed plan of God, inscrutable, unchangeable. The will of God is rarely a happy topic.

When you notice that one of the New Testament words for the will of God is "good pleasure," however, it begins to take on a different light.

Pretend you've never heard anything about the will of God. Here are some New Testament verses about it:

> It is not the will (*thelema*) of my Father who is in heaven that one of these little ones should perish. (Matthew 18:14)

> Fear not, little flock, it is the Father's good pleasure (*eudokesen*) to give you the kingdom. (Luke 12:32)

> Work out your salvation with fear and trembling [holy seriousness], for God is at work in you both to will (*thelema*) and to do God's good pleasure (*eudokia*). (Philippians 2:12-13)

God destined us in love to be God's sons and daughters through Jesus Christ according to the good pleasure (*eudokia*) of God's will (*thelema*) . . . having made known to us the mystery of God's own will (*thelema*) according to God's good pleasure (*eudokia*), which God set forth in Christ as a plan for the fullness of time *to unite all things in him, things in heaven and things on earth.* (Ephesians 1:5-10, author's translation)

There it is. That is God's will, and it is not natural catastrophe. Rather it is—and I use a word coined by J. R. R. Tolkien—a "eucatastrophe," a good catastrophe. The will of God is cataclysmically good.

In the New Testament the will of God is not some dark, inscrutable reality hidden from us to which we must blindly submit. It is the saving work of God to bring a kingdom good beyond our imagining: God's plan to save the world and unite all things. In the New Testament the will of God has a definite *content*, a content revealed in the preaching of the gospel of the kingdom. If the kingdom of God were a box of cereal, the list of ingredients on the back would read: feeding the hungry; forgiveness of sins; welcome of the outcast; sharing what you have; loving enemies; a community of friends; peace, righteousness, and joy in the Holy Spirit.

That's what Jesus proclaimed as the will of God and that's why God looked at him at his baptism and said, "This is my beloved Son in whom I am well pleased" (*eudokeo*, Matthew 3:17). And that is why on the Mount of Transfiguration God shone his glory in Jesus and said again, "This is my Son in whom I am well pleased (*eudokeo*), listen to him" (Matthew 17:5).

The will of God: not some dark hidden side of God. The will of God is the saving of the whole world, the uniting of all things. According to 1 Timothy 2:4, it is the will of God that all persons be saved.

And the will of God is not something to which we blindly and fearfully resign ourselves. It ought to bring *rising joy*. Like this verse from John Hay:

Not in dumb resignation
We lift our hands on high;
Not like the nerveless fatalist,

Content to trust and die,
Our faith springs like the eagle,
Who soars to meet the sun,
And cries exulting unto thee,
O Lord, thy will be done.[1]

III

If that is the case, then what is our struggle? Why do we need to pray every day, Thy will be done?

It is because sometimes our will and God's will are not in harmony. Sometimes there is an agonized struggle, a clash of will against will. Theologians debate whether our human will is by nature disposed toward the doing of God's will or opposed to it. But this is not a debate that can be solved theoretically; it is an issue that can only be resolved existentially. Every day we must grapple with the question, Is my will *this day* disposed toward the living out of God's will or opposed to it? On *this issue* am I in concert with God's will or raging against it? Or do I care?

There are those wonderful moments in life when what we want and what God wants are one. We feel at one with God and with the world. The psalmist's verse is our song: Delight yourself in the Lord and he will give you the desires of your heart (Psalm 37:4). Unmistakably you feel God's *eudokia*, pleasure.

There were many days like that for Jesus. I call them "Galilean days," days of his Galilean ministry where he taught and healed and forgave, befriended and loved; and every word, every deed, every gesture seemed like a river flowing from God through Christ to us, unhindered, powerful, and free. He was a pure prism of God's light. He could, to use the words from a Reynolds Price poem,

> . . . Speak any syllable that creased [his] mind
> . . . sleep in the dirt
> Where [he] happened to tire—raise a cold corpse
> Without its permission . . . [2]

Galilean days.

But there are other moments when the struggle is agonized and fierce because what we want and what God wants are not the same.

These are "Gethsemane times." I think we tend to minimize the struggle of Jesus in the garden because we deny that we must go through the same struggle. If the Son of God had an agonized struggle of wills with God, don't you think we will? What we want feels like what we desperately need. We do not think we can live without it, but what we want may not be what God wants.

The image of Galilean days is vivid to me. I remember seeing Galilee with all its stunning beauty and imagining Jesus growing up as a boy in the beauty of that world, and I think about the joyous stirring days of his early Galilean ministry. "Thy will be done" points to days of Galilean joy where following God's will seems as easy as falling off a log. It also points to those Gethsemane times where the struggle is agonized and fierce, and long. Hours long, days long, sometimes years long.

In south central Kentucky is the Abbey of Gethsemani where Thomas Merton lived. The brothers have built a garden of Gethsemane out in the woods. When you approach it, you first see a memorial plaque. The garden is in memory of Jonathan Daniels, a young seminarian murdered during the civil rights movement of the 60s. This is no sentimental journey you are on. Then you come to a sculpture, life-size, of three disciples asleep. They are reclined against one another, dead asleep.

Then you go around a bend in the woods and see the solitary, agonized figure of Christ, kneeling on hard stone. (How long could one kneel like that?) His head is not bowed in pious resignation, his hands not folded in proper prayer. His head is thrown back in agony, his hands cover his face. With his head thrown back you see his neck, a strong, sinewy neck, a strong neck exposed to heaven and earth in utter vulnerability. The strength of the neck and its naked vulnerability are set in stunning paradox.

John's gospel says that Jesus "went forth with his disciples over the brook Cedron where there was a garden." The garden was Gethsemane, no romantic prayer garden but a garden of agonized struggle. And the brook is the brook that all of us have to cross if we are to be all God made us to be.

It is only in the clash between our will and God's will where we truly discover who God is and who we are and who we can be. In Gethsemane God ceases to be a projection; in the garden our life ceases to be a romantic, self-serving illusion.

When Jesus knelt in that garden, he knew his preaching and his living of the kingdom had brought him to clash with the powers that be, and that death was imminent. Who wants to die, especially the Son of man who loved life as much as anyone who ever lived! But now to refuse death would be to deny everything he had lived for. God did not wish him dead, God forbid, but Christ's mission with God had led to a cross, and the cross would become the way God would save the world.

When Joan of Arc first saw the scaffold where she was sentenced to die by burning, she lost her courage. She was only seventeen years old and had a full life to live. She offered to recant her "heresy," and she signed a formal statement that she had done so. But three days later she recanted her recantation. Here, paraphrased, is what she said at that moment: "It is I who have failed, not my Voices. They have never deceived me. I signed that form because I was afraid of death, and my Voices have come to me in prison and have reproached me for my great treason. They have told me that I ought not to have been afraid, that I have indeed perjured myself when I said God did not send me, for in truth God did send me."[3]

She crossed the Cedron, knelt in Gethsemane, ascended the scaffold of wood, and became a saint. And Christ ascended his own scaffold of wood and became the Savior of the world.

IV

We all have our Gethsemane struggle. For some, any notion of surrender brings dark and sickening waves. We've been *made* to surrender and later felt violated, and it's all been justified in the name of religion or love.

Or we were taught a theology that said all of life was a Gethsemane, never any Galilee, and that our will was automatically turned against God. So how do we know God's will? Easy! It's the opposite of what we want or need.

Sometimes the crisis is not the clash of wills set in the garden, but the fact that you no longer have a will to exert. Your will has been disabled by sin or trauma or addiction or shame. You have no will; you've given it away and don't know how to get it back. Reinhold Niebuhr divided sin into two: the sins of *pride*, the arrogant exertion of the self, and the sins of *sloth,* the losing of the self in some impulse or vitality. In pride one thinks too highly of oneself, in sloth, too lowly. I'm speaking of the latter. Pain or abuse or despair have tempted you to give up your own capacity to direct your life. The boundaries are dissolved; you don't know who you are anymore. You feel cut loose from any connection with God. Obedience seems a lost cause because your will is enslaved, overwhelmed by some flood or shamed into nonexistence. Gethsemane is unimaginable because you don't have the will to even get across the Cedron. If this is you, then the beginning of the recovery of the will lies in telling the truth about yourself to God: God, my will is gone; help me recover my will so I may will what you will.

Psychiatrist and spiritual guide Gerald May has described our spiritual struggles as between *willfulness* and *willingness.* He said, "We all have secrets in our hearts. I will tell you one of mine. All my life I have longed to say yes, to give myself completely to some Ultimate Someone or Something."[4] That may be the secret of all our hearts. Perhaps a secret covered over by the scars of false surrenders, unwise surrenders, coerced surrenders. Perhaps our secret has been pushed down deep by the teaching of the world consumed by self-determination and self-assertion.

Willfulness is the spirit of self-determination. It is the urge for mastery, the desire to control the outer world and the inner world. It sees the answer to life's problem in an exertion of the will.

Willingness, on the other hand, is the spirit of self-surrender. It has to do with mystery, not mastery. Willingness is a surrendering of one's self-separateness and an immersion into the deepest processes of life itself. Surrender to God is not God breaking you like a cowboy breaks the will of a wild stallion. Life may break our will, but not God. It is more like your will merging with God's will as a flowing stream merges with the river.

Sometimes the journey from willfulness to willingness is as easy as diving rapturously into the river. Galilean days. Other times it leads through Gethsemane. The battle is fierce and hard, and it feels for all the world like our tears are our own blood.

It is in the garden where we are honest to cry, "If it be possible let this cup pass." We recognize the difference between what God wants and what we want. And it is in the garden where we are *given grace* to pray, as Jesus prayed, "Nevertheless, not my will, but thine be done."

Notes

1. John Hay, "Not in Dumb Resignation," public domain.
2. Reynolds Price, "Jesus," in *Laws of Ice: The Collected Poems* (New York: Scribner's, 1997), p. 181. His first-person rendering from the poem:

   I could speak any syllable that creased my mind
   (No family glares)—sleep in the dirt
   Where I happened to tire—raise a cold corpse
   Without its permission and then walk out.

3. This is a paraphrase of the actual transcript of Joan of Arc's trial. The English version of this portion of the trial is as follows: "My voices told me . . . [that] if I said that God had not sent me, I should damn myself; it is true that God sent me. My voices have since told me that I did a great injury in confessing that I had not done well in what I had done. All that I said and revoked . . . I did only because of fear of the fire." From Régine Pernoud, *Joan of Arc: By Herself and Her Witnesses*, trans. Edward Hyams (New York: Stein and Day, 1966), p. 221.
4. Gerald May, *Will and Spirit: A Contemplative Psychology* (San Francisco: Harper & Row, 1982), p. 6.

29

The Turn toward the Cross

At some point Jesus knew death was coming his way—death on a Roman cross—and he had to choose whether to accept or to flee this future. He had threatened the fragile peace of Israel by his large following and by his attack on the religious status quo and the temple system of purification by bought sacrifice.

For political and religious reasons, then, the authorities were conspiring to put him to death. Jesus chose to accept this death because he saw in it the larger redemption of the world. No doubt he knew the prophecies of the suffering servant from the scroll of Isaiah:

> Who has believed what we have heard? . . .
> He was despised and rejected by men;
>   a man of sorrows, and acquainted with grief;
> and as one from whom men hide their faces
>   he was despised and we esteemed him not.
>
> Surely he has borne our griefs
>   and carried our sorrows;
> yet we esteemed him stricken,
>   smitten by God and afflicted.
>
> But he was wounded for our transgressions,
>   he was bruised for our iniquities;
> upon him was the chastisement that made us whole,
>   and with his stripes we are healed.
>   —Isaiah 53:1, 3-5 RSV

He would choose this way as the suffering servant of God, and this would mean death by the most degrading of means, death by Roman crucifixion.

I

We moderns who wear the cross as jewelry cannot fathom the first-century horror it represented. This form of execution was reserved for the worst offenders, revolutionaries against the state, violent criminals, and low-class thieves. Roman citizens could be crucified only for high treason. Otherwise the cross was reserved for slaves and foreigners. The body was strung up on a cross of wood. The hands were nailed to the crossbar. The feet were joined together and a nail was driven through both feet at the heels to attach them to the wood.[1] It took a torturously long time for the person to die. The naked bodies would hang for days; the corpses would then be thrown on the trash pile to be eaten by scavenging beasts. No more hideous fate could be imagined.

No wonder the apostle Paul called the cross "a stumbling block to the Jews and folly to the Gentiles" (1 Corinthians 1:23). Justin Martyr, defender of the faith in the next generation, said, "They say that our *madness* consists in the fact that we put a *crucified man* in the second place after the unchangeable and eternal God. . . ."[2]

The Roman statesman Pliny wrote about the "perverse and extravagant superstition" of Christians—that a man honored as God would be nailed to a cross as a common enemy of the state.[3]

Some early graffiti discovered on a Roman palace wall near the Circus Maximus, dated 200 B.C.E., shows a man hanging on a cross, except that instead of a man's head there is the head of a jackass, and scribbled underneath in large letters are the words: "Alexamenos Worships God."

The cross remains a stumbling block (*skandalon*) to the Jewish mind. Elie Wiesel contrasts Mount Moriah, where Isaac was saved from slaughter, and Golgotha, where Jesus wasn't:

> . . . on Mount Moriah . . . the father did *not* abandon his son. Such is the distance between Moriah and Golgotha. In Jewish tradition man cannot use death as a means of glorifying God. . . . For the Jew, all truth must spring from life, never from

death. To us, crucifixion represents not a step forward but a step backward.[4]

In this light it is not hard to understand the dread that Jesus would feel as he faced the decision to die in this way, nor to understand the incredulity and horror his disciples would feel to think of this fate as their master's end.

The "hinge" of the gospel accounts of Jesus' ministry turns at Caesarea Philippi, where Jesus retreated with his disciples, revealed who he was, and then told them that he must die.

"Who do men say I am?" he asked. His disciples' hands shot up: "John the Baptist come back from the dead; Elijah returned; one of the prophets," they answered.

"But who do you say that I am?" Jesus continued. Peter was the one who answered, "You are the Christ, the Messiah, the son of the living God."

Jesus applauded Peter's answer: Flesh and blood has not revealed this to you; God has. Then Jesus began to teach them how he must suffer rejection and be killed.

It must have all been so strange, so horrifyingly strange. One moment to know they were in the presence of the Messiah, the next to hear him talking about rejection and death. The words "Messiah" and "suffering" did not compute. "Crucified Messiah" was a contradiction in terms, the oxymoron of oxymorons.

Peter rushed in again and began to rebuke Jesus. "Jesus, you've got it all wrong—this cannot happen to you; you're the Christ." And Jesus, just as swiftly as he had praised him, rebuked him and said, "Get thee behind me, Satan! For you are not on the side of God, but of men" (Mark 8:33).

It is almost impossible to understand how much Jesus' revelation of himself as suffering Messiah reversed all their ways of thinking, feeling, hoping. The Messiah must never suffer. When the Messiah comes, all will be right and all will be well. These were the centuries-old faith convictions of their people. But here, but now, Messiah has come and all is not right and all is not well, not yet. The Messiah is now saying to them that he has come to enter our suffering and to suffer himself.

Then Jesus added, looking at his disciples: This applies to you as well. If you follow the Messiah, you will suffer too. "If any want to become my followers, let them deny themselves, take up their cross and follow me. For those who want to save their life will lose it, and those who lose their life for my sake, and for the sake of the gospel, will save it" (Mark 8:34-5).

II

What does the preaching of the cross, the taking up of the cross, mean for those who follow Christ today? Those words of Jesus haunt us: "If any would come after me, let them deny themselves, take up their cross and follow me."

What does the cross mean for our world? Dietrich Bonhoeffer called it "the cost of discipleship." It is almost an embarrassment to the overly easy Christian lives found among the privileged classes of America. Being Christian in America apparently costs so little. Christian people endure their human share of suffering, but how much of it is a specifically *Christian* kind of suffering—suffering for Jesus' sake and the gospel's?

What does it mean to take up the cross and follow Jesus? Two images come to mind.

First, to bear the cross is to carry your own ordinary human suffering in such a way that it becomes vocation. You refuse the role of victim with its learned helplessness, its bitterness, and its despair. You pray, "God, forge from the fires of my own personal suffering a calling, a ministry to others. Help my suffering deepen my soul, enlarge my sympathy, increase my understanding, extend my arms, and move me into some meaningful action on behalf of others." Your suffering will rob you of some things, but it will give you some others. It will rearrange your capacities and your opportunities. It will give you focus and give you compassion. Your vocation as a disciple will come from the crucible of your affliction.

Second, to bear the cross of Christ is to take up the suffering of others as a ministry, a cause, an advocacy. You become a "person for others." The suffering of others becomes a sacramental meeting place where the passion of Christ and the passion of the world become one, where the sufferings of Christ and the sufferings of the world merge and move toward resurrection. You no longer run from the world's suffering. You take it up as a cross, you hold it like bread and wine. For Jesus' sake and the gospel's. You bring ointment and bandages; you do mercy; you work for justice, and cheer and scream for it.

This is not easy work. There's enough suffering in this world to take us all under. But the *koinonia* (community, companionship) of suffering is the *koinonia* of the Christ, and in the community of the cross, Christ-followers experience the power of Jesus Christ in them.

III

The Cost of Discipleship. That is the title of a book by Dietrich Bonhoeffer. On April 5, 1943, he and his brother-in-law were arrested for helping German Jews escape into Switzerland. On the same date, April 5, 1945, two years later, Adolf Hitler personally signed the execution order that condemned Dietrich Bonhoeffer to die. Bonhoeffer's last recorded words were, "This is the end— for me the beginning of life." He was hanged April 9, 1945, just days before U.S. forces arrived to bring the war to a close. He was thirty-nine years old.

He had struggled for years with what it meant to take up the cross of Jesus. His book *The Cost of Discipleship* warned the church that it had succumbed to the notion of cheap grace. The grace of Jesus Christ was a "costly grace," he asserted.[5]

He was the most brilliant young theologian of his country. At one point he came to Union Theological Seminary in New York City to study. As the crisis of his own German people intensified under Hitler's rise to power, Bonhoeffer found it impossible to stay in America. Although his American friends feared for his life and begged him to stay, Bonhoeffer felt he must go back and be with his people and resist the policies and power of Hitler.

There was a terrible night as Hitler's policies grew worse. It has come to be called *Kristallnacht,* the "Night of Broken Glass," November 9, 1938. This was the night the hidden and unofficial violence against the Jews turned open and official. Hitler gave orders for synagogues to be ransacked. There ensued a rampage of violence against Jewish holy places and homes and places of business. Synagogues were demolished, holy books burned, thousands injured and killed or shipped off to concentration camps. *Kristallnacht*, "Night of Broken Glass."

That night Bonhoeffer opened his Bible and read Psalm 74:

> O God, why do you cast us off forever? . . .
> Remember your congregation, which you acquired long ago. . . .
> Your foes have roared within your holy place;
>> they set up their emblems there.
> At the upper entrance they hacked
>> the wooden trellis with axes. . . .
> They set your sanctuary on fire;
>> they desecrated the dwelling place of your name,
>> bringing it to the ground.
> They said to themselves, "We will utterly subdue them";
>> they burned all the meeting places of God in the land.
> We do not see our emblems;
>> there is no longer any prophet,
>> and there is no one among us who knows how long.
> How long, O God, is the foe to scoff?

Bonhoeffer read that psalm that terrible night and wrote, in the margin of his Bible, his own completion of the question, How long? *"How long, O God,"* he wrote, *"shall I be a bystander?"*

Perhaps this is at the heart of the calling of the cross: it will not let us be bystanders.

IV

From a certain point Jesus took on the role of a suffering messiah in the midst of a suffering humanity and "turned his face toward Jerusalem" and the cross.

The final climactic week came in a sequence of events Christians call Holy Week. It began on Palm Sunday, when Jesus rode into Jerusalem on a donkey while onlookers spread palm branches on the road and cried, "Hosanna to the son of David! Blessed is he who comes in the name of the Lord!" It was a prophetic sign of immense irony: a servant king riding victoriously into his city to die.

He proceeded to the Temple mount, where he enacted another prophetic sign, the "cleansing of the Temple," where he drove out the moneychangers and sellers of animals for sacrifice and said, quoting the scriptures, "Is it not written,'My house shall be called a house of prayer for all peoples'? But you have made it a den of thieves" (Mark 11:17). It was the fulfillment of his repeated challenge: Go and learn what this means, "I desire mercy not sacrifice, says the Lord." He spoke words that referred to his own death but were later used by his opponents to convict him of high treason: "Destroy this temple and in three days I will raise it up" (John 2:19). He pointed to the grand Temple buildings and said, "You see all these, do you not? Truly I say to you, there will not be left here one stone upon another that will not be thrown down" (Matthew 24:2). He was to become the temple to whom all people could come as a house of prayer. And this new temple would outlive the Jerusalem Temple of stones. These words were indeed revolutionary, but not in the way they were taken to mean. Tragically, the Jerusalem Temple would forty years later (in 70 C.E.) be destroyed in the war with Rome.

In a quiet moment, while Judas was arranging to betray Jesus for thirty pieces of silver, a woman anointed Jesus during a meal with expensive perfume, itself a prophetic act of anointing his body beforehand for burial. Then came the last supper with his disciples; then the agony in the garden where he prayed, "*Abba*, remove this cup from me; yet not what I will, but what thou wilt" (Mark 14:36); then the arrest; Peter's threefold denial; the two trials—one religious, one officiated by the Roman governor Pilate; the crowd's mocking torture; and finally execution by crucifixion.

All this Jesus did not have to endure. It was his choice—for the sake of the world that he and God so loved . . .

Notes

1. For archeological research on and drawings of the act of crucifixion, see *Israel Exploration Journal* 20 (1970):8-29.
2. Justin Martyr, *Apologia*, 1.13:4. Cited in Martin Hengel, *Crucifixion* (Philadelphia: Fortress, 1977), p. 1. See also Hengel, *The Atonement* (Philadelphia: Fortress, 1981).
3. Pliny, cited in Hengel, *Crucifixion*, p. 2.
4. Elie Wiesel, *Messengers of God: Biblical Portraits and Legends* (New York: Random House, 1976), p. 76.
5. Dietrich Bonhoeffer, *The Cost of Discipleship* (New York: Macmillan, 1963), pp. 35ff.

30

The Passion of Christ:
Jesus, the One Handed Over

I was told, perhaps you were too, that if I was going to make a difference in this world it would come by my *action*, by what I did. But what we are not told—not even in church where the story of Jesus is told—is that God can make something of our *passion*, that is, what is *done to us*.

The week leading up to Jesus' crucifixion is sometimes called "Passion Week," the week of the passion of Christ. The word "passion" comes from the Latin word *pascho*, which means "to be done to." It is the opposite of *poio*, which means "to do." In this life there is action and there is passion.

This is the part of the story of Jesus that is often left out, but it is a part that must not be left out because our lives are at least as much made up of passion—that is, what is done to us—as action, what we do. And if God is redeeming us and our world, that redemption is happening through our passion as well as our action.

The New Testament underlines this truth by describing Jesus over and over as the one "handed over." Perhaps if we can explore the significance of Jesus as "the one handed over," we can better see God's way of redeeming us in *our* being handed over.

I

Priest and writer Henri Nouwen went to see a friend who was dying of cancer. The friend knew he was dying and said something like this to Nouwen: "All my life I've been an activist. My sense of self has been bound up in what I could accomplish. But now I can do very little, and I can do nothing to prevent my dying. Please help me to know how to live whatever life I have left." Henri suggested that they read and study together a book called *The Stature of Waiting* by W. H. Vanstone.[1] It dealt with Jesus' being handed over and how God redeems us in our passion—in what is done to us—as well as in our action.

II

Looking at the way Jesus faced his passion takes us to the core of our most challenging life experiences—not just facing death, which we all will have to do sooner or later, but facing all those times, conditions, circumstances of life where we are more *acted upon* than acting.

Illness strikes suddenly and you find yourself a patient in a hospital. Being a patient is humiliating. You are powerless. You are done to, handed over into someone else's hands. But other circumstances can thrust upon you the status of a patient: unemployment, retirement, poverty, divorce, mental illness. Consider the person in a nursing home. All her life long she has been active, independent, competent, unweary in well-doing. Now she is stuck in bed and wheelchair, afflicted with time, being done *to* far more than doing, a humiliation not unlike the cross. And she wonders why God is keeping her alive and wonders if there is anything left for her to do in this life.

In this world we are taught that dignity comes in acting, doing, being the subject of action. So when we are the receiver, the passive object of someone else's action, we feel indignity, even humiliation.

As for God? We picture God as the supremely active one, busy doing things, making things happen.

But the story of Jesus reminds us of a truth more profound: There is redemption in our passion, in what happens to us, as well as in our action. God is a suffering God who redeems us in what is done to us—and in what is done to God. Jesus tells Peter what will be Peter's future and how he will be redeemed in his own passion:

> Truly, truly I say to you, when you were young you clothed yourself and walked where you wanted, but when you are old you will stretch out your hands, and another will clothe you and carry you where you do not wish to go. (John 21:18, author's translation)

Then Jesus said, "Follow me."

These words do not just describe old age, which is where most of us will end up whether or not we wish to go there. They also describe what would eventually happen to Peter, that he would be led, bound, to a cross and die upon it. This death, Jesus said, would glorify God and work God's continuing redemption. In other words, God will use not only your courageous actions, Peter, but also your passion and suffering, your "being done to."

III

Vanstone's book provides a fascinating study of Jesus as "the one handed over." The New Testament word is *paradidomi*, to "hand over." Thirty-two times it is used to describe what Judas Iscariot did to Jesus, and every time we have mal-translated it as "betray." Only once (in Luke's description of the Twelve) is the *actual* Greek word "to betray," *prodidomi*, used to describe Judas. Thirty-two times the word used is *paradidomi*, "to hand over." Why has it been so often translated "betray" rather than what it literally means, "to hand over"? Why didn't the writers use the more familiar word, "to betray"? The reason is the extreme importance the phrase "to be handed over" had for New Testament writers as a description of the redemptive work of God in Christ. This is why over and over again the verb *paradidomi*, "to be handed over," is used. Something more sweeping than mere "betrayal" is happening. Jesus is being handed over, and "being handed over" has overtones of redemption.

The word, moreover, was not associated just with the act of Judas. The Jewish leaders are described as *handing Jesus over* to Pilate. And Pilate is described as *handing Jesus over* to the will of the people. In the words of institution at the Lord's Supper, Paul says, "On the night Jesus *was handed over.*" The phrase "handed over" is a phrase laden with the significance of redemption, God's redemption of the world.

But the New Testament doesn't just speak of Jesus' *enemies* handing him over. *God* is described as handing Jesus over too. Romans 8 in its hymn of redemption sings:

> If God is for us, who is against us?
> God who did not even withhold his own Son,
> but *handed him over* for us all,
> will he not also freely give us all things? (verses 31-32, GNB)

What can this mean—for God to hand Jesus over?

Often at Christmastime, in the context of the miracle of the Incarnation, I think of this story. David, our firstborn, was about six weeks old. On his first trip outside our home, we took him with us to the country church where I was pastor. In a country church the children belong to the whole community, and the church "nursery" is the collective lap of all the women in the church. I was leading worship while my wife, Cherrie, sat holding our newborn son in her arms. Suddenly a woman reached for David, and Cherrie, despite a new mother's natural reluctance, handed him over. Then to Cherrie's brief terror, David was handed to another, and then another. There I was, trying to preach, and there Cherrie was, pretending to be calm as we watched our tiny baby bounce from lap to lap.

Parents may feel something similar when they take their son or daughter to kindergarten the first day, or to college, and "hand them over" to people they don't even know and just leave the child there! Or when they sit and watch their own son or daughter at the wedding altar.

Such was the risk of the Incarnation, God handing his infant son to us. And this same God watched as Jesus set about on his mission to proclaim—and embody—the kingdom through healing, teaching, befriending, and prophetic action. Then one day his mission shifted from action to passion. He was handed over to the Jewish and Roman authorities, arrested, bloodied with a whip, interrogated, judged, sentenced, crowned with thorns, spat at, laughed at, stripped, and nailed to a cross.

The *Abba* God who handed Jesus over to Mary, into the family of Joseph and into the people called Israel, also watched his son handed over into the hands of those who killed him. It was unspeakable horror to the motherly/fatherly heart of God. And it was also, by way of a mystery beyond our comprehension, the redemption of the world.

But even that isn't the whole story. Jesus himself took on the dignity of suffering by *handing himself over.* He gave himself up. He chose to be suffering Messiah, Savior. John pictures Christ's death as the final exaltation and triumph, using the same word, *paradidomi,* to describe Jesus' own action at the moment of his death:

> Jesus took the wine [offered to him] and said, It is finished. Then he bowed his head and *handed over* his spirit.

And so this phrase becomes part of the Christian faith's language of adoration as we ponder Christ's selfless self-giving. For the apostle Paul, "The life I live now in the flesh I live by the faith of the Son of God who loved me and gave himself for me [that is, who loved me and *handed himself over* for me]."

This wording is not incidental to the gospel. It reminds us of this crucial truth: Jesus brought his mission to fulfillment not in action but in passion. Such is the way God worked redemption then, and the way God still works redemption in you and me.

Holy Week is the week Jesus moved dramatically from action to passion. It begins in climactic action: the triumphal entry; Jesus entering Jerusalem riding on a donkey; the crowd singing their hosannas, shouting in praise; "Hosanna, blessed is he who comes in the name of the Lord;" the cleansing of the Temple, and so on. From this day on, a life of action turns to a life of passion. Jesus becomes the one handed over, done to, acted upon.

But the New Testament does not consider this a misfortune without dignity and meaning. It is the redemption of the world. The work of redemption, which began in action, God completed in passion.

IV

The story of Christ's passion is crucial for us, for our own lives are a mixture of action and passion, of what we do and what is done to us.

Part of the task of life is to join our human action with God's activity in this world: by healing, teaching, loving, making justice and peace. But another part of our life task is to let God redeem us in our passion, in what is done to us, thereby joining our passion to the passion of Christ. We can, to be sure, let this take an unhealthy turn—looking for martyrdom, playing the victim, finding some gain in staying a victim. But understanding redemption through passion is not about looking for suffering but about living with the inevitable suffering of our lives and our calling.

Henri Nouwen says startlingly that most of our life is passion; only a small part is determined by what we think, do, or say. And he says:

> I am inclined to protest against this and to want all to be action, originated by me. But the truth is that my passion is a much greater part of my life than my action. Not to recognize this is a self-deception and not to embrace my passion with love is self-rejection.[2]

How can we embrace our passion with love? Not to do so is to live in angry, or guilty, rejection of what happens to us.

There is the passion of illness. You're in a hospital. Needles are put in your veins, thermometers stuck in your mouth, catheters applied where catheters are applied. You're given a gown to wear that never quite covers your backside. And nurses come in and ask questions not even your mother would ask. It's more than a little embarrassing.

Or you're fired or abandoned or divorced. You're stuck in a nursing home or in an unhappy job. Once you may have been in control, but now you're not. Your fate seems no longer in your hands. Your action can do very little if anything to change things. Your life is far more a *being done to* than a doing. Passion.

The challenge set before us by the death of Jesus is to see our passion as part of the redeeming passion of God. If your school or family or your business or your congregation is not in your hands, neither is it really in the hands of those "in power." It is—finally—in God's hands.

We are called to let God transform the indignity of suffering into the dignity of suffering and the humiliation of powerlessness into the posture of hopeful, faithful waiting.

The person facing surgery waits for the surgeon's hand to

remove whatever is impeding God's healing, then waits for the body to heal, waits with God, waits for God. Maybe that is why patients are called "patients." They must take the posture of waiting.

Like a naturalist waiting for nature to bring a bird, like a farmer waiting for the ground to be ready for planting, like an artist waiting for the creative moment, like a Savior waiting on a cross, we wait for God. We wait in our passion for resurrection.

Conclusion

In my work as a pastor I have seen too many die of cancer. And I have learned much from them as I've walked with them toward death and eternal life. Some of that walk has been obscenely painful and humiliating. Some deaths have been an unspeakable tragedy—a young mother, a young man, a young girl.

I've seen people be partners with God in *action,* in the courageous, valiant fighting of the disease. I've seen them bravely take on chemotherapy or radiation therapy; I've seen them gather their resources of prayer and spirit and love and extend the number of their days and years through courageous action and partnership with God in fighting the disease. And I've seen some conquer the disease.

And I've also seen something else: I've seen people use their time of suffering to show much love and be of great service to others, even making it a time of praise. I'll never forget a visit with a Kentucky woman, Jean Stout, who had been malformed and crippled all her life. As a young person, she had been too embarrassed about how she looked to be baptized, so, late in her life, I baptized her in her nursing home bed. Now she was close to death and taking massive doses of medicine to reduce the pain. One day she smiled at me and said, "The only thing that helps my pain is something they call liquid morphine. This may sound silly to you," she said with a radiant smile and pointing to the bottle hanging from the intravenous stand, "but that morphine is the most beautiful color of blue I've ever seen." Her improbable praise brought me tears.

I've seen fathers and mothers bless their children in their dying—and adult children bless their parents. And I've seen people use their passion to grow more intimate with those they loved the most, and I've seen estranged relationships healed and helped. Redemptive passion.

But I've seen them do something else. I've seen people come to a point where they knew (sometimes before anyone else knew) that their action would no longer make a difference in the fighting of the disease, and they moved from action to passion in their relationship to the disease. It is as if they saw a corner and turned it. They moved from fighting the disease to accepting what the cancer was doing to them, and in this movement they opened a door not so much to death, though death was part of it, as to God. And they've said, "God, you've been in my action, be now in my passion. O God, walk with me these last months, weeks, days until the day this body dies and you carry me in your arms into the heavenly dwelling place." At that moment some have said, "God, I can no longer take care of my family. I hate that worse than anything. I must leave them in your hands and in the hands of others."

When that happens, another healing happens—a healing deeper than the body that is destined for death, a healing that is a glimpse of final union with God. It is a kind of letting go, a kind of *paradidomi*, a handing over. It is abandonment into the Divine Love, into God. It's what Paul felt, I think, when he said, "As for me, I am already being poured out on the altar and the hour of my departure has come. I have fought the good fight, I have finished the race, I have kept the faith." He anticipates the reward of God not only for himself but for "all who have loved [Christ's] appearing" (2 Timothy 4:6-8, author's translation).

These people have taught me something holy: They have taught me not only how to die, but how to live, how to offer my passion as well as my action to God.

There are many things that happen in our lives; some happen by way of our initiative and our action. Perhaps more of life, however, is made up of what happens to us—our passion.

Jesus, the one handed over, is the one who teaches that God is working toward healing and wholeness in *all* things. This is the message of Holy Week and of Christ's passion that precedes the dawn.

Notes

1. W. H. Vanstone, *The Stature of Waiting* (New York: Seabury, 1983).
2. Henri Nouwen, *The Road to Daybreak* (New York: Doubleday, 1988), p. 156.

31

From Death to Daybreak: Easter in the Gospel of John

Easter begins in all four gospels with an empty tomb. When the women disciples (one in John, two in Matthew, three in Mark, and more in Luke) came to stand vigil at the tomb or to anoint his body, they found the body gone. There seems little ancient dispute over the fact of an empty tomb. The dispute was *how* the tomb came to be empty. The most prevalent theory among the opponents of the resurrection was that the body of Jesus had been stolen by the disciples in order to stage a mock resurrection.

Other than the empty tomb, the four gospels have remarkable divergences.

Mark's Easter gospel has an angel announce the meaning of the empty tomb, "He has risen," to Mary Magdalene, Mary mother of James, and Salome. Then they are commissioned to go tell the news. The gospel comes to a startling and shuddering end: "And they went out and fled from the tomb; for trembling and astonishment had come upon them; and they said nothing to any one for they were afraid" (Mark 16:8).[1]

Matthew's Easter gospel has the two Marys at the empty tomb. When the angel tells them the news, they go as commissioned by the angel to Galilee to tell the disciples. While they are on their way to tell, the risen Christ appears to them. They fall at his feet and worship him. Then Jesus appears to the eleven disciples in Galilee. The book ends as Christ, just before ascending into heaven, gives to his disciples what is called the "Great Commission":

> Go therefore and make disciples of all nations, baptizing them in the name of the Father and of the Son and of the Holy Spirit, teaching them to observe all that I have commanded you; and lo, I am with you always, to the close of the age. (Matthew 28:19-20, RSV)

Luke's gospel, highlighting the role of the women disciples, describes a larger circle of women at the empty tomb. They go to tell the other disciples what has happened, with mixed results: "These words seemed to them [the disciples] an idle tale" (Luke 24:11).

The risen Christ then appeared incognito to two of his followers trudging along the road to Emmaus. One of them is named Cleopas (possibly Jesus' uncle) and the other is unnamed (some scholars offer that he is James, the brother of Jesus).[2] The two did not recognize him as he explained scripture to them along the road. But later that night as they sat at table Christ took bread and blessed it and broke it and gave it to them. As he did, they recognized him. And as soon as they knew who he was, he vanished from their sight. Oh, the aching fleetingness of his presence! Then, Luke says, Jesus appeared to the rest of the gathered disciples and commissioned them to preach the gospel to all the nations. Luke's gospel ends with the disciples returning to Jerusalem and worshiping with great joy in the Temple.

All the Easter gospels emphasize two dimensions of Christ's resurrection appearances: (1) there was a forgiveness extended to the disciples who in their weakness had failed him, and (2) there was a commissioning, or recommissioning, to go into the world with the message of the good news of Christ.

John's Easter gospel, perhaps most vividly and poignantly of all the gospels, depicts these two dimensions. Here is Easter according to John.

I

After the crucifixion, friends of Jesus, with the help of a couple of Jewish noblemen, Joseph of Arimathea and Nicodemus, were able to place his body in a tomb. Jesus' disciples had mostly fled in fear.

Only the women followers—and the "beloved disciple," un-named in John—stayed close to watch him die and prepare his body for burial. And only the women were at the tomb in the early morning we now call Easter.

According to John, Mary Magdalene came alone to the grave in the dark before dawn. She was the follower whom Jesus had delivered of seven demons and one of the company of women disciples who supported his ministry out of their means.

When she arrived, she saw the stone rolled away and assumed with desperate grief that someone had stolen the body. She ran to tell Peter and the beloved disciple.

Peter and the beloved disciple ran to the tomb. Easter begins with running legs. People hear the hint of a miracle, miracle of miracles, and they run to see.

The beloved disciple outran Peter and reached the tomb first. (I think this detail is proof the beloved disciple wrote the book of John: he couldn't resist recording that he had beaten Peter in a foot race!) When he looked in and saw the graveclothes lying there, he believed immediately that resurrection had happened. The beloved disciple is an example of those Jesus meant when he said, "Blessed are those who have *not* seen and yet believe." For the beloved disciple the empty tomb was evidence enough for him to believe that the resurrection had happened.

II

But Easter is more than the story of an empty tomb. It is also the story of the risen Christ who began to make resurrection appearances to his friends. And the one to whom Jesus appeared first was Mary Magdalene.

In Paul's account of the resurrection tradition from 1 Corinthians there is no mention of women being among the witnesses of the resurrection:

> He appeared to Cephas [Peter], then to the twelve. Then he appeared to more than five hundred brethren at one time. . . . Then he appeared to James, then to all the apostles. Last of all, as one untimely born, he appeared also to me. (15:5-8 RSV)

That is because according to Jewish law, women were not allowed to bear witness. Paul and the new church, it seems, had not yet lived into their own proclamation that in Christ there is no Jew or Gentile, slave or free, male or female; and so they left out the *first* one Jesus made a witness to the resurrection, a woman named Magdalene.

But John is bold to preserve for us that the first to whom Christ appeared was Mary Magdalene. She was alone, weeping next to the empty tomb in the garden in that early morning quiet between dark and full dawn.

Two angels appeared to comfort her, saying, "Woman, why are you weeping?" Mary replied, "They've taken my Lord away and I do not know where they have laid him." Saying this, she turned around and saw Jesus standing there, but she didn't recognize him. She thought he was the gardener! I am always astonished by the lowliness of Jesus' resurrection appearances. I'd have him shining as bright as the morning sun, descending from the clouds with trumpets blaring and a thousand Mormon Tabernacle choirs.

Instead, he looks like the gardener. Mary did not recognize him until he called her name. There is something unique about the way people call our name, especially people who love us. "Mary," he said, and Mary answered in Hebrew, "*Rabboni*," which means "my dearest Master," her voice suddenly musical with cascading alleluias.

The first miracle of Easter is the message: *Death cannot destroy love.* It cannot extinguish it, and all that is holy in love survives the grave. We shall see one another face-to-face. Love is stronger than death.

"Mary," he said, and she *knew* him. "My dearest Master," she replied, moving quickly to touch him (embrace him, cleave to him: the Greek verb appropriates the language of love).

But Jesus said, "Do not hold onto me, cleave to me, for I am on my way to the Father."

The interchange gives us a glimpse into the mystery of the resurrection body of Christ. It was not a resuscitated corpse like that of Lazarus. It was a new, transformed, spiritual body that could not hold or be held. *The resurrection body is at once wondrously different and wonderfully the same.* We will know one another, but we will no longer be bound by space, time, and physicality.

Jesus said to her, "Go to my brethren and tell them I am ascending to my Father and your Father, to my God and your God." Mary Magdalene then went and told them the exultant news: "I have seen the Lord!" Mary's is the first witness to the resurrection. Early church theologian Hippolytus named her *Apostola Apostolorum*, "the apostle to the apostles." She is the first one sent (which is what apostle means, "one sent") with the gladdest news in all the world: *Christ is risen.*

III

But Easter is far from over for John. Later that day, Easter evening, the disciples were huddled together in fear behind locked doors.

Suddenly Jesus appeared to them. "Shalom," he said, "peace be with you." Then he showed them his hands and side, his scars discernible there in his eternal body. Again we see the resurrection body, wondrously different, wonderfully the same. The scars visible, they recognized him. But he needed no door to enter the room. He just appeared.

Jesus spoke again, "Peace be with you." Then he commissioned them. "As the Father has sent me, so send I you." Then he breathed on them God's breath and said, "Receive the Holy Spirit."

The second message of the Easter miracle is that *the Spirit of Christ survives death.* Christ breathes into his followers his own spirit as they follow him. They are not left with their own fickle and fragile spirit but are given Christ's own spirit. With that spirit they can live the abundant life he came to give. "I came that they may have life and have it abundantly," were his words (John 10:10). This abundant life is characterized by at least these two things, *love* and *truth*: love that makes us servants and truth that sets us free.

As the risen Christ appeared to them, he "apostled them." "As the Father has sent me, so send I you." He breathed into them his own Spirit. And then he defined their mission as his apostles: *Go and forgive sins.*

"If you forgive, or loose, people's sins, they are *loosed*. If you hold onto people's sins, they stay bound," he said. (The forgiveness we keep, and which keeps both us and the one who has harmed us bound, is our last illusion that we have control.) Go and set people free, Jesus said as he sent them, free from their sins and free from their hounding guilt and binding shame. A most essential meaning of our apostleship is to go into the world with Christ's forgiveness. Religion in every age tries to make the free forgiveness of God a commodity to be bought and sold, whether the means of exchange is money or institutional loyalty or some human code of conduct. But Christ still comes to cleanse temples, saying, "My house shall be called a house of prayer for *all people.*" The beginning of the new life is forgiveness, the grace of God, and it is as free as the sun and the rain, as free as wildflowers that spring unbidden from the earth, as the wind on which birds catch their flight. Live in that freedom, Jesus said, and be God's givers of that freedom. The third message of Easter is about being loosed from sin, about freedom and forgiveness.

IV

John has two more scenes that complete his Easter story. Thomas, the "doubter," was not among the disciples to whom Jesus appeared on Easter evening. He said when he heard of Christ's appearance, "I'll not believe until I see it, not till I touch his hands and side and feel the wounds."

A week later, the next Sunday, Christ obliged. He appeared again to the disciples, this time with Thomas *there.* He turned to Thomas. "Put your finger here in my hand, in my side. Doubt no longer, but believe." Thomas knelt in worship and said, "My Lord and my God."

We do not know whether Thomas in fact touched Jesus' wounds. What we do see there is the spirit of Christ who did not begrudge him his doubt but did all he could to help him believe. So Christ comes to our reluctant hearts today, that we may more fully believe.

V

The last scene in John happened soon after, at the Sea of Tiberias in Galilee. The disciples had gone back to fishing. Peter said, "I'm going fishing," and the others followed: Thomas and Nathanael and the two sons of Zebedee, James and John, and two others not named. (Maybe they are your names.)

They had fished all night and caught nothing. A stranger appeared on the seashore and yelled out, "Boys, caught anything?" Here is Jesus the risen Lord looking like some curious vacationer. "No," they answered. He then said, "Cast the net on the right side." The voice, the words, seemed oddly familiar. They threw the nets starboard, and the nets were soon full to the breaking.

The beloved disciple cried, "It is the Lord!" Impetuous Peter did not wait for the boat. He stripped, dove overboard, and thrashed his way to shore.

When the others got there, Jesus was cooking breakfast— bread and fish—over a fire. He asked them to bring more fish to cook, and Peter ran and dragged the whole net filled with 153 large fish. One hundred fifty-three large fish, the text says with startling exactness. I wonder who counted . . . and who weighed!? (Scholars have debated at great length the meaning of the 153 fish. Why were there 153? Did the number have a hidden, symbolic meaning? World-renowned New Testament scholar Raymond Brown, who has written the definitive commentary on John, says he's had this vision of dying and going to heaven and professorially asking Jesus, I've studied and studied and haven't figured it out. Why did the text say there were 153 fish in the net? And Jesus will answer, Because that's how many were there!)

VI

After breakfast we have the last scene. Peter and Jesus are now alone. It may be the first time they've been alone together since the terrible night of Jesus' arrest, when Peter three times denied he even knew Jesus.

Now three times Jesus asks Peter the question, "Do you love me?" Three times. One would have been enough, but after the second, the third was inevitable. Three times Peter had denied him, now three times Jesus asks, "Do you love me?" And three times Peter says, "Yes, I love you . . . *Yes*, I love you . . . Lord, you know everything; you *know* that I love you."

And three times Jesus replies to Peter's profession of love with these words: *Feed my sheep.*

This final resurrection scene is marked—as most of the other scenes—by forgiveness and by a new commission. But this one also clearly marks the *way* of Christ's mission, that is, one of service to others.

Apostles of Christ bear the news of resurrection and offer the freeing power of God's forgiveness. But finally what they offer the world in Christ's name and Christ's spirit is *the service of love.* Love that takes the form of a servant. There was, says Hans Küng, a "downward bent" to the way of Christ. And so also to his apostles' way. Mother Teresa, minister to the Untouchables of Indian culture, described it this way: "Do small things with great love."

The risen Christ at the same moment blesses and commissions. This is a remarkable grace, for we need not only to be loved but to be able to love others—not only to be served but also to serve. It's all bound up in the way of the crucified and risen Lord, the way of service. Francis of Assisi caught the Christ-spirit in his own way of joyful poverty and service:

It is in giving that we receive,
It is in pardoning that we are pardoned,
It is in dying that we are born to eternal life.

It is an Easter faith that let Francis write this hymn:

All creatures of our God and King
lift up your voice and with us sing
Alleluia, Alleluia.
O burning sun with golden beam
O silver moon with softer gleam
O praise him, O praise him,
Alleluia, Alleluia.

*   *   *

And all of you with tender heart
forgiving others, take your part
O sing ye, Alleluia.
You who long pain and sorrow bear
praise God and on him cast your care
O praise him, O praise him
Alleluia, Alleluia.

Alleluia, Alleluia, Alleluia—on Easter the alleluias never seem to stop. They go on forever . . . like the *hesed* of God.

Al-le-lu-ia, meaning "praise-*Yah!*"
Praise Yahweh, the *Abba* of Jesus—
Creator and Redeemer of all the world.

As God has stamped the throat of every bird with its own unique song—the bobwhite, the robin, the whippoorwill—God has stamped each of our hearts with its own unique song. Four notes. Al-le-lu-ia. When we sing that song, we are most fully who God made us to be: joyous servants of God in love with God and God's world, enlisted in the service of love.

Conclusion

John ends his gospel with the words "But there are also many other things which Jesus did; were every one of them to be written, I suppose that the world itself could not contain the books that would be written" (21:25).

They are still being written, even this one, seeking in its halting way to give expression to the grace and truth of Jesus. Easter is completed in the pouring out of the Spirit on all flesh at Pentecost. The Christ-spirit is alive in the people who follow him. Luke's Acts of the Apostles chronicles this next chapter of the biblical story.

Notes

1. All manuscript traditions demonstrate that verses 9-20 of Mark were added later. Explanations of the abrupt end of Mark range from the pedestrian (the end of the scroll was broken off and lost) to the literary (Mark wanted to throw the ball to the readers to end the gospel: the women were too afraid to talk; what will you do with the gospel?).

2. Robert Eisenman, *James the Brother of Jesus: The Key to Unlocking the Secrets of Early Christianity and the Dead Sea Scrolls* (New York: Viking, 1996). He compares Luke with Josephus's quote of Jesus' appearance to James in the lost Gospel of the Hebrews.

32

The Acts of the Apostles:
The Unhindered Gospel and
the Spirit-Formed Church

The Acts of the Apostles was written by the writer of Luke's gospel
as the sequel to his gospel and the first chapter in the life of the
new church, the community of those who follow Jesus as Christ
and Lord.

Its theme is captured in the very last word of the book, an
adverb, of all grammatical things! *Akolutos.* "Unhinderedly." The
book ends with the apostle Paul under house arrest in Rome,
awaiting his eventual execution under Nero. But these last verses
burst with the theme of freedom:

> And he lived there two whole years at his own expense, and
> welcomed all who came to him, preaching the kingdom of
> God and teaching about the Lord Jesus Christ quite openly
> and *unhinderedly.*(28:30-31 RSV, altered)

New Testament scholar Frank Stagg, who labored all his
scholarly life in the southern United States and observed the ways
culture hindered the gospel by its racial barriers, saw in this final
adverb the major theme of both Luke and Acts. "Throughout his
two volumes, Luke never lost sight of his purpose, and he planned
well the conclusion to it all, achieving the final effect by the last
stroke of the pen. 'Unhinderedly,' Luke wrote, describing the
hard-won liberty of the gospel."[1]

I

Actually, the theme is also announced at the beginning of Acts. The risen Christ is about to end forty days of resurrection appearances and ascend to heaven, leaving his followers so that he might return to them in the Holy Spirit. The Spirit, the promised Paraclete, will take Jesus' place in the believing community. The disciples ask, "Lord, will you at this time restore the kingdom to Israel?"—meaning the final restoration at the end of time.

Jesus replies, "It is not for you to know the times or seasons which the Father has fixed by his own authority." (Which ought to have, but has not, quelled the presumptuous pursuit of identifying these times and seasons into fixed dates.) Then he added, "But you shall receive power when the Holy Spirit has come upon you; and you shall be my witnesses in Jerusalem and in all Judea, and in Samaria, and to the ends of the earth" (Acts 1:8).

This verse becomes the outline for the book as well as the trajectory of Christ's mission. Acts begins, then, with the risen Christ promising the Holy Spirit to his followers and telling them when it falls upon them to go with the gospel into all the world, even to "the uttermost part of the earth." The book chronicles how the church on mission struggles to be as free as the gospel it proclaims.

II

Chapter 2 begins with these portentous words: "And when the day of Pentecost had come." The Jewish Pentecost celebrated the harvest and the giving of the Torah on Mount Sinai. John Calvin caught the significance: As fifty days after the original Passover and the Exodus the law of God was given to Moses on tablets of stone at Sinai, so fifty days after the death and resurrection of Jesus Christ, which was the new Passover for the world, the Spirit was given who writes God's law on our hearts.[2]

It happened amid rushing wind and "tongues as of fire." The Spirit of God that moved across the face of the deep and created the heavens and the earth, that overshadowed Mary's flesh and brought forth Jesus, that descended upon Jesus at his baptism, announcing his sonship and anointing his mission, now let itself loose upon the church.

As the Spirit descended, the disciples found themselves speaking in other tongues. Then the Spirit swept out of the house and into the streets, rushing out amid Jews of all nations who had come for the Pentecost celebration of the Torah. By the miracle of the Spirit's presence, though the crowd was composed of many different languages, they could understand what the disciples were saying. (I often prayed for such a miracle in German class.)

The miracle of Pentecost is more, however, than the miracle of *speaking* in different, unknown tongues: It is the miracle of *hearing*, that is, hearing and understanding:[3]

. . . each one *heard* them speaking in his own language. (v. 6)

. . . how is it that we *hear?* (v. 8)

. . . we *hear* them telling in our own tongues the mighty works of God. (v. 11)

. . . give *ear* to my words. (v. 14)

People can hear and understand what God is trying to say through the apostles. It is a sign that the gospel of Christ will be spoken and heard in all the nations and in all tongues.

Pentecost is also the reversal of Babel. In the story of the tower of Babel humankind tries to build a tower to heaven. At Pentecost heaven comes down to us. Instead of the prideful exertion of human will and power, we have the outpouring of God's spirit and power upon us. Instead of Babel's unity based on centralized control that conscripts everyone and everything in its totalitarian project, we have a unity in diversity based on the spirit of love poured into our hearts. Note, at Pentecost the languages are not all made one language—that is the conformity of Babel. At Pentecost the languages remain colorfully different, but now we can hear and understand each other. We can *shema* again, hear again:[4]

Shema Y'Israel	Hear, O Israel
Adonai Eloheinu	The Lord is our God.
Adonai Echad	The Lord is One.

And hearing God, we hear one another and become one, as God is one.

Instead of, therefore, the judgment of Babel—the confusion of tongues and the scattering of the people—we have the blessing of

Pentecost: people hear and understand though they speak differing tongues, and they are *sent* out through the world with the gospel of God.

People looking on at what was happening thought Jesus' followers were drunk. But Peter replied, "We are not drunk on wine. What you see is the fulfillment of the prophet Joel":

> And in the last days it shall be, God declares,
> that I will pour out my Spirit upon all flesh,
> and your sons and your daughters shall prophesy,
> and your young men shall see visions,
> and your old men shall dream dreams;
> yea, and on my menservants and my maidservants in
>   those days
> I will pour out my Spirit; and they shall prophesy.
>   —Acts 2:17-18 RSV

The Spirit is pouring itself out not on some, but on all flesh; not on an elite corps of leaders (male, of course, by custom and tradition), but on all the people of God, young and old, male and female.

What Pentecost tells us is that the church is *Spirit formed*. It was brought into being by the Spirit, and it takes on the character of the Spirit. Can spirit have form? Its *character* is its form. For two thousand years the church has been trying, with varying degrees of success, to match its corporeal form to the Spirit's character.

The Spirit-formed church has love that takes the form of a servant. It lives in the righteousing power of God that is making things right, and it has freedom for its song. The Spirit is poured out on all flesh; all are anointed to lead and to serve—male and female, young and old. The "truth of the gospel" has this message: "There is neither Jew nor Greek, there is neither slave nor free, there is neither male or female, for you are all one in Christ Jesus" (Galatians 3:28).

And there is neither "clergy" nor "laity" either. The word *laos* means the whole people of God. An unfinished dimension of the Protestant Reformation is the "priesthood of all believers," where all believers are made priests of God and priests to one another. In the church of Pentecost, Spirit and authority are poured out on the whole people (*laos*) of God. The church is, says the epistle of

Peter, a "kingdom of priests." "Once you were not a people; but now you are God's people; once you had not received mercy, but now you have received mercy" (1 Peter 2:10).

The book of Acts records that Peter preached and that three thousand in Jerusalem were converted: "They *heard* and were cut to the heart" (2:37).

The church was born at Pentecost. Its new life together is described in these lovely phrases:

> And they devoted themselves to the apostles' teaching, to fellowship, to the breaking of bread, and to the prayers (2:42).

And with these words:

> And all who believed were together and had all things in common; and they sold their possessions and goods and distributed them to all, as any had need. And day by day, attending the temple together and breaking bread in their homes, they partook of food with glad and generous hearts, praising God and having favor with all the people. And the Lord added to their number day by day those who were being saved. (Acts 2:44-47 RSV)

III

In the next chapters Peter and John began preaching in Jerusalem. And not only did they preach; full of the power of Christ's spirit, they also healed. One day on the way to the Temple they met a crippled man who asked for alms. Peter replied, "Silver and gold have I none, but such as I have, I give to you; in the name of Jesus of Nazareth, walk" (3:6). And the man got up and began leaping about and praising God. (As noted by McClendon, Christ is present to the church in *worship*, *witness*, and kingdom *work* in the same way as in this miracle of healing and hearing the *word*.)

Their preaching and this miracle set up tension with the authorities. They were hauled before the leaders and told to quit preaching. They continued to resist this demand: "We cannot but speak of what we have seen and heard" (4:20). Brought in again for the "crime" of preaching, Peter and John defend their act of civil disobedience. "We must obey God rather than men" (5:29). These words have echoed throughout history on the lips of men and women who have defied human authorities in their obedience to God and in their singular desire to act for the sake of God's kingdom of justice, love, and peace.

The next turn in the story begins with the killing of Stephen, the first martyr of the new movement. As he was being stoned to death, he saw a vision of heaven with Jesus at God's right hand, and he prayed aloud for God to forgive his killers. Acts adds an important detail: the killers' coats were laid at the feet of a young zealot for God named Saul of Tarsus, who evidently orchestrated the execution.

As persecution of Jesus' followers in Jerusalem began to intensify, the new believers scattered through Judea and Samaria, and their scattering became the occasion for the spread of the gospel.

The gospel had been preached in Jerusalem. It now moved throughout Judea and Samaria. Philip the apostle preached in Samaria and many believed. As they were baptized, the Holy Spirit descended upon them. The Samaritan Pentecost! One has to be familiar with the racial and theological animosity between Jews and Samaritans to appreciate how radically this expresses the dramatic, new freedom of the gospel. It would not be hindered by racial hatred or theological dispute.

As Philip was returning from Samaria back south to Jerusalem, an angel told him to keep on going past Jerusalem along the south road to Gaza. Philip did so and "happened upon" an Ethiopian eunuch in a chariot who was traveling back from Jerusalem to Ethiopia, where he was in the service of the queen, Candace. When Philip neared the chariot, he saw that the eunuch was reading the Hebrew scriptures. Philip asked if he understood what he was reading, and the eunuch asked for his help. As Philip climbed into the chariot, the eunuch showed him what he was reading from the scroll of Isaiah:

> As a sheep led to the slaughter
> or a lamb mute before its shearers
> so he opened not his mouth.
> In his humiliation justice was denied him
> and as for his genealogy he was cut off
> with no offspring
> for his life was taken up from the earth.

Why has this Ethiopian eunuch been to Jerusalem and why is

he reading the Hebrew scriptures that so explicitly exclude him?[5] Deuteronomy 23:1 states that "a eunuch shall not enter the assembly of the Lord." He is a foreigner, foreigner of foreigners. (Ethiopia was considered the farthest away of faraway lands, the dropping-off place of the universe, in the imagination of first-century people, the uttermost of the uttermost parts of the earth.) He is a man of African pigment, darker than the darkest Bedouin; he is a Gentile and he is a eunuch.

He has been to Jerusalem to a place that so clearly marked his manifold exclusion from the "people of God." Now he is reading about the suffering servant of God, one despised and rejected, one from whom people hid their faces, one cut off without children.

"Who," the eunuch asked, "was the prophet referring to? Himself or some other?"

Philip, the text says, "beginning with this scripture . . . told him the good news of Jesus" (8:35). As he explained this passage from Isaiah 53, did he give the scroll a few turns to Isaiah 56 and read these words to the eunuch?

> Let not the foreigner who has joined himself to the LORD say,
> "The LORD will surely separate me from his people";
>> and let not the eunuch say,
> "Behold, I am a dry tree."
> For thus says the LORD:
> "To the eunuchs who keep my sabbaths
>> who choose the things that please me
>> and hold fast my covenant,
> I will give in my house and within my walls
>> a monument and a name
>> better than sons and daughters;
> I will give them an everlasting name
>> which shall not be cut off.
> And the foreigners who join themselves to the LORD
>> to minister to him, to love the name of the LORD,
>> and to be his servants, . . .
> these I will bring to my holy mountain,
>> and make them joyful in my house of prayer; . . .
> for my house shall be called a house of prayer
>> for all peoples.
> Thus says the Lord GOD,

who gathers the outcasts of Israel,
I will gather yet others to him
besides those already gathered."
—Isaiah 56:3-8 RSV

Did Philip tell him how all these scriptures found fulfillment
in Jesus Christ, suffering servant of God, who turned over tables
in the Temple and quoted, "My house shall be called a house of
prayer for all people"? Did he tell him Jesus was the new temple
to whom all are invited—even foreigners and eunuchs? Did he
tell him that Jesus had no children but that God was giving him
a family too many to count? Did he tell him that he, the eunuch,
could become part of this everlasting family?

Whatever Philip said, the words cut to his heart; for when they
passed some water, the eunuch took the initiative and asked,
"Look, here is water! What *hinders* my being baptized?" (8:37).
(*Hinder* is used again in adverb form as the last word of the book.)

Philip had to decide what to do. All the baptismal regulations
had not yet been clarified by the church back in Jerusalem. Should
he baptize this man on the spot? A foreigner, an African, a eunuch?
Philip, led by the freedom of the Spirit, baptized him then and
there. Philip, as we are seeing, is becoming one of the most creative
missioners in the new movement. We learn elsewhere that his four
daughters will become preacher/prophets! The gospel really does
mean freedom.

As they came out of the water, the text says that the Spirit
"caught up Philip" (was this confirmation of Philip's decision?).
And the eunuch went on his way home "rejoicing" (8:39).

IV

The gospel has gone from Jerusalem, throughout Judea, to
Samaria, to the uttermost parts of the earth. But there were more
barriers to cross, not so much geographical as racial and religious.
They pertained to the evangelization of the Gentiles who were
uncircumcised and did not observe the ritual regulations of the
Jewish faith. These were the great unwashed, unclean of the
world. Would they have to become Jewish before they became
Christian?

A turning point came when Peter met a Greek Gentile named

Cornelius (Acts 10). Cornelius was eager to hear the gospel of Jesus. A vision told him to send messengers to get Peter and bring him back.

At the same moment Peter was receiving a vision. He went out on a rooftop to pray. He was hungry and fell into a trance. He saw a vision from God of a great sheet being lowered from heaven that was filled with all kinds of unclean animals—reptiles, birds, pigs, and so on. A Voice said to Peter, "Take and eat." Peter protested, "No, Lord, I've never eaten anything unclean!" The Voice then said, "What God has cleansed, you must not call common" (10:15).

While Peter was trying to figure this out, the messengers came to Peter and invited him to the home of Cornelius. (It was very much against kosher regulations to enter a Gentile home.) Peter went. When he met Cornelius, Cornelius asked that he tell him about Jesus.

Peter began with new words coming from his heart, "Truly, I perceive that God shows no partiality" (10:34), and announced the gospel he was just beginning to understand. As he preached, the Holy Spirit fell on all who were in the house. Would Peter baptize them? Peter said, "Can anyone forbid [the word "hinder" again] water for baptizing these people who have received the Holy Spirit?" Baptism has replaced circumcision (a rather male mark of inclusion) as the sign of the covenant.

This experience of Peter would lead to the creation of a council in Jerusalem to decide on the matter of the evangelization of Gentiles. After heated argumentation they ruled that circumcision was not required of new converts, and that Peter and Paul and Philip and all the apostles could preach to the Gentiles without forcing them first to become Jews. Paul would later say to the Galatian church, which was embroiled in the circumcision issue, "Circumcision is nothing; uncircumcision is nothing; the only thing that counts is new creation!" (Galatians 6:15 REB).

The prophecies of Isaiah were being fulfilled, the freedom of the gospel was winning, and, in the words of author Larry Woiwode, "the blasted bunch of mixed beasts in that sheet—the Gentiles of every nation on earth—have been added by their action to God's Israel."[6]

V

I need to catch you up, for this council was preceded not only by the experience of Peter but by the most unlikely of all conversions—the conversion of Saul of Tarsus into Paul, Christ's apostle to the Gentiles.

Saul was on his way to Damascus to persecute Christians. "Breathing threats and murder," he was ready for his next round of assaults against the fledgling church.

Then it happened. Light flashed from heaven. Paul fell to the ground, blinded, and heard the voice of a risen Christ saying, "Saul, Saul, why do you persecute me?" Flannery O'Connor once commented, "I reckon the Lord knew that the only way to make a Christian out of that one was to knock him off his horse."[7] Amid blinding light and amazing grace Saul was called to be an apostle of the very one he was persecuting. Led "like a blinded horse,"[8] Saul came to Damascus. A Christian named Ananias came to the house where Saul was staying. Calling this feared enemy of his people "Brother," Ananias laid hands on him and Saul regained his sight. He never got over the grace of it all: While we were yet sinners Christ died for us, he said. While we were weak God died for the ungodly; while enemies of God we were reconciled to God by the death of his son (see Romans 5:6-10). Paul knew most of all he was talking about himself.

Over the next years Paul discerned God's call to him to be the apostle to the Gentiles. Sent by the church at Antioch, he set off on three "missionary" journeys.

One of them took him to Philippi in Greece. The beginning of the Christian mission there is a cameo of the spread of the gospel to the Gentile world (Acts 16:11-40).

As Paul entered this Roman-ruled city, he went first to find a synagogue. Finding none, he went to a river, which was where places of prayer could be established when there was no synagogue. There he met a wealthy, competent businesswoman named Lydia, who dealt in fine purple cloth. She was a God seeker, but had not heard of Jesus Christ. Paul introduced the gospel, God opened her heart, and she believed. Then she offered her home to be the house church for the fledgling Christian community in Philippi.

Another day on the way to town, Paul and his companion Silas began to be followed by a slave girl. She had a "spirit of divination" that gave her soothsaying powers and made considerable money for her owners. Paul exorcised this demon, a deliverance that gave the slave girl spiritual freedom but ruined her fortune-telling powers. This angered her owners, who used anti-Semitic cant to rouse the authorities and crowd against Paul and Silas. (No wonder there was no synagogue in Philippi!) They were beaten and thrown into prison.

As Paul and Silas were in chains, singing psalms, an earthquake shook the prison, springing open the doors and breaking their chains. The jailer awoke, saw the open door, and was about to kill himself when Paul intervened and said, "Stop, we are all here." The shaken man cried out, "What must I do to be saved?" And they replied, "Believe in the Lord Jesus and you will be saved."

The man did believe, he and his family. In beautiful and poignant reciprocity, he took water and bathed Paul and Silas's wounds, and they took water and baptized him.

The next day the authorities discovered they had beaten and jailed Paul, who they did not know was a Roman citizen, without a trial! This was a terrible breach of law. They wanted to sneak him out of town quietly, but Paul insisted on an apology and a VIP parade. He did not want the beginning Christian witness to be compromised by a less-than-honorable exit. On the way out of town they stopped and encouraged the new community at Lydia's house. Such is how the mission in Philippi began.

VI

Paul's dream was to take the gospel to Rome, the empire's great capital city, and he got his heart's desire, even though it turned out he arrived in chains. A trip back to Jerusalem had led to his arrest, and he was taken on a ship to Rome as a prisoner.

The book of Acts reaches its bracing and stirring climax with its last sentence: *"And so we came to Rome"* (28:14).

When Paul landed there, he was surprised and gratified to be met by Christian brothers and sisters who had traveled from all over Italy to greet him. The gospel of Christ had preceded even its premier gospeler!

Paul was placed under house arrest for two years and was able even in that situation to make witness to many who came to see him. And Paul, as the last sentence goes, gave witness boldly, openly, freely—and *unhinderedly*.

From Jerusalem and Judea to Samaria and to the uttermost parts of the world—the Spirit-formed church and the unhindered gospel were on their way. Over the next few decades the Christian movement left the safe confines of being a sect of Judaism, which was a "licit religion" in the Roman Empire, and became an "illicit religion."

In 64 C.E. Rome would burn and Nero would lay the blame on Christians. Sporadic persecution would continue until the time of Domitian (81-96 C.E.), when the persecution would become systematic. A failed military uprising against Domitian led to his unleashing the full fury of the state against two defenseless opponents—Jews and Christians. This widespread persecution sets the stage for the last book of the Bible.

Notes

1. Frank Stagg, *The Book of Acts: The Early Struggle for an Unhindered Gospel* (Nashville: Broadman, 1955), p. 1.
2. See Larry Woiwode, "The Acts of the Apostles," in *Incarnation: Contemporary Writers on the New Testament* (New York: Viking, 1990), p. 76.
3. Walter Brueggemann, *Genesis* (Atlanta: John Knox, 1982), p. 103.
4. Ibid.
5. I am indebted to Fred Craddock for his interpretation of this encounter, which now follows.
6. Woiwode, "Acts of the Apostles," p. 94.
7. Flannery O'Connor, *The Habit of Being,* ed. Sally Fitzgerald (New York: Farrar, Straus & Giroux, 1979), p. 355.
8. Martin Luther's image.

33

Revelation: The End of the Story

It is important to know how God's story begins: with a Creator God who scooped us out of the clay, blew into us his own breath, and called us good.

It is important to know the crux of the story, when God became a man named Jesus who died on a Roman cross to show us a love so high and so broad and so deep that not even this death could stop God from loving us.

But it is also important to know how the story ends.

David Buttrick tells the story of a family (his own) whose guest room was always filled with guests. One day the children in the family played a practical joke. They sneaked into the guest room, took the mystery novel off the bedside table, tore out the last chapter, and returned the book to its place.

The next morning the guest came to the breakfast table bleary-eyed and curious. What happened to the last chapter? How did it turn out? Who dunnit? He went home, found the mystery in a second-hand bookstore, and finished it. To his great surprise, some things he thought were important turned out to be irrelevant and some things he had ignored became most important in the end.

In the same way, we need to read the last chapter of God's story. "For," as David Buttrick says, "if God's story will end in a world reconciled, with New Humanity engaged in grave, glad courtesies of love, with 'the sound of them that triumph and the

shout of them that feast,' with the City and the Lamb and wiped-
away tears, then all our stories must be revised."[1]

Revelation, or the Apocalypse of John, tells how the story of
God ends.

I

The story comes from the very mind and heart of God to a man
named John. He is a prophet and he is a prisoner (in the darkest
of times the two often go together). Because he has refused to bow
down and worship Rome and call Caesar Domitian "Lord," John
has been banished from Ephesus and imprisoned on an island
named Patmos. His brothers and sisters in Christ whom he had
to leave back in Asia Minor—they are in great danger. If they
refuse to bow down, they too risk persecution, imprisonment,
and even death.

Isolated in his exile, John is consumed with terrifying questions. Why is Domitian so powerful? Why does God allow the
forces of evil to be so strong? Why does he let evil persons prosper
and good persons be persecuted? Who is in control after all? Who
will win out? What is to happen to the churches?

Then God gave John a story. It came from visions brought by
an angel. It is a wild, fantastic story filled with terrifying animals
and mysterious persons, glimpses of heaven and hell, the darkest
of darkness and eternity's own light.

The story operates on two levels. On the first level it is a
survival document for a persecuted church. It is God's message to
the downtrodden. It is a secret document written in codes—an
animal code, a number code, and a color code.[2] It is an underground document written to reveal the meaning of history to the
persecuted people of faith and to conceal it from their persecutors.
At this level it has also been an important word from God to the
people of God undergoing persecution throughout history. It
belongs to a genre of sacred literature called "apocalyptic." Apocalypse means "unveiling" and, like the book of Daniel in the
Hebrew Bible, Revelation is an unveiling of the meaning of history
during dark and terrible times and of God's final victory to come.

Modern fundamentalism, following the lead of John Nelson
Darby, nineteenth-century founder of the Plymouth Brethren,

interprets the book of Revelation as a linear blueprint of prophecies leading to doomsday. Scofield's edition of the King James Version promulgated this mode of interpretation to millions through its notes at the bottom of each page. Elaborate charts have been set up to pinpoint when various parts of the book are being fulfilled, and dates are projected for when the End will come. Hal Lindsay's hugely successful book *The Late Great Planet Earth* adopted this approach and led large numbers of people down this road of dubious interpretation. Since his book's original publication in 1970, Lindsay has revised and revised again the dates he set for the end of the world (necessity being the mother of inspiration).

Jesus spoke plain words that warn against such calendarizing of the end times: "But of that day or hour no one knows, not even the angels in heaven, nor the Son, but only the Father" (Mark 13:32). History is replete with Christians who claim to know more than Christ.

This mode of interpretation has displayed a rather uncharitable habit of assigning absolute evil to one's earthly adversaries. The Antichrist, Beast, and Dragon of Revelation have been identified variously throughout history as the pope or the papacy in general, Napoleon, F.D.R., the Soviet Union, and even Ronald Reagan (each of his names, Ronald Wilson Reagan, contains six letters—"666"!). And it has gloried in the "Tribulation," which the enemies of God and unbelievers will suffer while believers are whisked away in the so-called Rapture. It seems so far away from the spirit of Christ, who is supposed to be the center of the book.

The misplaced literalism of fundamentalism and the cognitively distorted literalism of mental illness have often combined to produce pathological readings of Revelation that have led to such tragedies as the April 19, 1994, Waco inferno, where David Koresh led his cult into a suicide mission designed to inaugurate a countdown to Armageddon.

The Heaven's Gate cult of Marshall Applewhite, which tried to hook onto the tail of a comet, is the latest example of apocalyptic prophecies gone awry. Applewhite grew up listening to his father preaching often from Revelation in the fundamentalist, premillennial vein. This preaching, coupled with Applewhite's deep inner conflicts and mental illness, led eventually to his forming the

Heaven's Gate suicide mission of March 1997—thirty-nine dead on a California estate, each hoping to catch a ride on a spaceship that was supposedly following along behind the Hale-Bopp comet—a poignant and tragic story.

Revelation has been ignored by some who are turned away by its bizarre and sometimes violent imagery. Yet it has been hotly debated by others. It was one of the last of the books of the Bible to be admitted to the final canon of scripture and has remained one of the most difficult to interpret. Jerome, the first great translator of scripture, who translated the entire Bible into Latin (the Vulgate), said of this book: "Revelation has as many mysteries as it does words."[3] And Cotton Mather, American Puritan clergyman, wrote, "I confess Apocalyptic Studies are fittest for those Raised Souls, whose Heart Strings are made of a Little Nicer Clay than other mens."[4]

I offer here a proposal to read the book on two levels. The first level is, as described above, a survival document for a persecuted church, written first to those undergoing persecution under Domitian, but available to persecuted people of God throughout history.

On a second, deeper level it is a book that reaches to a region deeper than the conscious mind, a level of archetypes and symbols where God still walks with us in the cool of the day. In the mysterious unfolding of images and characters is the message that the forces of good will not be defeated, that God will win the final victory, and that there will be a final healing of all things.

It resembles in some ways the stories we call fairy tales, which themselves are filled with as much darkness and light as we can stand. The gospel story is, to use J. R. R. Tolkien's phrase, a *eucatastrophe*, "the good catastrophe, the sudden joyous 'turn' . . . and sudden miraculous grace." And Revelation, again to use his words, "denies (in the face of much evidence if you will) universal final defeat . . . , giving a glimpse of Joy, Joy beyond the walls of the world. . . ."[5]

II

The story begins in heaven—at God's throne. That's where everything begins. That is where the universe began and the stars were flung into space. That is where history begins—and ends. As one great historian, Herbert Butterfield, put it, "If God stopped breathing we would all vanish."

John sees the throne, and the face of God gleams like all jewels in the world shining together. Around the throne are twenty-four elders singing songs of praise. And four strange flying creatures—one like a lion, one like a bull, one with a man's face, and one like an eagle—are flying around the throne beating their wings and singing, "Holy, Holy, Holy."

Then there appears a Lamb. He has suffered a mortal wound yet is alive. His secret name is Jesus Christ. Thousands, no, millions break forth in joyous song: "Worthy is the Lamb who was slain, to receive power and riches and wisdom and strength and honor and glory and blessing." The Lamb goes to the throne and takes a scroll on which is written all of history. The scroll is bound together by seven seals, and now the Lamb begins to break open the seals.

As the scroll opens, we see history happening before our eyes, history we know like the back of our hand.

First we see the white horse of conquering, and on that horse we see a parade of conquerors: Alexander the Great, Julius Caesar, Napoleon, Hitler, Stalin, and on and on.

Then we see a red horse of war. Its rider has a sword and on the sword is the blood of a thousand wars: Trojan wars, Gallic wars, civil wars, world wars, Vietnam, Afghanistan, El Salvador, Bosnia, Liberia, the Persian Gulf.

Then comes the black horse of famine, and we see the long cruel line of parched lips and bloated stomachs from Egypt to Central Africa, to Ireland, to Bangladesh, to the inner cities of the United States.

Finally the fourth horse comes and its color is pale green. It is the horse of death, and on that pale green horse ride plagues and diseases, malaria, smallpox, cancer, and AIDS.

We know that to be the way of human history. Then as all of the seven seals are broken and the scroll is opened up, all of history is unveiled, and we see that it is beset by even more calamity—persecution of Christians, earthquakes, volcanic eruptions, hurricanes ravaging coastlines, invasions of insects, and on and on. And we are terrified to look and wonder why it is all happening.

Then the story gives us the answer. There has been a revolt

against God, and it began in the very throne room of heaven: "war in heaven" between God's forces and the forces of evil, led by the Dragon. Unable to defeat God in heaven, the Dragon flees to earth and carries on his war there—against God's people on earth.

The secret name of the Dragon is Satan. He is the reason for the revolt and for the chaos and calamity throughout the course of history.

History is the story of a fight to the finish between the forces of good, led by God, and the forces of evil, led by the Dragon. The forces of heaven are led by a holy Trinity: God, God's Son, Jesus Christ, and the Holy Spirit. The forces of darkness are led by three great enemies. The first and foremost has already been introduced—the Dragon. John described him this way: he is a huge, red dragon with a long tail. He has seven heads, and on each of the heads are ten horns and a crown (Revelation 12:3). All of this is code language.

But the Dragon is not alone. He has two partners in darkness. Just as there is a Holy Trinity, there is also an unholy trinity made up of the Dragon, the Beast, and the False Prophet. The Beast comes from the sea. He also has seven heads and ten horns on each head, and on each horn there is a crown, and on each head there is a name insulting to God. The Dragon gives to the Beast of his own authority and power and throne, and the Beast accepts it. When the Beast from the sea accepts the power and authority from the Dragon, all the world bows down and worships the Beast, saying, "Who is like the Beast?" In the Old Testament that is what the psalmist says about God: "Who is like Yahweh? Who can compare with the Lord?" You see, the Beast has become like a god. And his number is 666.

Revelation 13 and Revelation 17 contain a number of allusions to Rome and Caesar Domitian. (The woman of Revelation 17 even sits on seven hills, perhaps an allusion to Rome's seven hills [17:9].) The code language is meant to suggest who Domitian is as the enemy of God's people in the late first century. It is also meant to refer to others throughout history who presume to take God's place and thereby become demonic in their pretensions of power. Paul Tillich once defined the "demonic" as anything finite that presumes to become infinite.[6] Such is the role of the Beast in Revelation 13.

Who is the Beast? Anybody or anything that accepts power
and authority offered by Satan. Jesus was offered it in the wilderness. But he said no. Each generation has those who have said yes.
The Dragon has his partner the Beast, and the Beast changes faces
in every generation.

But those are only two members of the unholy trinity. Who is
the third? He is the False Prophet—the beast "from the land." The
False Prophet goes all over the world persuading people to bow
down and worship the Beast. As the chief propagandist of the
unholy forces, he performs miracles and gives gifts. He will use
any device available to persuade us to fall down and worship the
Beast. The false prophet is pictured with two horns like a lamb; he
speaks like a dragon, and he gives the mark of the beast to all who
are willing to fall down and worship him. With that mark comes
the promise of special powers and privileges.

There it is—the story, history, your story and mine. A battle
between the Holy Trinity—God, Jesus Christ, and Holy Spirit—
and the unholy trinity—the Dragon, the Beast, and the False
Prophet. And the battle is carried on among human beings, those
who follow God and those who follow the Dragon. John calls the
followers of God "heaven dwellers," and he calls the followers of
the Dragon "earth dwellers."[7]

III

The story is true of the past. It describes the present. But it also
unveils the future. The title of the book of Revelation means
"unveiling," and that is what God gives us—an unveiling of past
and present, and now the future. The future is not in our hands,
not even in the hands of those who wield earthly power, but in
God's hands.

Who will win? God or the Dragon? Christ or the Beast? The
Holy Spirit or the False Prophet? Who is in control? Who will win
the final victory?

Seven bowls of wrath are poured out that stand for historical
judgments against the evil pretensions of nations like Rome. A
battle at "Armageddon" is fought where the kings of the earth
coming from the east (actually, about four centuries later the

invasion would come from the north) are arrayed against the evil power of Rome (16:16).

The name "Armageddon" has spawned a number of theories about its location, some trying to locate the place at Megiddo, a plain in the Middle East that is famous for its battles. Literally "Armageddon" means "Mount of Megiddo," which suggests a composite image: Mount of Zion and battle plain of Megiddo. It is a symbolic, not a geographical, place, and it refers to a place of final battle between the nations of the earth, where great and evil powers meet their fate.[8] When the evil of history has been exhausted and is extinguished, then shall come the final outworking of God's salvation.

This is what the story tells: At a time in the future, which nobody knows, Christ the Messiah will return. Only this time he will not come as we first saw him, the Lamb slain for our sins. This time he will come as a glorious figure on a white horse. His name is "Faithful and True." He will come in power and glory, with "King of Kings and Lord of Lords" emblazoned on his robe. He will gather all the forces of good and meet the monster and all the forces of evil at the final climactic battle (Revelation 19). The battle is fought and Christ is triumphant. He then throws the Beast and the False Prophet into the lake of fire that burns forever.

The Beast and the False Prophet are taken care of, but one member of the unholy trinity is left—the Dragon. Now the story reminds us of an old western. It is the final showdown at the O.K. Corral. While the good guys are taking care of the bad guys, the chief villain sneaks away and the hero goes after him alone. God alone now goes to take care of the Dragon once and for all.

First he sends his angel, and the angel throws the Dragon in a deep pit and chains him there for one thousand years (symbolically, a perfect or complete length of time). During that period Christ sets up his kingdom on earth with all God's people.

Then the Dragon will make his last-ditch effort to defeat God. God sets him loose and he roams the whole world, deceiving the nations and recruiting them to join him in his effort to defeat God and God's people. The great nations are called Gog and Magog. (These are symbolic names taken from Ezekiel's prophecy [chapters 38–39] that represent the worst of evil nations, in other words, "Evil and Evilest" or "Dumb and Dumber.") They gather to defeat

God's people, but this time God takes care of them personally. He casts down fire from heaven and destroys them; then he throws the Dragon in the lake of fire along with his cohorts in darkness, the Beast and the False Prophet.

Now is the final judgment, when every person shall rise and stand before God. The "earth dwellers," those who have worshiped the Beast and have fought against God, will join the Dragon, the Beast, and the False Prophet in the lake of fire and suffer what is called "the second death," or final extinction. However, all of those whose names are in the Lamb's Book of Life, those who have been faithful to God and God's way—each one will be given a smooth, white stone. And on that stone, which you hold in your hand, will be written a secret name, perhaps your own secret name, for then you will know yourself completely as now only God knows you. Or perhaps it is the secret name of Christ, for he will stand by you and for you on that day and will claim you as his own. God will say, "This stone is your entrance into my kingdom. Come, enjoy the feast which I have prepared for you since the foundation of the world."

And then a new heaven and a new earth will appear, replacing the old heaven and earth. The New Jerusalem will come down from heaven, adorned as a bride for her husband, a city too wonderful to describe in human words. There God will live with us and we with him. God will wipe away every tear from our eyes and death will be no more.

A river of life will flow through the center of the city. Trees will line both sides of the river; their branches will bear fruit all year around and their leaves will be "for the healing of the nations" (22:2).

There will be a great multitude there from every tribe and nation, class and tongue, too numerous to count. Who are the "few" who shall be saved? A multitude too great for the human mind to take in! They will be wearing clean white robes and singing praise to God. How did they get such gleaming white robes? "These are they," says an elder from the throne, "who have come through the great tribulation of life and have washed their robes and made them white in the blood of the Lamb" (Revelation 7:14).

"The blood of the Lamb" is our human poetry pointing to the

ineffable, the self-emptying love of God poured out on the cross. It points to the grace of God: What we could not do for ourselves God has done for us. *Hesed.* Jesus, Messiah and Lord, bore our sins and bore them away. He was broken on a cross, and from his breaking has come our healing. We cannot wash away our sins nor can we rid the world of its tired and terrible sins, but he is "the Lamb which taketh away the sin of the world."

The Supper of the Lamb is the joyous feast of the people of God through all the ages. Adam and Eve are there, the distortion of desire finally healed, and Abraham, Sarah, and Isaac, Hagar and Ishmael side by side. Tamar is there and Miriam and David and Mary and Martha and Lazarus and Augustine of Hippo and Patrick of Ireland and Hildegard of Bingen and Francis of Assisi and Toyohiko Kagawa of Japan and Dorothy Day and Martin Luther King and . . . time and imagination and love would fail us to name all who will be there, joining in the great feast of the kingdom of God. It is a picture of the Final Blessing where, in the words of Julian of Norwich,

> All shall be well
> and all shall be well
> and all manner of thing shall be well.[9]

IV

There the story ends, and John the storyteller turns to you and me and asks, in effect, Do you believe the story? Do you believe it enough to stake your life on it? In the final analysis this is the crucial issue of the book. Not, Do you understand it all? or What is its historical meaning? or Who is 666? or When is Christ coming? or When is the Rapture—before or after the Tribulation? All these are questions adults argue over because they have lost the child's capacity simply to believe it. John says, "Don't add anything to the story, or leave anything out of it." He wants us simply to believe it, to hear it and obey.

When we ask, Do you believe it? we do not mean, Do you believe in seven-headed dragons? We mean, Do you believe that evil is terrible and real and so is God's judgment on evil? Do you really believe, despite appearances sometimes to the contrary, that

God will conquer all evil and that the darkness will not overcome the light?

The book of Revelation is, as God's Word often is, a two-edged sword. It cuts two ways. It is warning and it is promise. The warning is this: you must choose whose side you will join. You must choose today if you have not already. It makes a difference whose side you are on, a real historical difference and a real eternal difference. So do not dally.

The promise is this: God will win the final victory. Regardless of how things seem, God is in control and the final victory is assured. And you as God's children will share the victory.

Revelation is the story that God's love, which in history becomes a suffering love, will finally become a triumphant love—and that Christ's love made eloquent in suffering shall prevail and bring to completion the redemption of the world.

"Blessed, happy, is the one who tells the words of this prophecy," says John at the beginning of Revelation (1:3), "and blessed are those who hear and keep what is written therein."

To "keep what is written" means to live by the faithfulness and goodness of God, regardless of the times, and with faithful endurance to look forward to the final healing of all existence, the victory of all that is true and good and beautiful.

What is the true, the good, the beautiful? Israel, from its beginnings, saw it originating from the mouth of Yahweh, and Christians have glimpsed it in the figure of Christ, who lived all too short a time to show us the face of God.

From sacred texts, Jewish and Christian, this is the story of God.

Notes

1. From an unpublished manuscript by David Buttrick; author's files.
2. James Blevins, from a lecture on Revelation at the Southern Baptist Theological Seminary, Louisville, Kentucky.
3. Jerome, Letter 53.8, as cited in Bernard McGinn, "Revelation," in *The Literary Guide to the Bible*, ed. Robert Alter and Frank Kermode (Cambridge: Harvard University Press, 1987), p. 523.
4. Cotton Mather, cited in McGinn, ibid.
5. Quoted in Buechner, *Telling the Truth*, p. 81.
6. Paul Tillich, *Systematic Theology, I* (Chicago: University of Chicago Press, 1967}, p. 134.

7. See Paul Minear, *I Saw a New Earth* (Washington, D.C.: Corpus Books, 1968), p. 261ff., for his interpretation and translation of "earth dwellers."
8. See G. B. Caird, *The Revelation of St. John* (London: Adam & Charles Black, 1966), pp. 200-210.
9. Author's adaptation into modern English. See chapter 1, note 12 for Julian's original statement.

Epilogue:
The Star Thrower

He was a scientist on vacation roaming the beach of Costabel, seeing what the ocean had offered up onto its sandy shore during the night. Loren Eiseley was his name, and he looked with a scientist's cold eye at natural selection at work. "In the end," he mused darkly to himself, "the sea rejects its offspring."[1] He saw shells with their tiny animals inside, he saw a small octopus dying on the sand, and he saw hundreds of starfish the stormy waters had washed ashore.

I

He had awakened an hour before dawn to go to the shore. Walking along, he saw another kind of death at work: the flashlights of professional shellers as they greedily gathered the starfish from the sand and stuffed them into their bags. Bags full of dying starfish.

He walked on around a bluff. The rising sun behind had projected its rim of light onto the stormy sky ahead, and there before him "a gigantic rainbow . . . had sprung shimmering into existence." Then he looked and saw in the distance near the foot of the rainbow, just within its circle of color, a human figure. He could hardly make it out. The figure was looking down. It stooped and flung some object beyond the breaking surf. As Eiseley drew close, he saw the man reach down again and pick up . . . a starfish.

"It's still alive," Eiseley offered.

"Yes," said the man, and he took the star and spun it far into the sea. "It may live if the offshore pull is strong enough," he said gently.

"Do you collect?" Eiseley asked.

"Only for the living," he said, and he stooped and threw another star. "The stars," he said, "throw well. One can help them."

Eiseley walked on. As he reached a bend in the shore he turned, looked back, and saw the man toss another star. "For a moment," Eiseley wrote later in his famous essay, "The Star Thrower," "in the changing light, the sower appeared magnified, as though casting larger stars upon some greater sea. He had . . . the posture of a god."

But then Eiseley's eyes refocused and his scientist's mind startled back into motion, and he reconsidered. "No, he is a man . . . the star thrower is a man, and death is running more fleet than he along every sea beach in the world."

As Eiseley walked along the beach, he pondered Darwin and nature's law of tooth and claw, where death is some sad rule of progress. He pondered Freud and the inner struggle between darkness and light in the human soul. He pondered the twisters that roared across the plains in his boyhood, wreaking destruction, and he saw again in his mind's eye the old photograph of his mother as a child clinging to her sister, her eyes already troubled. He remembered the biblical injunction, "Love not the world . . . neither things that are in the world."

And he thought to himself, "But I *do* love the world. I love its small ones, the things beaten in the strangling surf, the bird, singing, which flies and falls and is not seen again . . . I love the lost ones, the failures of the world." And he said to himself, "I must go back and find the star thrower."

As he returned down the beach, far ahead in the "rain-swept morning" he saw the star thrower still flinging stars beneath the rainbow.

Eiseley reached the man, picked up a still-living star and spun it himself far out into the waves.

"Call me another thrower" was all he said to the man. And he picked up another and flung it into the sea, and another. "Perhaps," he thought, "far out on the rim of space a genuine star was similarly being seized and flung." He could feel the movement of his body in the repetition of throwing. It felt good. "It was like sowing—the sowing of life. . . ."

He walked on, then looked back and saw the star thrower once more, "small and dark against the receding rainbow." He saw the man stoop and fling once more. And Eiseley picked up a star and flung and flung again, sowing life against all the death in the world. A sower, sowing life. Flinging life like a fool in love with the world. And as he flung, he felt as though he and the man were casting stars on some infinite beach "beside an unknown hurler of suns."

There the famous essay ends.

II

So the God of the universe spins worlds into existence. And so this same God sent into our history of tooth and claw and endless human struggle, a star thrower.

His name was Jesus from Nazareth, a tiny town in a tiny occupied country. And we, at first, thought him a fool, flinging stars into the sea, sowing life in the face of so much death. Jesus, the Star Thrower, came and said, "I *do* love the world. I love every small one, every bird that sings and flies and falls. I love every creature great and small, and every human child, star of God, washed on life's shore."

He went to the synagogue and opened the Hebrew scriptures and read:

> The Spirit of the Lord is upon me
> because he has anointed me
> to preach good news to the poor
> to proclaim release to the captives
> and recovering of sight to the blind
> to set at liberty those who are oppressed.

And he saw a man with an unclean spirit and said to the spirit, "Be silent and come out of him." And out the spirit came. Liberty! And he spun the man back into life and said, "Live!"

And he saw Simon's mother-in-law with a high fever and he rebuked the fever and immediately it left. "Live!"

And he went by the Sea of Galilee and saw two men washing their nets and he said, "Put your nets out into the deep and let them down for a catch." And they protested. Simon said, "But we've been at it all night and caught nothing, but at your word, I will." They did, and their nets were full to breaking. And Jesus said, "Don't be afraid of this miracle; this is a sign of God's kingdom. From now on you will be catching men, saving women and men. Sowing life."

And a man came to Jesus full of leprosy and when he saw Jesus he fell on his face and said, "Lord, if you want, you can make me clean." And Jesus touched this untouchable man, so long untouched, and said, "I want. Be clean. Live!"

And four men brought their crippled friend to Jesus on a pallet and Jesus said, "Your sins are forgiven," and then he said, "Take up your pallet and walk." And he flung another star and said, "Live!"

And he went to the office of a tax collector named Levi. And he said, "Your job is your death, come follow me. And live!" And the man left everything, rose, and followed.

And this same Levi threw a party for Jesus and invited to his feast other tax collectors and other sinners and outcasts. And the Pharisees and scribes grumbled and said, "Why do you eat and drink with such?" And Jesus said, "Those who are well need no physician. I have not come to make the righteous more righteous, the respectable more respectable, but to call sinners to repentance and to life!" And he spun another star into the sea.

And he saw a man with a withered hand. It was the sabbath. Jesus knew he had an audience waiting to see if he'd break the sabbath law and heal on that holy day. And he said to his audience: "What is the Lord's sabbath for but to do good! Would the Lord of the universe save life or destroy it on his sabbath of joy and rest?" So he turned to the man and said, "Stretch forth your hand." And God healed the man's hand on God's own sabbath.

And the star thrower called others to cast with him, the Twelve: Peter, Andrew, brothers James and John, Philip, Bartholomew, Matthew, Thomas, another James, Simon the Zealot, and two named Judas.

"Follow me and let's sow life," he said. And they did.

And he taught to us the way of peace. A crowd gathered and he said, "Love your enemy, for God is kind to the ungrateful and the selfish." (Perhaps we too have a chance.) "Give to everyone who begs, for God is merciful to all." And he said, "Judge not and you will not be judged; forgive and you will be forgiven."

The way of peace. Foolish to the world of tooth and claw, but the wisdom and power of God to those who are being saved.

And he healed the centurion's slave, and he raised to life the son of the widow of Nain. "Live!" he cried. Two more stars hurled into the sea.

And he had dinner with a Pharisee, and while they were eating, a woman who was a sinner broke into the men's company carrying a box of perfume. As she reached Jesus, tears were already falling, tears that wet his feet, and she let down her hair and wiped his feet with her hair and anointed them with her perfume.

The Pharisee host was predictably outraged and grumbled at the woman's outlandish behavior. But Jesus said, "One who is forgiven much, loves much." The Pharisee grew silent. And he looked at her and said the words she'd already heard, words that had brought her there and brought her tears, words that had let down her hair and poured perfume on his feet. Words that were *life* to her: "Your sins are forgiven," was what he said.

And he went through the cities and villages and the Twelve were with him. And also some women, women given life now sowing life, women healed of evil spirits and disease: Mary Magdalene healed of seven demons, Joanna, wife of Chuza (Herod's steward), Susanna, and "many others" who provided for Jesus and his mission of *life.*

And all I've recounted is but a summary of four chapters of one gospel, Luke, a thimbleful of God's ocean of love and light. As John's gospel says at the end, "What is written here is just a start. If we remembered all that Jesus did, the books would fill the world."

III

Who is this man spinning stars back to life? This single, solitary man on one small beach, who came to one tiny country and for three short years taught and healed and forgave and lived a kindness that brought people life. Was he a fool, sowing life against so much death?

Was his mercy a fool's gesture in the face of nature's chaos and "man's inhumanity to man"? Was his an ineffectual, mutant love standing on the shore of evolution's faceless sea? Or was it God's *new thing* redeeming our laws and ways? A sign, like the rainbow, of the sureness of God's love and of its final triumph? Yes, I think that's it. God's new thing. A sign. The future we now see.

Has the star thrower found you cast upon the shore and spun you out into the waves to live?

He comes to those who are walking in the shadow of death and says, as he lifts them from the sand, "Live! Live all the days this world has to give you and then all the life God's eternity has for you."

He says to those for whom life has been too strong, those bearing life's killing burdens, "Live!"

And he comes to those caught in their sin, sick with shame, dying in their self-imposed exile, and says, "Come out of hiding. Your sins are forgiven. Come join the family of God and live."

And he comes to those who look on the outside for all the world like they are living but on the inside feel like they are dying and he says, "It is time to live. Live!"

He says to the poor in spirit, sometimes disheartened by themselves and by the world, "Live! Yours is the kingdom of God."

And he comes to hungry children and to those lost without home and without God, and he comes to the teenager addicted to alcohol and drugs, and to the mother trapped in poverty and to the mentally retarded son and to the prisoner and to the bored high school student and to the alcoholic and to the ghetto youth and to the hungry readers of books and he says, "Live!"

And he comes to you and hands you a star and says, "You are a thrower too."

Note

1. All quotations are from Loren Eiseley's essay "The Star Thrower," in *The Star Thrower* (New York: Harvest Books, 1978), pp. 169-85.